In The Light Of His Resurrection

The Post Resurrection And Post Ascension Appearances Of Christ In Scripture

Bonnie J. Smith

In The Light Of His Resurrection
The Post Resurrection And Post Ascension Appearances Of Christ In Scripture
© 2024 Bonnie J. Smith, LLC

ISBN: 978-0-9890467-8-7

Cover Credits:
Front Cover / Collaborative Concept: Bonnie J. Smith; Eileen M. Posadny
Front Cover Illustration: Eileen M. Posadny

Back Cover / Collaborative Concept: Bonnie J. Smith; Maria A. Smith
Back Cover Illustration: Rachel T. Royer

Dedication

Two special friends have been with me on the long writing journey of this book since the 1980's. They are: Betty S. Everett of Defiance Ohio, and Richard E. Wilkin of Findlay Ohio. Around that time I discussed my earliest written concepts for the book and for years thereafter throughout its evolving stages.

Betty was a prolific writer having written over 4500 published articles and 9 books. She co-founded the Northwest Ohio Christian Writers in 1979. A group for aspiring writers which thrived until 2015. She encouraged and mentored many potential writers on their journey of exploring writing as a ministry. I met her in January 1980 and shortly thereafter we started discussions about my writing underway and my interest in the scenes in the garden at the tomb of Jesus. She has been faithfully there over the years reading select chapters now-and-then and continually expressing her encouragement to finish this book. Always asking, "Are you writing?" She passed away in January 2022.

Richard was a retired minister; a former pastor, previous denominational president, a respected statesman of many years, and was a seminary professor too. I met him in that latter vocation in 1987 while I was attending Winebrenner Theological Seminary.

He and I went up, over, and down the back side of various mountains in theological discussions. As an encourager, who became a trusted spiritual mentor; he showed special interest in many chapters in this book. He passed away in June 2021.

The two Christians named above (who never met and were both born around 1929-1930) were brought across my path and spiritual journey by the Lord Jesus Christ. They were amazing sounding boards for me early-on and always remained interested in my thoughts, perceptions, and direction for the manuscript; but never judgmental about my conclusions. Therefore, I take full responsibility for any composition or theological errors in the book.

Finally... because of their longstanding and treasured friendship, and their valuable time so freely and graciously given... I was blessed beyond measure.

Contents

Section Fifteen: Post Ascension Appearances Bring Change

Section Sixteen: God's Promise, An Eternal King

About This Book

How it started for me…

While reading the Gospels in the mid-1970's I became fascinated with the scenes at Jesus of Nazareth's garden tomb. There appeared to be discrepancies between the gospel writers information, but as a believer in the Bible I knew there had to be spiritual answers to my troubling questions. Therefore this book simply started as a personal Bible study search. What was the chronology of the scenes, along with the presence of those angels and human characters? I took a major step in looking through the fifty-two verses and discovered more. Along the way I discerned and believed the seven sepulcher scenes were a possible book. However… too small in size to be practical so that thought was set aside.

Through the years of daily devotional reading and those on-and-off major study times throughout the Bible… this chronology format for a book idea started to germinate. It kept expanding. Nevertheless education, ministry vocation and leadership involvement, posting on my personal ministry website, *Touch Eternity Teach*, and starting and completing the writing of another book titled, *Biblical Drama Ministry*, all took precedent at various times. Plus along with those natural human intervening circumstances including… family graduations, weddings, births, deaths, involved health complications and medical crises, and the moving to five different residential locations; all of which caused the writing to be set aside time-after-time and for long durations.

Being an avid reader for many, many decades I gleaned direction from research while reading resources including articles and books. This led to my collective thoughts expanding, the germinating of multiple ideas, perceived chronological insight explored, while selecting and studying Bible passages… all from here, there, and everywhere. Notes with verses and paragraphs filled with thoughts… written on sheets of paper or scribbled on scraps of paper, spare restaurant napkins, backs of offering envelopes from church pews, and hundreds-upon-hundreds of index cards; all which became scattered about since the mid-1970's. All the while… half-believing the thought it would finalize in book format.

It should be understood without much explanation that the many years involved in writing resulted in drawing my own conclusions from resources read, then many thoughts used as a composite on various themes. I have chosen not to cite any references for lack of having kept correct documentation of them. Therefore my desire is for the reader to focus on the Lord Jesus Christ and the Scripture references included.

Along the way I sensed and discerned the Lord's direction for the book had to be a chronological focus solely on the Resurrection of Jesus, His following post Resurrection appearances, and His post Ascension appearances recorded through the remainder of the New Testament. The book's front cover was designed in 2013; the back cover idea kept evolving into 2022. Throughout 2020-2022 I set my heart, mind, and hand toward completing a draft manuscript.

Discover what is here for you…

A reader will find I have not focused on Greek and Hebrew language meanings because most readers would not be interested in their descriptive inclusion. My narrative teaching format used here is one reason many will select to read this book. It includes the straightforward presentation of themes surrounding Jesus Christ, the Son of God / Son of Man.

Limiting paragraphs on Scriptural backstory from the Old Testament has been intentional. A few chapters about Christ before His actual death on the cross have been included. My attempt at chronology from His burial and forward without an abundance of distracting side trips kept the concept focused.

Quoted Bible verses are referenced within the narrative content of the paragraphs. Many ideas drawn from verses have their Bible reference included also for easy reader verification. This purposeful decision allows one to have immediate Scriptural access information; and after a few pages soon the reader adjusts and passes over it unless one wants that specific information at that moment. Throughout the book a sentence might have a break identified by … so hopefully the reader slows down for a second.

Readers will discover a thorough, thought-provoking chronology, without being overwhelmingly provocative; which enables one to discover some treasured insights. To the best of my ability and understanding I have put forth what I believe is a sound chronological order. I make no claim what you are reading is 100% accurate. Will readers agree completely on everything? Absolutely not.

My prayer for you the reader… that this book will be a blessing to you on your spiritual journey.

Bonnie J. Smith

February 2024

Section One

Three Days And Three Nights

1
Burial Before Sunset

A mysterious darkness shrouded the scene. The King of the Jews silenced. A horrific crucifixion finished. Death prevailed. Breaking the tempo on Golgotha, the soldiers' armor rattled and clanged as they moved about beneath three crosses. Spectators who had come to witness the crucifixion of Jesus depart accompanied by their various moods. Foes with gleeful hearts whisper words of victory. Others shrouded in fear rushed back to Jerusalem. Confused disciples mourn in disbelief. Those who cared with unconditional love stand motionless in shock with tear-streaked faces. The only thing left... a burial. Placing the body, Jesus of Nazareth, inside a tomb to decompose.

The four gospel writers in the New Testament... Matthew, Mark, Luke, and John, give specific reference to Jesus' burial. They move from the crucifixion site to the tomb and garden scene pre Resurrection. During this timeframe there were many unfulfilled expectations concerning the coming of the kingdom of God. Their writings grasp the mood on the timeline up to the Resurrection. Though the garden location remains the dominate descriptive scene for three days, human characters come and leave, and events change.

The burial procedure and post death scenes allows one to center on the controlled chaos prior to Christ's Resurrection. Information cloaked in the burial passages sets up not only a timeline, but a power line. Besides... references in some Resurrection verses refer back to the burial. Below the Scripture verses from the New International Version of The Holy Bible (NIV) are referenced with their captions related to the burial of Jesus of Nazareth, the King of the Jews.

The Burial of Jesus
Matthew 27:57-61

The Burial of Jesus
Mark 15:42-47

Jesus' Burial
Luke 23:50-56

The Burial of Jesus
John 19:38-42

The heightened drama in the crucifixion scene took place on the cross between the sixth and ninth hours. (Luke 23:44) The twenty-four hour daily timeframe started for the Jews at sunset and went to sunset the next day. At sunset, a new day began Jewish time; this in contrast to the Gentile time with days identified from 12:01 a.m. to 12:00 p.m. midnight. For Gentiles, the crucifixion happened between 12:00 noon and 3:00 p.m. Those were the eighteenth to twenty-first hours for the Jews.

Who are the characters involved center stage in the burial passages? The predominate person taking leadership responsibility for Jesus' bloody corpse is Joseph of Arimathea. For him, this might not have been an easy stance. On the other hand, a spontaneous decision made during the crucifixion.

Being a prominent member of the Sanhedrin (aka ruling council), but also a good and upright person, Joseph neither consented to their decision to condemn Jesus, nor took action toward affirming an unjust and horrific crucifixion. (Luke 23:50-51) However, this secret follower who feared the Jews now becomes bold and forthright. He opted to take a public stand. Joseph had several roles during the immediate hours after the death of Christ.

First... Someone had to claim the mortal body of Jesus soon because the count down to sunset was imminent. The crucifixion was on the afternoon of Passover, Wednesday (fourteenth) just hours before sunset and start of the holy day... Feast of Unleavened Bread (fifteenth). Jewish custom demanded the corpse be removed from the cross and the crucifixion site before the special Sabbath. Those engaged in this active procedure would be unclean for seven days according to Jewish law. (Numbers 19:11) Joseph's decision precluded him from participation in the Jewish Convocation's ceremonial worship. The initial timeline falls during Passover and the seder meal was imminent.

Minutes and hours, accompanied with foot-travel, pushed the sequence of events along. In mid-afternoon, Joseph went to Jerusalem and negotiated permission from Pilate for the corpse.

Second... Pilate needed confirmation that Jesus was dead. This required the summons of the centurion from the crucifixion site at Golgotha to confirm death had indeed taken the Crucified One. (Mark 15:44-45) Once this military official with first-hand knowledge delivered it to Pilate, Joseph responded accordingly.

Roman soldiers would have had the responsibility to remove the body from the cross, the first to touch the corpse. Nevertheless, two gospel writers, Mark and Luke, make a clear distinction Joseph took the body down. Somehow, someway, he had active involvement which solidifies first-hand participation. A centurion present at the crucifixion had a revelation about the dying Christ, and may have granted compassionate permission to assist at the ground level. (Matthew 27:54; Luke 23:47)

Prior to the crucifixion, and for himself, Joseph had a burial site hewn out of stone and fully prepared in a garden. (Matthew 27:57-61) Being a wealthy and prominent man, he would have given special attention to the new sepulcher in a select place. Undoubtedly it had more than one burial shelf; some probably with a raised headrest also. A virgin tomb, not inhabited by any other corpse would have been at a premium. Multiple bodies often were clustered together for burial. The Israelites did not use coffins.

The available tomb near the crucifixion site made transporting the body easier than some other location might have provided. Customary procedure consigned burial outside the city limit. Only the respected and highly honored, such as King David had distinction for burial inside the city of Jerusalem. Joseph's sepulcher in the garden offered a practical and dignified final resting place for Jesus of Nazareth.

Third… The burial procedure required a linen cloth and embalming spices. Joseph, accompanied by Nicodemus, joined in partnership during the crisis. Only John's gospel mentions Nicodemus' participation. He gives indication that Joseph and Nicodemus devised a plan that kept pace with rapidly moving events on the timeline. Before nightfall they removed Christ's body from the crucifixion site; sharing and fulfilling the responsibilities for the burial. Nothing recorded in the gospels of a brier used; nor anyone else named who might have assisted in transferring Jesus. These two became the compassionate pallbearers.

Coming in secret at night early-on in Jesus' itinerant ministry, Nicodemus, a Pharisee, became a follower of Jesus. (John 3:1-21) He had received specific instruction about natural birth versus spiritual birth. This disciple becomes instrumental in dealing with death in the blood-stained and nail-scarred presence of the Crucified One. Again, first-hand, Nicodemus, will learn a spiritual distinction now between womb and tomb.

Nicodemus was not the only secret disciple. Others, along with him and Joseph of Arimathea, had been members of this incognito religious grouping. (John 12:42) Nevertheless, these two specific men as believers and out-of-sight followers of Christ took a bold and open stance on a sad, but historic day.

The body was naked not only as a symbol of shame; but also Roman protocol for a crucifixion. Immediate removal from the cross would mandate covering Him. Those everyday clothes that Jesus had been wearing when arrested were tattered and torn.

An alternative solution evolved to remedy the need for cloth to wrap the body of Jesus in preparation for removal from Golgotha in order to transport Him to the sepulcher in a nearby garden. The God-given lot fell to Joseph of Arimathea.

Fourth... While in Jerusalem and in the timeframe when Joseph was negotiating with Pilate, he probably bought some linen cloth. Waiting for the centurion's travel to Pilate, Joseph had time to steal-away moments in the marketplace. (Mark 15:46) The clean cloth used to wrap the corpse after the immediate removal from the rugged wooden cross was the wealthy man's second tangible gift. No polyester or cotton here. No wool either, even though Jerusalem and surrounding villages had shepherds. Wool was taboo for burial clothes. Only fine linen held the place of material choice.

They would not have stood at the base of the cross tearing a white linen cloth into strips. Therefore, likely two linen cloths were used in the burial preparation. Or one large solid piece first torn into two sections. Maybe exact, possibly not. One half used at the foot of the cross. Later, the other torn into strips for the procedure. One strip after another wrapped around the corpse produced folds into which the embalming spices were packed.

Lots of material, pure white to start. Remaining that way would have been a challenge. No table at the crucifixion site. On the ground just rocks, dirt and whatever else the earth offered. Inside the tomb, perhaps a cleaner surface for preparations.

Nicodemus, meeting up with Joseph, brought a mixture of myrrh and aloes weighing seventy-five pounds. (John19:39) Inside the tomb at the sepulcher site, in privacy, the two men wrapped the body of Christ along with the spices in strips of linen torn in accordance with Jewish burial customs.

Fifth... Joseph rolled a big stone across the entrance to the tomb. How large depends whether he had assistance from Nicodemus. Effective ways could be devised when chiseling the entrance of a potential tomb, for the moving, shoving, or rolling of the stone as a tomb closure. Being a wealthy man Joseph probably had spared no expense to provide the best possible means for closing a tomb.

The physical stature and endurance of these two men requires them to have been able to manage the weight of a dead male body, a seventy-five pound mixture of spices made specific for burial purposes, and a big stone. Mandated by time, swiftness of foot-travel sapped energy. These two hours had been labor intensive. Emotionally drained, their fear dissolved, replaced with self-esteem drawn from true character. They believed they provided Jesus of Nazareth's final resting place. Inside the tomb, however one wants to imagine it, drab or stone elegant, death prevailed.

2
Respectful Mourning

When Joseph left the burial site, Mary Magdalene and the "other Mary" were sitting in the garden opposite the tomb. No folding lawn chairs; just large stones, or stone ledges, or the ground served as seating. No guard stationed nearby at this point either. The female counterparts, to the Joseph and Nicodemus male partnership, were finally alone. The males had exited the scene separately, because the focus seems placed upon Joseph's departure. Perhaps Nicodemus waited at the entrance of the garden and then accompanied Joseph back to Jerusalem.

This location of the women seems indicative of privacy granted to the naked Christ's initial preparation for burial. Also, not having physical contact with the corpse allowed them to participate in the impending Jewish feasts. Grief has left them immobile as they sit stationary in the fading daylight like two statues carefully placed in a garden.

When these two women are named in the burial passages, both a geographical and universal understanding verifies Mary Magdalene, from Magdala, the region of central Galilee. She was the female from whom seven demons were cast during the Lord's itinerant ministry. (Mark 16:9)

The "other Mary" could be one of several women. Many females followed Jesus from Galilee. They met His daily financial needs and those of His disciples throughout their travels.

Mary, a common name or derivative of other names, allows an uncertainty of the person. The word "other" prefixes the name of Mary in Matthew's gospel twice; once each in burial and Resurrection scenes. A Jew, writing to Jews, and the only gospel writer who makes reference to the "other Mary" by closing chapter twenty-seven, and opening chapter twenty-eight with this distinction. (Matthew 27:61; 28:1)

A verse in Matthew 27:56 tells of Mary, the mother of James and Joses, watching the crucifixion with the women from Galilee. These sons, James and Joses, had a father named Alphaeus. A name tag for the son, James, called the younger or the little, became an important identity extension for his name. A distinct setting apart as being younger than James, the brother of John, (sons of Zebedee and Salome), because both James were in the Lord's band of Twelve disciples.

Alphaeus, their father, had a double reference in name too, known as Cleopas. Adding to this complexity, his name Cleopas is spelled three ways in Scripture: Cleopas, Cloas and Clophas. (Luke 24:18)

However, Mark says, Mary the mother of Joses. This parallels Matthew's crucifixion observance, because one does not always refer to all siblings when calling a parent in the family by name.

Early in his gospel, the Apostle John incorporates specific data like Mary as the wife of Cleopas and her being a sister of the mother of Jesus. (John 19:25) Important to note also... an additional and influential scene has this "other Mary" and Mary Magdalene being two witnesses, to the transfer of responsibility at the crucifixion site, by Jesus, for His mother to John's permanent care. (John 19:26-27)

Nonetheless, the topic of the "other Mary" will be revisited later and brought to the forefront again in the Resurrection scenes.

3
Twelve Are Missing

Early in His ministry, Jesus of Nazareth chose Twelve disciples from all of those who followed His teachings; whom He later called apostles. He gave them authority to preach, and power to drive out evil spirits, and to heal every disease and sickness.

In Matthew 10:1-4, they are listed as:
"Simon (who is called Peter) and his brother Andrew;
James son of Zebedee, and his brother John;
Philip and Bartholomew;
Thomas and Matthew the tax collector;
James son of Alphaeus, and Thaddaeus;
Simon the Zealot and Judas Iscariot, who betrayed him."

Additional information for clarification:
Simon, aka Cephas; aka the rock; aka son of John (Jonah);
Andrew, aka Simon Peter's brother;
James and John, aka Boanerges / Sons of Thunder;
Philip, (no other personal name in Scripture);
Bartholomew, aka Nathanael;
Thomas, aka Didymus (the twin);
Matthew, aka Levi;
James, aka James the younger; aka the little;
Thaddaeus, aka Lebbeus; aka Judas son of James;
Simon, aka the Canaanite;
Judas Iscariot, aka son of Simon Iscariot.

The names above are the original Twelve. The gospel writers also used the numbers Eleven and Ten. (Matthew 20:24; Mark 10: 41) However, when the writers in the Bible used the numerical Twelve in what might seem out of context, or appears no longer applicable in totality, their probable intent was to distinguish the Twelve from other disciples in situations on the timeline.

Where were these Twelve in the immediate timeframe following the death of Jesus on the cross? Actually, Eleven. Judas Iscariot had completed suicide before the crucifixion because of being overtaken by guilt for having betrayed Jesus of Nazareth to the elders of the people and the chief priests. (Matthew 27:1-5)

The beloved disciple, John, had been assigned a son's duties to take care of Mary, the mother of Jesus, as his own. (John 19:26-27) This charge given by Jesus during the crucifixion and accepted by John would allow genuine dismissal from attending to the body of Jesus at the conclusion of the crucifixion. Domestic arrangements were first on the agenda because from that day forward Mary went to John's residence. Not likely in Galilee at the moment, but nearby in John's father's residence; wealthy Zebedee's second home located somewhere in the Jerusalem area.

Jesus' six half-siblings were not followers of Him on this immediate timeline. (Matthew 13:55-56; Mark 3:20-21; John 7:5) Those half-sibling brothers were: James, Joseph, Simon, and Judas; plus at least two half-sibling sisters who remain unnamed in Scripture. (However in Acts 1:14, it appears Luke writes the brothers were in the upper room at Pentecost; as the Resurrection must have created a dramatic change in their belief about Jesus.)

Silence cloaks the whereabouts of the remaining Ten disciples, from the chosen Twelve. They ignored compassion and responsibility because of their fear of the Jews. Jewish burial custom should have produced an entourage of people which included these disciples following the body of the deceased to the tomb. This official practice involved wailing mourners, sometimes even hired to signify extraordinary grief surrounding the death and the importance of the deceased loved one. Not so in the entombment of Jesus. Fear of man overruled love and social responsibility because of the looming and threatening repercussions from the current religious and political systems.

Fear drives one either into a fight pattern towards truth, or a flight pattern that feigns comfort and peace. The disciple's emotions were ruled by unbelief, fear, and grief. They lacked what should have been a healthy fear of God coupled with a reverent respect of Him to challenge and guide each of them. Instead they were disillusioned. After the crucifixion His disciples fled, when they should have led.

4
Religious And Political Reflections

Following the first process of preparation for the burial attended to by Joseph and Nicodemus, Pilate's involvement continued beyond the day of crucifixion. Distinguished visitors came to Pilate, namely the chief priests and the Pharisees. Matthew's writing chronicles the initial steps for the setting up of a plot to unfold later.

The Guard at the Tomb
Matthew 27:62-66

Reading the above Scripture reveals this feast day brought more than worship on the part of the Pharisees as they approached Pilate on the Feast of Unleavened Bread. They briefed the Roman governor on their concerns that the Deceiver, now buried, had declared earlier He would rise again. Furthermore, they believed His followers would steal the body; thus maintaining a Resurrection had indeed happened.

Due to Pilate's culpability in agreeing to have Jesus crucified and as governor of Judea he appeased them and ordered that the tomb be secured at least until the third-day prophecy was beyond fulfillment. (Matthew 27:64) The guard would sustain the serenity and stillness of death at the sepulcher. A seal was put on the stone along with the soldiers being posted. That official procedure would provide sustaining evidence of any unwanted or unlawful entry. If anyone entered the guards would be aware of it.

Like the military procedure at a crucifixion, a guard consisting of four or five men including a centurion would take position in the garden near the tomb. These Roman soldiers had jurisdiction, authority and capability to carry out their assigned task. Nevertheless, Pilate and the guard would soon learn that the best of their intentions could not be laid to rest no matter how secure the stone appeared.

Section Two

The Resurrection Story Told

5
The Gospel Writers

The thoughts and words of the four gospel writers are pertinent to the Resurrection story. Their individual purposes too.

Matthew simply wants the reader to know a Resurrection took place. The gospel writer deals less with the Resurrection in and of itself, but strives to convey truth by giving the reader a perspective through a focused window on the religious and political systems.

Mark wrote the first of the four gospels included in the New Testament. Chronicled in his Resurrection passages he informs the reader Mary Magdalene was the first to see, to eventually recognize, and to communicate with the risen Christ. (Note: these verses, Mark 16:9-11, are believed by some theologians to have been added as a latter section of Mark's work. Referenced and used here as the complete work of Mark because they are included in the canon of Scripture... The Holy Bible.)

Luke starts with a stoic scene where the women entered the empty, silent tomb. He writes of sudden activity; and later alludes to a vision of angels, thus providing another window into the Resurrection through his gospel.

John opens by setting the drama as if only four human characters were on the stage. He eliminates mentioning all humans except Mary Magdalene, Peter, and himself; plus the Son of Man (aka Son of God... the Eternal One, the Lord Jesus Christ).

Important to document at this junction is the sequence of how the writers wrote and the suggested timeline of their manuscripts. As for these four books in the New Testament the accuracy for the timeframe of the dates has been speculation by theologians; but here "approximate dates" used are: Mark, 60 A.D., the earliest of the four to set the information in writing. Matthew and Luke followed later, 65-75 A.D., gleaning some information on their own, but they pulled documentation from Mark's gospel too. John wrote his gospel to the Church later, approximately 80 A.D.

Matthew was a disciple, one of the Twelve, known previously as Levi the tax collector, when Jesus called him. Mark, the younger of the four writers, had a solid Jewish upbringing and was a wholehearted follower of Jesus even though not one of the Twelve. Luke, a physician, traveled with the Apostle Paul during the early missionary beginnings of the fledgling New Testament Church as it flourished in fruitfulness and spiritual power. However, Luke was not an eyewitness of Christ; therefore never hearing His teachings first-hand. John, a former fisherman, became one of the Apostles like Mathew. Though exiled on the Island of Patmos off the coast of Greece in his later years, John's love for and devotion to Christ continued to develop further in faithfulness for decades.

Each gospel writer approaches the Resurrection giving different pertinent facts and conveys descriptions necessary to invite the reader into their scenes. Nonetheless, one thing about the post Resurrection remains clear. The mood and mode... He is risen! Christ appears, disappears and reappears numerous times after His initial Resurrection.

6
Wrapped In Duty

The reader becomes reacquainted with Mary Magdalene and the "other Mary" plus those additional named and unnamed women when they go to the tomb on Sunday morning. They are connected to the events at the Resurrection scene out of love and a sense of duty. This same motivation caused them previously to follow Jesus throughout His itinerant journeys in Israel.

These women "bought" the spices likely on Friday morning (having followed the timeline of feast restrictions for the Convocations); in preparation for the burial anointing of the corpse of Jesus early on Sunday morning. Therefore, Wednesday (fourteenth) and Thursday (fifteenth) would have been on the Jewish timeline of no financial transactions on a holy day. Later, the women "prepared" those spices and perfumes on Friday (sixteenth) before sunset and rested on the Saturday Sabbath (seventeenth). (Luke 23:56) They had the spices and perfumes with them when they went to the tomb on Sunday (eighteenth) morning.

A reader of Scripture gleans information from Mark that these individuals who "purchased" the spices were Mary Magdalene, Mary the mother of James, and Salome. Luke tells the reader the women were Mary Magdalene, Mary the mother of James, Joanna, and the others. Joanna appears to now step into Salome's responsibility for some reason. Did she prepare a specific type of spice? Four females are named so far who bought and prepared. The "others" Luke refers to are forever left unnamed. However, the numbered is at least six. Before dismissing the number count, perhaps the "two" others were young female servants from Zebedee's residence who carried the spices.

Too late for these Jewish women to be involved in the purchase on Wednesday (fourteenth) afternoon because of Passover day. (The crucifixion and the entombment had taken place that afternoon). Allowing one exception to this purchase timeline might be Joanna's ability to go to the marketplace. If so, money could have exchanged hands between the two Marys and Salome which gives credit to the three of them having bought the spices. (Mark 16:1) Perhaps Salome passed the money to Joanna who actually purchased. Not farfetched. Lots of restrictions and traditions involved.

A special Sabbath... the holy day of Passover ended on Wednesday (fourteenth) sunset. As assigned on the Jewish calendar that season... the three Convocations, the Lord's Passover (fourteenth); then the Feast of Unleavened Bread on Thursday (fifteenth) started at sunset as previously discussed... but not the upcoming Saturday Sabbath at this point.

After the Saturday Sabbath, at "dawn" on the first day of the week, Mary Magdalene and the "other Mary" went to look at the tomb. Only two? This proves to be a purposeful and distinct setting apart in Matthew's gospel. Why? Were they interested in confirming the rumor-fact-fiction-tales about the sealed tomb? Or... to affirm they remembered the correct location in the garden? Did they go to determine if they needed additional female assistance to remove the stone? Did they know about the guards? If so, would the soldiers be helpful?

Out of curiosity, or because of the possibility of an actual "earthquake" rumbling on the ground under their feet earlier, did this duo set out on a head-start? (Matthew 28:1-2) Fear may have caused them to keep their distance. Due to the semi-camouflage of darkness they could not see anything out of the ordinary. Or did they hear the awakened guard of soldiers ahead in the distance? Uncertain and edgy in mind and heart, perhaps they start back toward the city.

What if by chance, they halt and encountered the other two women (Salome and Joanna) who were attempting to catch up to them? Perhaps in the stillness of the diminishing nighttime, voices had echoed softly behind them. Collectively the four and two unnamed others continued on as if this truly were the first trip to the tomb. Speculation only, but it helps to evaluate apparent inconsistencies where some women are named, and others not.

While on their way to the tomb just "after" sunrise, they began questioning each other about who will roll the stone away from the entrance of the tomb. (Mark 16:2-3) Why at this point on their task-oriented journey that question comes up remains mysterious. Two women could not roll the big stone; but four would have a better collective strength that would allow them to go ahead with their anointing task. A stone at the entrance would have been a familiar custom. Sealed and guarded, on the other hand, not common.

7
Serving In Love

Before moving into the sequence and characters involved in the seven scenes related to the Resurrection in the garden, the women by name, discussed in the previous chapter, should be further identified both from the four gospel accounts and their presence at the tomb. Identification and timing are crucial for an attempt at chronological proof. In the New Testament a reader gleans a brief cameo of four of the six.

Mary Magdalene's presence is acknowledged and it is she who seems to head the lists. Before this subject is broached, John's record needs to be looked at for any significant details. The beloved disciple, John, leads the reader to believe Mary Magdalene was the only female of importance to initially see the astonishing scene at the empty tomb. This gospel writer states it was still "dark" that Sunday morning. Did she start out at first to mourn alone? How early had she gone there? How many trips did she make on Sunday morning? Was it more than one?

Mary, the mother of James and Joses, and wife of Cleopas, bears repetition thus placing her second in the grouping. She is the "other Mary" and the identity marker Matthew uses to set her apart from some women also named Mary in the New Testament. It was her husband, Cleopas, and his companion, who later experienced a post Resurrection appearance of Jesus on the Emmaus Road. (Luke 24:13-32)

Next, mentioned once each are: Salome, by Mark; and Joanna, by Luke.

Salome, is well-known as the wife of Zebedee and the mother of their sons, James and John. She places third on the list. The three males from her household owned and actively pursued the fishing industry for their livelihood until Jesus called the two sons to be His disciples. They lived as a family near Capernaum, not far from Bethsaida where their fishing partners Peter and Andrew resided, on the coastal northern part of the Sea of Galilee. (Mark 1:16)

Joanna, the wife of Cuza, the manager of King Herod's household in the region of Galilee, had received a healing from some disease in the presence of Jesus, the healer. (Luke 8:1-3) By name, she would be considered fourth on a compiled list. Her involvement with Jesus must have produced unsettling political entanglements for her spouse because of his professional position. Perhaps not an Israelite, but a Roman woman (heritage) and the reason she "purchased and prepared" spices; because she had no Jewish Saturday Sabbath to honor.

Luke complicates the process by writing "others." Even if he mentally included Salome; others being plural, still leans toward a count of six. There are four named women.

Does this list come in a neatly wrapped package? Actually, no. The bow is not there yet. The mystery needs to be explored further if six is the number of attending females; by names or indirect association.

Mary of Bethany holds no place of prominence at the crucifixion, burial and Resurrection. Does it not seem strange? She, the person who sat at Jesus' feet, thirsting after and drinking in His teachings of the kingdom of God; and who also anointed His feet for burial prior to His being sentenced to death by crucifixion. (John 12:1-8)

She had been the first authentic believer of Christ's impending death, documented by her anointing procedure. This same female had experienced first-hand the resurrection of her brother, Lazarus, through the power of the Lord Jesus Christ. Could she be the "other

Mary?" Probably not. Her signature title, Mary of Bethany, lacks its distinct prominence here. Her valued revelation and honorable participation came pre crucifixion. Leaving for her a lasting memorial of her love for Christ who had become their family friend. Through spiritual perception and revelation she knew Jesus would die, but appears to have had an abiding faith and belief in His well-defined and proclaimed future Resurrection.

Mary, the mother of Jesus, remains isolated from public view. Secluded in John's protection she mourns the loss of her son, the Son of God / Son of Man. This pattern of mourning was normal for the culture. Could it be she, who is the "other Mary?" Not likely, because her signature title of distinction, mother, would certainly apply. On the one hand, Matthew's avoidance to name, could be considered a specific, or speculative neglect of reference to her. On the other hand, maybe respect is given to her wish to remain unnamed because she desired to escape isolated mourning protocol by slipping away to the tomb with Mary Magdalene. Not wanting anyone to know, including John, that she had been there. Restless and not able to sleep, did she need to be near her deceased son for comfort? Unlikely, but in probing the subject of these six women various options need to be contemplated.

Mary, the mother of John Mark, becomes well-known in the early Church. Her son, John Mark, is Mark, the gospel writer. As for her, Mark himself makes a clear distinction in his writing about Mary, the mother of James and Joses. His purpose? To clarify the female is not his own mother. If the "other Mary" is Mark's mother, then for whatever reason Matthew, too, chooses to classify her with this simple, but preferential distinction of "other." Again, not likely.

Mary, of Rome, is the final Mary referenced in the New Testament. This woman resided in Rome at the time of the early Christian Church and many years after the Resurrection of Jesus. Unlikely the "other Mary" because the timeline does not fit.

These options needed explored to learn why apparent inconsistencies exist. The writers tell bits and pieces of the Resurrection story, but not necessarily in exact order because the four distinct individual accounts were written for different purposes and times.

A flashback to the closing scene of the burial proves valuable as a chronology becomes established. Immediately after the burial, Mary Magdalene and the "other Mary" sat outside the tomb with a big stone closure covering the entrance; placed by Joseph of Arimathea (and Nicodemus). No guard present.

Fast forward. On the timeline... Jerusalem had swelled with hundreds of God-fearing Jews, a great crowd, who had come for the feasts. (John 12:12) Word spreads about a guard being posted and the stone sealed. The seasonal gathering of families and pilgrims for the cluster of three holy Convocations... the Lord's Passover, the Feast of Unleavened Bread, and the Feast of Firstfruits, provided ample opportunity for words of truth and speculative rumors to evolve about the sealed tomb.

Truth-fact-fiction-tales become blurred. When in crises, people stay up at night. Families cluster. Tears flow. Communication falters. Silence can often muffle love, admiration, and trust. Or... allow denial, anger, and fear, an opportunity to fester.

By the time the gospel writers introduce the reader to the women a couple days later on Sunday at the tomb, they are there to "look." (Matthew 28:1) What have they come to see? Reaffirm memory of tomb location in the garden?

Will guards really be present? Will the anointing for burial be delayed? More important, who will roll that stone away? Could they count on the Roman guards to assist this one time for final Jewish burial preparations? Did these thoughts loom foremost in the minds of the women?

8
Resurrection Scriptures

The order of the tomb scenes in the Resurrection passages in the New Testament begins at specific chapters in the gospels: Matthew 28; Mark 16; Luke 24; John 20. The verses in the Bible continue to the conclusion of each writer's book. John's gospel has an additional chapter covering a later post Resurrection appearance of Jesus.

In God's sovereign plan, as in one's daily life, rehearsals are non existent. The same was true for His Son's mission throughout the land of Israel. Also true of those first moments and early morning hours immediately following the Resurrection. The supernatural production unfolding on the garden stage left no time for a dress rehearsal.

From all indication, the four gospel writers try to expound on multiple events and experiences in the garden at the tomb as the predominate location. When humans engage in storytelling, starts and stops, even lines of conversation, take the listener around corners which crisscross paths throughout the message conveyed.

To complicate matters, to be immersed in the framework of an "eternal" existence, one experiences events as if happening all at once. An important truth! In readingthe gospel accounts of the Resurrection, this eternal power of God breaking into the earthly existence of human beings… produces in writing what could appear to be inconsistencies. This type of Spirit breakthrough is new to the disciples; and still unfamiliar to the reader in the twenty-first century. Simultaneous, thus making chronology somewhat difficult to explain through events because of eternal boundary lines. As in Matthew's account, Chapter 28:2-4. (More on this later.)

Toss in vision too, as stated in Luke 24:23; one might have another level of revelation. Visions see into the eternal side as if crossing over, while leaving the person stationed on the earthly side. When referring to the angels at the sepulcher in the garden one must attempt to reconcile how the power of God interacted with humanity through the angelic beings in the various scenes.

The following Scripture selections tell of the supernatural phenomenon unfolding at the Resurrection on the first day of the week... Sunday, Resurrection Morning:

The Resurrection
Matthew 28:1-11

The Resurrection
Mark 16:1-11

The Resurrection
Luke 24:1-12

The Resurrection
John 20:1-18

Another important sequence surfaces concerning the actual time-of-day for the departure to and the arrival of the women who went to the tomb. Inconsistency appears to spring forth. Going step-by-step what are the gospel writers conveying... with their timeline in the sky?

How light was it? Below is the phrase each gospel writer uses to describe the time of day:

John's reference... early while still dark
   Matthew's reference... at dawn
      Mark's reference... very early after sunrise
         Luke's reference... very early in the morning

The five words below and their practical definitions, alert a reader to potential and useful information.

Dark... entirely without light; almost black; night
Dawn... the time in the morning that light first appears, when daybreak slowly begins
Sunrise... the appearance and time the sun rises above the eastern horizon
Sunset... the disappearance and time the sun sets (dusk) below the western horizon
Twilight... the subdued light just after sunset (or sometimes just before sunrise); often called the period of sunset to dark; a gradual decline of light; as the day fades before the dark of night

Therefore the timelines of sunset and twilight written above can be eliminated as not relevant to the garden scene at the tomb. Or are they? Remember how the Jews defined a 24 hour day... from sunset one day to sunset the next day. When the gospel writers are talking about the timeline, one might be suggesting any time in-between.

As for daybreak... the first glimpse of daylight actually would be different in the four seasons. This would include twilight often mentioned in Scripture verses throughout the Bible.

(Note: Anyone reading the above timeline in the twenty-first century has the ability to notice on a clear night, an hour before sunrise, dawn's light starts to break forth on the eastern horizon.)

Looking at each writer again, a thoughtful consideration for a conclusion follows:

John is specific; the time is early while still dark.
Matthew is specific; the time is dawn implying darkness transitioning to daybreak.
Mark is specific; very early after sunrise.
Luke is specific; very early in the morning.

What might one conclude from these references? Importance related to who (women) and when (time) their journey began. Are these times closer to arrival at the tomb or departure times from residences? If the latter, did one woman go to another's house and the times correspond to whomever in the group is the final person to join-in thus setting a departure time. These variations leave space once again that the women came in two or more groups. Or even that Mary Magdalene made more than one trip. Nevertheless the entire garden scene unfolded on Sunday in the early morning hours.

9
Four Writers, One Story

The four gospel writers proclaim the Resurrection story. Factual, but neither chronological with one another, nor intended to be. Fragmented segments of the Resurrection at the tomb come forth as each tells his story. However, the way opens for potential mental and spiritual fill-in portions to unfold.

They recorded what was appropriate for their reading audience and at the time of setting the information in writing. Again, Mark wrote first, then Matthew and Luke, and finally, John.

Since no one really knows for sure, let's suppose the reader in the twenty-first century can glean important bits and pieces from what appears as either inconsistencies or discrepancies. Such as those angels; here, there, everywhere. Sitting. Standing. Only once alluded to as walking... the angel who rolled the stone away. How many? One? Two? Five? A possible count of seven, if no repeat appearances.

A rather simplistic chronology can unfold through a valid, but provocative step. Nonetheless, this procedure needs to be incorporated and explored here before one gleans a purposeful understanding of the seven post Resurrection scenes at the tomb.

How can one do that process? If each of the Resurrection passages of Scripture are typed, with the author's name along with chapter and verse; then clipped apart and arranged as a whole unit, an insightful opportunity presents itself. When placed in a possible sequential order the result gives a simplistic look into a practical perspective on chronology.

Obviously, no one knows for sure, but given the potential format described in the paragraph above, along with a sincere attempt to clear up pesky questions in interpretation, the result gives a valuable methodology. There may be objections to this idea and procedure, but Christians are taught, instructed, and admonished to look at the whole council of the Word of God. (2 Timothy 3:16-17) This should include these seven Resurrection scenes as a unit. Therefore the important passages need to be meshed together for an essential and valid earthly timeline.

The passages in their entirety are from: Matthew 28:1-11; Mark 16:1-11; Luke 24:1-12; and John 20:1-18. This chapter, shows how the gospels might look verse by verse as they are interwoven into a possible sequence. One soon realizes there are repeats in some places when listed, but keeping all fifty-two verses together from the four gospels takes priority for Scriptural continuity.

There are seven scenes at the tomb. A time lapse (obedient interruption), takes place between scene four and scene five when the women leave (run) to tell the disciples Christ is risen! Also incorporated here for reading continuity are "preliminary and concluding events" acting as bookends which round out the information from beginning to end. The following probable divisions reveal how it unfolded according to the four gospel writers:

Preliminary Events

Initial events before and during the women's preliminary preparations to purchase and prepare the spices for burial; along with their journey to the tomb which recognizes a morning departure timeline on Sunday, the day of the Lord's Resurrection.

Mark 16:1
When the Sabbath was over, Mary Magdalene, Mary the mother of James, and Salome bought spices so that they might go to anoint Jesus' body.

Matthew 28:1
After the Sabbath, at dawn on the first day of the week, Mary Magdalene and the other Mary went to look at the tomb.

Luke 24:1
On the first day of the week, very early in the morning, the women took the spices they had prepared and went to the tomb.

Sepulcher - Scene One
One Angel Sitting Outside

Matthew 28:2-4
There was a violent earthquake, for an angel of the Lord came down from heaven and, going to the tomb, rolled back the stone and sat on it. His appearance was like lightning, and his clothes were white as snow. The guards were so afraid of him that they shook and became like dead men.

Sepulcher - Scene Two
One Angel Sitting Outside

John 20:1
Early on the first day of the week, while it was still dark, Mary Magdalene went to the tomb and saw that the stone had been removed from the entrance.

Mark 16:2-4
Very early on the first day of the week, just after sunrise, they were on their way to the tomb and they asked each other, "Who will roll the

stone away from the entrance of the tomb?" But when they looked up, they saw that the stone, which was very large, had been rolled away.

Matthew 28:5-6
The angel said to the women, "Do not be afraid, for I know that you are looking for Jesus, who was crucified. He is not here; he has risen, just as he said. Come and see the place where he lay."

Sepulcher - Scene Three
Young Man (Angel) Sitting Inside

Luke 24:2-3
They found the stone rolled away from the tomb, but when they entered, they did not find the body of the Lord Jesus.

Mark 16:5-6
As they entered the tomb, they saw a young man dressed in a white robe sitting on the right side, and they were alarmed. "Don't be alarmed," he said. "You are looking for Jesus the Nazarene, who was crucified. He has risen! He is not here. See the place where they laid him."

Sepulcher - Scene Four
Two Men (Angels) Standing Inside

Luke 24:4-8
While they were wondering about this, suddenly two men in clothes that gleamed like lightning stood beside them. In their fright the women bowed down with their faces to the ground, but the men said to them, "Why do you look for the living among the dead? He is not here; he has risen! Remember how he told you, while he was still with you in Galilee: The Son of Man must be delivered into the hands of sinful men, be crucified and on the third day be raised again." Then they remembered his words.

Matthew 28:7

Then go quickly and tell his disciples: "He has risen from the dead and is going ahead of you into Galilee. There you will see him. Now I have told you."

Mark 16:7

But go, tell his disciples and Peter, "He is going ahead of you into Galilee. There you will see him, just as he told you."

Obedient Interruption
No Nonsense At The Tomb

Mark 16:8

Trembling and bewildered, the women went out and fled from the tomb. They said nothing to anyone, because they were afraid.

Matthew 28:8

So the women hurried away from the tomb, afraid yet filled with joy, and ran to tell his disciples.

Luke 24:9-11

When they came back from the tomb, they told all these things to the Eleven and to all the others. It was Mary Magdalene, Joanna, Mary the mother of James, and the others with them who told this to the apostles. But they did not believe the women, because their words seemed to them like nonsense.

John 20:2

So she came running to Simon Peter and the other disciple, the one Jesus loved, and said, "They have taken the Lord out of the tomb, and we don't know where they have put him!"

Sepulcher - Scene Five
Race To Believe

Luke 24:12

Peter, however, got up and ran to the tomb. Bending over, he saw strips of linen lying by themselves, and he went away, wondering to himself what had happened.

John 20:3-10

So Peter and the other disciple started for the tomb. Both were running, but the other disciple outran Peter and reached the tomb first. He bent over and looked in at the strips of linen lying there but did not go in. Then Simon Peter, who was behind him, arrived and went into the tomb. He saw the strips of linen lying there, as well as the burial cloth that had been around Jesus' head. The cloth was folded up by itself, separate from the linen. Finally the other disciple, who had reached the tomb first, also went inside. He saw and believed. They still did not understand from Scripture that Jesus had to rise from the dead. Then the disciples went back to their homes.

Sepulcher - Scene Six
Two Angels Sitting Inside

John 20:11-13

...but Mary stood outside the tomb crying. As she wept, she bent over to look into the tomb and saw two angels in white, seated where Jesus' body had been, one at the head and the other at the foot. They asked her, "Woman, why are you crying?" "They have taken my Lord away," she said, "and I don't know where they have put him."

Sepulcher - Scene Seven
Christophany - Lord Jesus Christ Standing Outside

John 20:14-17

At this, she turned around and saw Jesus standing there, but she did not realize that it was Jesus. "Woman," he said, "why are you crying? Who is it you are looking for?" Thinking he was the gardener, she said, "Sir, if you have carried him away, tell me where you have put him, and I will get him." Jesus said to her, "Mary." She turned toward him and cried out in Aramaic, "Rabboni!" (which means Teacher). Jesus said, "Do not hold on to me, for I have not yet returned to the Father. Go instead to my brothers and tell them, 'I am returning to my Father and your Father, to my God and your God.'"

Mark 16:9

When Jesus rose early on the first day of the week, he appeared first to Mary Magdalene, out of whom he had driven seven demons.

Concluding Events

The events after the Lord Jesus Christ appeared (Christophany) at the empty tomb when He gave the command and commission to Mary Magdalene.

Mark 16:10-11

She went and told those who had been with him and who were mourning and weeping. When they heard that Jesus was alive and that she had seen him, they did not believe it.

John 20:18

Mary Magdalene went to the disciples with the news: "I have seen the Lord!" And she told them that he had said these things to her.

Matthew 28:9-11

Suddenly Jesus met them. "Greetings," he said. They came to him, clasped his feet and worshiped him. Then Jesus said to them, "Do not be afraid. Go and tell my brothers to go to Galilee; there they will see me." While the women were on their way, some of the guards went into the city and reported to the chief priests everything that had happened.

10
Camouflage Timeline

Was the crucifixion on Friday? Neither Scripture in general, nor the four gospel writers give a precise statement to Friday as the crucifixion day of Christ. In contrast, a clear distinction is given to the first day of the week for Jesus' Resurrection which was Sunday. (Luke 24:1; John 20:1) Friday, was the sixth day; before the Saturday Sabbath, the seventh, and last day of the Jewish week. Therefore, it cannot fulfill the prophetic deceased timeframe of Jesus even though labeled and called Good Friday by Christians several centuries later.

Exploring theological controversies should not be threatening to foundational Christian tenets of faith. It would be amiss at this juncture to ignore taking one of those controversial side trips centered on Good Friday. Key are Christ's own words.

Remember three days and three nights, the precise pre crucifixion declaration from Jesus. The Word of the Lord is flawless; then, now, and forever. (Psalm 18:30) Jesus always spoke truth; therefore, His prophetic timeline of three twenty-four hour cycles necessitates exploration. When the Pharisees, in confrontational mode, asked Jesus early in His ministry for a miraculous sign He said, "...the Son of Man will be three days and three nights in the heart of the earth" (Matthew 12:40). Later, in an explanation to His own disciples, Jesus stated that He, "...must be killed and on the third day be raised to life" (Luke 9:22).

Simple enough? Maybe not. Was it clear? It was to the Jews in that century. They had a complete concept of the timeframe because the Convocation practices of the Feasts of the Lord gave impeccable boundaries in the Torah, the first five books of Moses writings in the Hebrew Bible. (Exodus 12:1-30; Leviticus 23:1-14; Numbers 28:16-31)

When reading the four gospels, and about the times and events of the Passion week of Jesus and His being in the heart of the earth three days and three nights between His death and His Resurrection; a Friday calculation as the crucifixion day, and the first day of the week being Resurrection Sunday, does not fit into a practical and reasonable time slot together.

Theologians, scholars, and students of the Bible… including Jewish and Gentile, vigorously debate their views about these days in the Lord's Passion week. Even in large and small study groups they cannot agree. What does that mean overall? Why does it matter? In truth, they do not know the chronology timeline; and sometimes fess up to that fact in humility too.

In fairness, a few thoughts in relationship to those who attempt with sincerity to have a starting point for accuracy. They have to deal with moving targets which are allusive free-floating variables; there are several leap years in a generation, lunar adjustments, and no Passovers on Thursdays.

The theory as to which day of the week the Lord died becomes complicated through language interpretations such as Aramaic, Latin, and Greek. Add in traditions, rituals, cultural practices, and legalistic restrictions centered around days of the week causes various events to fluctuate too.

Puzzle pieces, used as signposts, in locked-step formation when selected as an initial timeline date "move forward" for a systematic premise. Some calculated choices within different timelines have virtue for accuracy; others not so much. Many chronology insights promote one or more views.

To declare error-poof strategy, along with theological correctness, and chronological perfection, would be difficult in methodology to pin-point in exactness. Chronology remains all over a range of possibilities; hence the title of this chapter… Camouflage Timeline.

Readers who go to Scripture for personal comfort, intellectual understanding, and spiritual revelation of Jesus' life as the Son of God / Son of Man… observe His habits and listen to His words. One thing which troubles novice Christians (new Christians) are what become apparent as inconsistencies from one gospel to another. The four gospel writers appear to give disputable facts in their writings one-with-another through language translations for what Jesus experienced during Passion Week and the timeline of calendar events.

Then Christians either move on by ignoring their own unresolved questioning thoughts; letting them fester and cause escalating doubt. Leading to increasing uncertainty or major unbelief about the authentic validity of Scripture.

Important chronology explored below; many insights have one or more views.

Jesus' Birth Date… No one knows the exact date of Jesus of Nazareth's birth on earth. There are speculations, educated guesses, astronomical observation and predictions (star), and historical political governing information related to Jewish and Roman facts. However, no precise proof of the date for His birth in Bethlehem of Judea. Only angelic proclamation given to the shepherds as confirmation of the Savior's birth, "Today in the town of David a Savior has been born to you; he is Christ the Lord" (Luke 2:11).

Jesus' Crucifixion Date… No one knows the exact year of the Lord's death. What complicates arriving at a definitive answer involves calendars. There were: Galilean, Judean (ecclesiastical and civil), lunar, solar, Roman, Gregorian, and many others different from each another. To use a solar calendar (sun in relationship to the stars) versus using a lunar calendar (phases of the moon); when tossed into the mix produces problematic and vast challenges of incorporating spiritual chronology.

Authoritative Accuracy... The largest connecting puzzle piece which floats along is "complete accuracy" and it remains allusive. Tangents for imposing strict timelines cannot loosen the Father's sovereign control. Amazing and awesome spiritual fact... the unknown years and date in the months for each... the Lord's birth, His crucifixion death, and His future Second Coming. Even the angels do not know the day of His return. (Mark 13:32) The mystery remains within the Godhead, Three-in-One of the Trinity. Incontestable Truth!

Friday, as the crucifixion day, was determined and "set in historical stone" so to speak, three centuries later. Relinquishing the Friday theory requires little intellectual insight, spiritual energy, and common sense.

Exact proof of the crucifixion year is unknown. Speculation for the year includes anywhere from 30-34 A.D.; for the crucifixion of the Messiah's death. Based on assumptions, Convocation schedules, historical hearsay, and governmental leadership, vast differences reign because of the evolving Spring seasonal and yearly information; leaving the years, dates, days, to remain in question.

When interpreters search various years, those from 30-34 A.D., for the Lord's crucifixion... Passover lands on different days of the week year after year. Therefore, any chronology challenge undertaken must attempt to align everything together.

Nonetheless, the Jewish ecclesiastical lunar calendar reveals the first month of Abib / Nisan places the Passover on Wednesday (fourteenth) and thereby tends to affirm the year 34 A.D.; for the crucifixion of Jesus. (More on this later.)

Important Chronology Note: The Jewish historical writings... along with Christian traditions and spiritual beliefs... related to information, knowledge, and facts, often agreed upon in general consensus about the Lord's Passion week in Jerusalem. However, the greatest variation in belief, of course, centers around the Jews believing Jesus was a prophet, but not the Son of God; whereas Christians believe Jesus is the Messiah.

Therefore with that difference acknowledged… the high points about the Lord's Passion Week are: Jesus' Triumphal Entry into Jerusalem, His Last Supper with the Twelve Disciples, the Eleven's final moments accompanying Jesus in the Garden of Gethsemane; and later along with Judas' betrayal leading to Jesus' arrest, trial, crucifixion, death, and burial. Also, the Lord being in the heart of the earth three days and three nights, and the Resurrection on Sunday morning establishes the basic timeline. There may be slight variations and thoughts, but the conceptional belief of this chronology is accepted concerning the Lord's important and resilient week in the Spring of that historical and world changing year.

Moving on.…. Deciphering a more detailed chronology takes extensive effort and determination. Below a premise unfolds in a futile attempt to describe how difficult the process to set in order a timeline remains after centuries of effort by those interested. Therefore this chapter, and the next, as written, cannot be "set in stone" either! Looking at a timeline for the crucifixion of Christ remains theory. Intellectual and spiritual intentions can miss the target. However it clears up a couple apparent discrepancies.

Premise… The following premise used for a timeline presented in this chapter includes Scripture, rationale, common sense, and theory; along with a composite of some Hebrew traditional beliefs and the first three holy Convocations in the Spring of Abib / Nisan on the Jewish calendar. Based on informative facts and taking into consideration the many free-floating variables; a flawed human attempt still seeks potential answers. Therefore the premise used here, as being valid, could be correct or incorrect. Nevertheless… important to be used because it validates how difficult proof-positive remains allusive.

The premise idea starts with Scriptural affirmation of the Lord's Resurrection on Sunday. Angelic proclamation also affirms the day, as the women went to the tomb on the first day of the week. (Luke 24:1; John 20:1) The angel announced to them, "He is not here; he has risen, just as he said" (Matthew 28:6).

Backstory... The sequence unfolds with the first month of the year being Abib / Nisan, March-April on the Jewish ecclesiastical calendar. Forty years after Jesus' initial post Resurrection appearances, the name of the month changed (after the uncivil Babylonian captivity of southern Israel / Judea around 70 A.D.) from Abib... a Hebrew name, to Nisan... a Jewish name.

Based on Jesus' earthly timeline in the year 34 A.D.; a brief outline of ten days below provides a narrative format which includes three holy Convocations honored, in the Spring season, in obedience to God by the Jews.

Some references clearly point to a timeline in Scripture of "6 days" and "2 days" before the Passover. (Mark 14:1; John 12:1-8) The documented betrayal behavior of Judas Iscariot unfolds too. (Matthew 26:14-16) John's passages about Preparation Day along with the arrest of Jesus and His trial keep the reader of Scripture informed of Jesus' location day-by-day. Also, included on the timeline are days revealing the Lord's corresponding death, burial, three days and three nights in the heart of the earth, and His Resurrection.

By following John's gospel it provides a dominate and specific outline. Used here because of the sanctioned documentation of his three epistle writings (letters) along with his writing of the Revelation included in Scripture... The Holy Bible.

In retrospect... All five years from 30-34 A.D., the three Spring Convocation timelines were calendar reviewed for this chapter. Taking into account the measure of three days and three nights, looking for Passover on a Wednesday (fourteenth) became key. The first month of the calendar year, Abib / Nisan 34 A.D.; became the selected choice. Therefore, using the Jewish Ecclesiastical Calendar (lunar) from that year, along with some of its unfolding days, from Thursday (eighth) through Sunday (eighteenth), proved best for the speculative chronology timeline.

Three Days and Three Nights... The timeline spoken by Jesus, three days and three nights for His being in the heart of the earth, provides the closest authenticity. Who would doubt His Word?

A starting point allows for either "moving forward from" or "back up from" and in this premise "backing up from" the Resurrection on Sunday led in the search for the actual day of the crucifixion of Jesus on the chronology timeline; it came to rest on Wednesday of the preceding week. The days align. After the horrific crucifixion and before an amazing Resurrection, on the timeline from Wednesday Passover (fourteenth), to the Saturday Sabbath (seventeenth), involved the calculated three days and three nights closest in hours. Sunday, the Feast of Firstfruits (eighteenth) commences at sunset on Saturday (seventeenth.)

Calculating those hours in complete accuracy hedges because the exact time of the Resurrection remains unknown.The words of Jesus are the factual starting point. However the crucifixion death being at 3:00 pm it was still day. Does that count as the first day in the heart of the earth even though only a few hours? This is an example of irregularities when searching for an accurate timeline.

Scripture is definitive in proclaiming the Resurrection happened on Sunday. Why is this particular Sunday (eighteenth) especially important in the Spring of that year? (More on this later.)

Twenty Four Hours... The Jewish feasts and their timeframes goes back to the Old Testament sunset to sunset. Two twelve hour blocks of time... a 24 hour daily cycle. A theoretical timeline, sunset to sunset, referenced as a logical boundary. Nevertheless, God's days were not necessarily 24 hours in total conformity. Nothing was rigid, there were variables. Convocation days each year as well as the daylight hours involving the seasons too. Therefore, the seasons, days, and hours fluctuated both on the calendar and on the proverbial clock (sunset / sunrise).

To complicate matters... when the hours in a day are referenced as a group, as a day, it does not mean a complete timeline of 24 hours.

In Jewish belief, a day as referenced could have any amount of hours. This provides a huge variable that intersects the definitive timeline spoken by Jesus of three days and three nights in the heart of the earth. Was it seventy two hours to the precise minute? Not likely!

On one level, the day of the week for the crucifixion, and on another level, the three days and three nights calculation cannot be locked in solid. If the Lord's death transpired at the twenty-first hour in Jewish time, (3:00 pm Gentile) then a corresponding exact Resurrection seventy two hours later does not fill-in with anything else in Scripture. (Luke 23:44-46)

The last few paragraphs above were used to set the stage for relaying other events and days in the mission of Jesus during Passion Week. However, for ease in reading, the written narrative format here unfolds through a forward chronology timeline.

Many beliefs and ideas are taught in the Christian Church about the Passion Week of the Lord Jesus Christ and a major emphasis starts with His Triumphal Entry to Jerusalem from the Mount of Olives. (Christians honor the Triumphal Entry… known in tradition as Palm Sunday… one week before they celebrate Easter as the Lord's Resurrection.)

Important backstory happened for Jesus before His Triumphal Entry. Two major events have unfolded several days prior to the Lord's Passion Week schedule or any Convocation celebrations starting. One of those important and often overlooked sequences of time was the raising of Lazarus from the dead. (John 11:38-44)

Jesus left Jordan; and returned to the area of Bethany of Judea, less than two miles south of Jerusalem, where the all-powerful resurrection of His friend, Lazarus, took place. (John 11:43-44) Many Jews were privy to the miraculous event before their eyes which happened four days after Lazarus' death. (John 11:39) This overt demonstration of the Lord's power either brought out the best, or the worst, in those threatened by Jesus of Nazareth's presence. As a result, dramatic effects unfolded in the life of Jesus, and His followers, and the ruling Jewish authorities; and most of all the timeline leading up to the pending three feasts.

Many Jews present believed and put their faith in Him. Others, after Lazarus' resurrection, went back to Jerusalem informing the Pharisees and the chief priests of the miracle. A meeting called by the Sanhedrin (aka ruling council) reached intense fury where they finalized their plot. The males holding authority positions included the high priest, chief priests, elders, and teachers of the law. (Mark 14:53) Determination to arrest and kill Jesus hindered only because of the hundreds of Godly people who were in Jerusalem for the first three Convocations in the Spring of that year.

In his writing, John tells his readers that this fermenting religious uproar caused Jesus to leave Bethany of Judea and head to the desert area around the village of Ephraim north of Jerusalem. (John 11:54) In this second, of the two backstories… Jesus goes into seclusion with the Twelve disciples. How extended is their time together? Likely a couple days. Nothing definitive in Scripture.

Jesus spent valuable moments with the Twelve who accompanied Him to this place of seclusion. Many teachings are recorded in the Bible in this block of time.

These precious hours and days became the final alone time together unhindered by the immanent threat of death toward Christ. It was from this area they departed and headed for Jerusalem, on His last journey… in the Triumphal Entry.(Matthew 21:1-11; Mark 11:1-10; Luke 19:28-38; John 12:12-15)

11
Triumphal Entry / Passion Week

In the Triumphal Entry Jesus and His Twelve disciples returned to the city of Jerusalem one day before Passion Week commences. The calendar days, dates, and events in Abib / Nisan in "brief highlights" possibly looked something like the following; taking into consideration many events are not included here in keeping with the main topics related to this chapter.

Thursday (eighth)
This day and date chosen as the first one in this premise because a revelation point in Scripture acknowledges it as "six days" before Passover. (John 12:1) Jesus and the Twelve arrived at the home of Martha, Mary, and Lazarus where they had dinner; Martha served. Mary of Bethany anoints the feet of Jesus for His burial. (John 12:1-3)
Sunset: Friday commences

Friday (ninth)
The reference "next day" signifies their departure for Jerusalem. (John 12:12)
Meaning of "on the morrow" not necessarily the exact next day.
Jesus and the Twelve return to the Jordan area likely on this day or next morning.
Sunset: Saturday Sabbath commences

Saturday (tenth) Saturday Sabbath / **Triumphal Entry**

On Saturday (tenth) in the mountainside descent Jesus came not only as the Unblemished Lamb of God being set apart; but as the King He rightfully had been since His birth as Son of God / Son of Man in Bethlehem of Judea. (Matthew 2:2)

This important scene, the public verbal praising event on a Saturday Sabbath transpired within the two mile walking restrictions. (John 12:12-13) The Triumphal Entry revealed His resilient determination to fulfill the Father's will of redeeming humanity from their sinful state.

Why both a donkey and her colt mentioned as being ridden by Jesus? The word "them" referenced in Matthew 21:1-7 indicates He rode both; not meant to be at the same time. (John 12:14-15) Spiritual meanings might be indicative of a transfer too. The Lord traveled on different terrains… desert and hills. Jesus probably rode on the donkey in His descent from the higher elevation. Closer to Jerusalem, did He transferred to the colt on the more level ground…which offered a better stable footing for the young animal? Cloaks had been on both. (Matthew 21:7)

The prophetic Bible verse, Zechariah 9:9, tells of the Messiah riding on a colt. Jesus fulfilled many Old Testament prophecies. The tenth day of the month, an important date, because the Lamb of God was set apart in preparation for the Convocation of the Passover. (Exodus 12:3)

Sunset: Sunday commences

Sunday (eleventh)

Simon, the former leper, in whose home the unnamed woman anointed the head of Jesus for His burial. (Matthew 26:6-13) Residence known as Bethany of the Jordan.

Sunset: Monday commences

Monday (twelfth)

The acknowledgement of "two days" before Passover (John 12:1-8); Mark 14:1. (In Luke 22:1 he writes… "Now the Feast of Unleavened Bread, called the Passover, was approaching.")

Sunset: Tuesday commences / Fast of the Firstborn begins

Tuesday (thirteenth) / **Fast of the Firstborn**

Preparation Day… In a section on the death of Christ in John's gospel he informs the reader, "Now it was the day of Preparation, and the "next day" was to be a special Sabbath" (John 19:14, 31, 42). Therefore Preparation Day finalized on Passover day. (Mark 15:42) In the year 34 A.D., the Fast of the Firstborn would have also been on Preparation Day. In the words "Preparation Day" used in Scripture, note the capital "P" and "D" used by John. (NIV) The other three gospel writers each have Preparation Day capitalized also in their passages. (Matthew 27:62; Mark 15:42; Luke 23:54) Nowhere else in Scripture before or beyond this point does specialized capitalization appear for these two words in mid-sentence. Emphasis in capitals possibly used because "prior" to the Feast of Unleavened Bread. (The crucifixion took place on Passover… Wednesday (fourteenth) being finalized with the death of Jesus at 3:00 p.m. a few hours before sunset. A seder meal as part of the Jewish celebration of the Convocation that evening would be imminent and included unleavened bread.)

What was Preparation Day? All preparations, according to Jewish customs, were finalized on this day (thirteenth) in the first month in the year, Abib / Nisan, so every devout, religious Jewish person could conform to the resting measures required on a holy Sabbath… the Lord's Passover (fourteenth). When the household made prior preparation for the Convocations… especially for the upcoming Feast of Unleavened Bread (fifteenth), it required tedious effort to remove all traces of yeast, and to clean, and to bake the unleavened bread. Portions of the seder meal dishes were prepared too; as only minimal cooking was permitted on Passover. The roasting of the sacrificial lamb at twilight always an important part of the seder meal.

Fast of the Firstborn…. Galilean Last Supper

The terminology "Last Supper" likely held by John, one of the Galilean Apostles, attributes to his intentional reference to the two words having a regional connotation of importance for him. Being Jewish in Galilee meant they observed the thirteenth day of Abib / Nisan with an old traditional emphasis.

These regional Jews honored the thirteenth day (the day before Passover) by fasting sunset (twelfth) to sunset (thirteenth). Known as the Fast of the Firstborn. As a firstborn son in the family, males remembered how the firstborn Hebrew sons at the time of the Exodus from Egypt were spared death at midnight by the lamb's blood seen on the doorframes. (Exodus 12:7,12,13) Jesus would have participated; being a Galilean and the firstborn son of the virgin Mary, from Nazareth. Several of the Twelve disciples were firstborn sons too. Eleven of the Twelve were Galileans.

A common practice… the Jews did not fast on a holy day. Jesus and the disciples finalized the Fast of the Firstborn with a "simple meal" prior to Tuesday (thirteenth) sunset. The fast ended early because of the sunset being imminent and Passover commences.

At this time in Jesus' final week in Jerusalem He ate this "symbolic" Passover meal with His Twelve disciples (on the eve of the thirteenth before sunset) where previous preparation plans were made by Peter and John in a pre-designated large upper room for their last meal together. (Matthew 26:17-19; Mark 14:12-15; Luke 22:7-13)

The celebration meal taking place twenty-four hours earlier than the seder meal on the Jewish Convocation schedule. Therefore no mention of any traditional passover foods eaten, like bitter herbs, nor the inclusion of the traditional roasted lamb. Also, what happened to the setting aside four days prior (on the tenth) of an unblemished lamb by the two disciples; and nothing of the slaughter of the lamb at the nearby temple, nor roasting it? Then what preparations did they make? Likely removal of yeast from the household. Baking of the unleavened bread and food purchased for breaking the fast with the Twelve.

No females mentioned anywhere in or near the upper room. Two connections happened. A man with a water jar, possibly the household servant. Unusual, as women performed this task. The owner of the house a male... another notable, distinct and specific reference. (Mark 14:12-16; Luke 22:10-13)

Therefore a simple meal along with focus on the bread and cup. Does it truly become the Galilean Last Supper? This last meal took place prior to the betrayal by Judas Iscariot, with him also participating at the table; but departing alone (after dark, thirteen sunset) and earlier than the others. (John 13:30)

At the Last Supper, Jesus through the breaking of the unleavened bread which He gave to theTwelve disciples, and with the cup following; appears to end the meal. They sang a traditional hymn and departed for the Mount of Olives. (Matthew 26:30; Mark 14:26) Something else of importance helps to tie this Galilean view together. Prayers were especially important that evening. Therefore, Jesus during Passion week immediately took the Eleven following the Last Supper to the Garden of Gethsemane to pray.

Later that evening, now the fourteenth, Judas finalized the betrayal in an olive grove on the opposite side of the Kidron Valley at a place called, The Garden of Gethsemane; otherwise known as the Mount of Olives. (Matthew 26:47-50; Mark 14:43-54; Luke 22:47-48; John 18:1-3)

For Christians, the tradition of celebrating a symbolic type Passover... became a sacrament in the early beginning of the Church and known as the Lord's Supper; the Lord's table / Communion (bread and cup) in the New Testament Church. (1 Corinthians 11:17) Still respected and honored by present-day Christians in the twenty-first century; and normally partaken in a Sunday worship service. Jesus told His disciples, "...do this in remembrance of me" (Luke 22:19). Years later... the Apostle Paul chides the Corinthians for eating communion as if it were a meal; they were to eat before coming to the Lord's table. (1 Corinthians 11:20-22)

Important Note: Matthew, Mark, and Luke... their writings are referred to as synoptic gospels because they parallel in many ways in their content. Whereas John's gospel does not conform. In his consistent point of reference he portrays the Messiah as a heavenly Christophany, the eternal Christ. Emmanuel... God with us. Incarnate... in the flesh. (John 1:-5,14)

John writes that Jesus ate the Last Supper with His disciples before Passover, thus in sovereignty He remained the sacrificial Passover lamb. In the Old Testament, the Passover defined and referenced as the Lord's Passover. (Leviticus 23:4) Jesus, the Savior, truly became the authentic Passover Lamb. The God-link between the Old and New Testaments. His eternal redemption... salvation timeline fulfilled. It Is Finished!

The breaking of bread provides a key toward locking in chronology proof. Was it a loaf of bread or unleavened bread at the Last Supper? In preparation, yeast was removed from households prior to Passover and the Feast of Unleavened Bread. (Leviticus 23:6) Therefore Jesus broke unleavened bread at the meal in the upper room with His Twelve disciples. Baked without yeast and not in a loaf formation. How spiritually appropriate and accurate His words, "This is my body given for you: do this in remembrance of me" (Luke 22:19). Jesus, without sin, for the sinners. The cup with wine followed... the new covenant in His shed blood. (Luke 22:20)

Sunset: Wednesday commences... Passover

Wednesday (fourteenth) Passover
Garden of Gethsemane... On the way to the Garden of Gethsemane with the Eleven, Jesus still used every available moment as a teaching opportunity. Upon their arrival Jesus took the inner circle of three... Peter, James, and John to be nearer to Him; however the Lord went on further. During this time frame the three slept because of exhaustion from sorrow (Luke 22:45) and probably the other eight too. Nonetheless, God the Father proved attentive and compassionate... as an angel came and strengthened Jesus for His crucial pending hours ahead. (Luke 22:43)

66

While they were in the garden... Judas Iscariot, the soldiers, officials of the chief priest, elders, Pharisees, and others, came and arrested Jesus. (Luke 22:47; John 18:1-3) His disciples fled, all except Peter and John. These two followed close behind the Lord to where the pending religious trial would start. (John 18:15-16)

Trial... A many-phased trial proceeded; filled with abusive events, legalistic hassles, and the eventual chaos of moving to a different location too. The sacrilegious event went on for hours. Actions and speech from the participating characters violated Jesus' personhood with disrespectful treatment. The Pharisees charge of blaspheme relayed to Pilate later at the civil trial through their argumentative dispute was that Jesus claimed to be the Son of God. They asserted this made Him deserving of death by crucifixion. Crucify reigned in loud chorus. (Luke 20:20-23; John 19:15) When Jesus seldom spoke, His truth-telling changed nothing; not even the heart of Pilate who gave the final order for the crucifixion of the Lord Jesus Christ. (Luke 23:23-25; John 19:16)

Jesus' Crucifixion... Why was Jesus crucified on the fourteenth? He needed to claim His rightful "unblemished lamb" responsibility being the Passover lamb pre-designed and thereby establishing the precedent He was truly... Lord of the Lord's Passover. Not just in memorial tradition which honored the protection on the Jewish firstborn of all in Egypt. (Exodus 11:4-8) The blood covering... Jesus' blood sacrifice came (12:00-3:00 p.m. Gentile time) because of the Jew's Passover lambs being slaughter in the courtyard of the temple in Jerusalem. Setting as a precedent at the crucifixion He would be the firstborn in blood sacrifice of redemption; and the Feast of Firstfruits at the Resurrection.

In the timeline, Jesus' crucifixion "death" at 3:00 p.m. on the fourteenth, was before the Jewish sunset and not yet the start of the next day.

Roman Crucifixion... The crucifixion taking place on Wednesday afternoon (12:00-3:00) brings complications and tends to be unreasonable. Why would the governor of Judea risk an uproar and a riot breaking out from Jesus' disciples and the hundreds of His followers who were in Jerusalem for the three Convocations? The governor accommodated the local Jews implored twofold request; the release of Barabbus and the crucifixion of Jesus. Also, Pilate being intentional and steadfast on the written message he ordered placed on the cross above the Lord's head... Jesus Of Nazareth The King Of The Jews. This criminal charge locked in spiritual truth, unknowingly by him. (John 19:19-22)

Burial.... In Jerusalem the Romans honored the burial preference of the Jews in relation to their holy days. At the crucifixion site, the Jews did not want those crucified to remain on their crosses after dark on a special Sabbath. The Roman soldiers accommodated this religious alternative. To enhance a criminal's death the legs were broken; as Jesus had already died, His side was pierced as a substitute procedure. (John 19:31-35) In the Old Testament when sacrificial lambs were roasted their legs were not broken. (Exodus 12:46)

Joseph of Arimathea took responsibility for the burial; assisted by Nicodemus. These two secret disciples now on public display as Jesus' compassionate pallbearers.

Two women, Mary Magdalene and the "other Mary" sat outside the tomb mourning. Overwhelming grief reigned, they stayed. Being expected soon at the pending Passover seder meal at sunset; they placed themselves in a timeline crunch within Jewish pre-established tradition.

Important backstory... Old Testament Scriptures give precise information for the total of seven holy Convocations commemorated yearly throughout the generations by the Hebrews; after their flight from Egypt and giving them freedom from 430 years of slavery. (Exodus 12:40-41) Three are pertinent to this chapter.

The Israelites practiced yearly, the Lord's Passover immediately followed by the Feast of Unleavened Bread and then also by the Feast of Firstfruits, as one group of three holy Convocations covering eight days total in the Spring. Celebrated in the month of Abib / Nisan during March-April, the first month of the Jewish ecclesiastical year and chief of months. Passover began on the fourteenth day commencing at sunset the evening before. Therefore the official start of the Convocation of three, commenced at sunset on the thirteenth. An annual family seder meal celebration on Passover (fourteenth) at sunset. Also, a second seder-type meal often followed on the eve of the Feast of Unleavened Bread (fifteenth.)

Sunset: Thursday commences... Feast of Unleavened Bread

Thursday (fifteenth) Feast Of Unleavened Bread

The fifteenth day of the month was the Feast of Unleavened Bread commencing the evening before at sunset. The date of the month never changes. Aways the fifteenth and follows Passover every year.

Beginning on this day Jews were required to eat unleavened bread (made without yeast) for seven straight days; the first of seven celebrated with unleavened bread in the holy Convocation. The unleavened bread was prepared on Preparation Day.

Important Note: Decades after leaving Egypt and wandering in the desert forty years; then after the Jews had planted crops / harvested them... they ate the memorial bread at Passover too. Until that timeline... God had miraculously fed them with manna for forty years in the desert wilderness. (Exodus 16:31-36)

Side Story... For the chief priests and Pharisees this particular Thursday (fifteenth) a holy Convocation did not appear to matter. (Matthew 27:62) Unprecedented insistence and timing. Amazing! They went to Pilate and requested that he seal the tomb. They did not want the Lord's followers stealing the mortal body of Jesus; thereby claiming a Resurrection had taken place. Pilate agreed to the procedure, but only until the third-day passed. (Matthew 27:62-64)

Sunset: Friday commences

Friday (sixteenth)

Friday was the day the women "bought" and "prepared" spices before sunset and the beginning of the Saturday Sabbath. At least four women either purchased and/or prepared the burial spices and perfumes on Friday. The only day available and void of Convocation restrictive limitations of no financial transactions or servile work projects.

Sunset: Saturday Sabbath commences

Saturday (seventeenth) **Saturday Sabbath**

Would God the Father break His own sacred plan? Would He resurrect Jesus just after sunset on Friday as the Sabbath commences? Of course, He could. God is omnipotent. From 3:00 p.m. on Wednesday to 3:00 p.m. on Saturday would account for 72 hours. However, then where is Jesus for the next few hours?

Sunday was never considered a weekly Sabbath day in Israel. Only the weekly Saturday Sabbath… God's own "Creation Sabbath" since the time of Genesis 2:1-3, and Leviticus 23:3. Going on further, in the New Testament, Jesus said He was Lord of the Sabbath. (Luke 6:1-5) Jesus said, " The Sabbath was made for man, not man for the Sabbath. Therefore the Son of Man is Lord even of the Sabbath" (Mark 2:27-28).

Sunset: Sunday commences… Feast of Firstfruits

Sunday (eighteenth) **Feast of Firstfruits / Lord's Resurrection**

Scripture appears to reveal the Lord's Resurrection happened in the early morning hours… actual time unknown. Prior to this moment in time Jesus had been in the heart of the earth three days and three nights. The revelation plan of the Resurrection begins unfolding. (Understandably no human knows this on their present timeline; only the reader of Scripture.)

Double Sabbath…

During this weekend a Double Sabbath unfolded because a combined weekly Sabbath and the next day, Sunday morning, a Jewish Convocation also ties into the chronology timeline. The Resurrection of Jesus and the third of the three Convocations have dual significance because the Convocation days align in 34 A.D.; as stipulated.

Feast of Firstfruits... Initially the Feast of Firstfruits did not have a designated day of the month. However this offering of firstfuit... a new "sheaf of grain" could not be chosen and presented until "after" a Saturday Sabbath had "followed" the Feast of Unleavened Bread on the fifteenth. The Feast of Firstfruits in the month of Abib / Nisan, 34 A.D.; a predetermined day of the week... Sunday. The day remains correct in identification for the Messiah... Jesus being the firstfruit of divine redemption. The Resurrection is again affirmed on Sunday.

In name, also referred to as the Feast of Weeks in the Old Testament because the count forward was seven weeks with the fiftieth day being Pentecost the fourth of seven Convocations celebrated by the Hebrews. (Exodus 34:22)

Post Resurrection Appearances...

The Lord's post Resurrection appearances starting in the daylight hours on Sunday included revealing His resurrected presence first to Mary Magdalene in the morning, and her counterpart, Peter in the afternoon; also two women in the morning, and their counter part, the two Emmaus Road travelers in the afternoon.

Those daylight hours complete, Jesus' sudden final appearance to the Ten (and others) on Resurrection Day happened in a locked house in Jerusalem, after the participants evening meal. Jesus showed His nail-scarred hands and ate fish to prove the reality of His Resurrection. He departed suddenly after His important teaching on forgiveness. (John 20:23) The restraints of physical boundaries no longer had control over His immortal body. Where did Jesus go next?

Scripture offers no further information until Sunday, one week later after the Resurrection, when Jesus stands suddenly in the same house, with locked doors again. Eleven disciples, includes Thomas in this scene. (John 20:26)

A few decades after the Resurrection, the Apostle John's precise, written documentation covers special times only when he was present and saw the risen Christ. Therefore he names three... one each in the same house a week apart (John 20:19, 26) and the early morning fishing and breakfast scene, near the shoreline at the Sea of Tiberias. With a group of seven disciples, after the all-night laborious and catch-less fishing trip (John 21:1-14); and where the Lord reinstates Peter. (John 21:15-19)

The Scriptures are ever-new to the reader through the power of the Holy Spirit. A seeker searching for the living God, and the Christian believer desiring to serve Him should come to the Word of God daily, unbiased and willing to become aware of truth therein. Therefore, one's personal and ingrained theological beliefs may be set ajar at times... while reading and meditating on the world-changing miraculous events completed through the Savior as described in the Bible.

Is anyone advocating changing Good Friday? Of course not. For Christians, prophecy relayed and fulfilled has utmost importance. However, for the Messianic Jews... who believe the Lord Jesus Christ is their Messiah... something different evolves because of their yearly calendar schedule. They still honor and practice the Holy Convocations in reverence to God and their Jewish faith.

For believers, the crucifixion day of the week on the calendar becomes secondary as celebrated tradition. It is neither about a Friday crucifixion and burial; nor Wednesday, or Thursday, or any other day of the week. Whatever day and date, one believes concerning a perceived timeline... it does not change the Christian belief about the basic natural and spiritual implications surrounding Christ's life. The divine purpose remains... to acknowledge Jesus as the Son of God / Son of Man... conceived through the over-shadowing power of the Holy Spirit, born of the virgin, sacrificial crucifixion death for sinners, burial, three days and three nights in the heart of the earth through descending into Hades (hell), and His glorious Resurrection... on Sunday the first day of the week.

Jesus' final words on the cross at His crucifixion "It Is Finished" proclaimed in the appropriate spiritual moment. (John 19:30) His overwhelming faith and trust in His Father evident because He had committed His Spirit into the Father's hands. (Luke 23:46) Amazing grace exemplified by the Lord.

Faithfully resurrected by God the Father, through the power of the Holy Spirit; Jesus fulfilled the three Spring seasonal Convocations in Abib / Nisan for Jew and Gentile alike… the Lord's Passover, the Feast of Unleavened Bread, and the Feast of Firstfruits.

Section Three

Backstory Timelines

12
The Rooster Crows

The four chapters in this section allows one to focus on looking for additional answers in the New Testament... on the biblical timeline. Also leaves areas open for speculation sometimes. Backstory included in the Bible filled with insightful details gives the reader of Scripture an opportunity to pose challenging questions of those unfolding scenes. Therefore important side trips are taken in this section because without them being included as a part of the historic chronology timeline, prior and up to the crucifixion of the Lord, they would remain camouflaged... or hidden; thereby causing an incomplete picture because each leads to other important events.

This chapter focuses on the rooster's crow... and Peter's denials. The backstory used from the chronology for this chapter starts after the arrest of Jesus in the Garden of Gethsemane. It unfolds in thirty verses through the four gospel writers: Matthew 26:69-75; Mark 14:66-72; Luke 22:54-62; John 18:15-18; 18:25-27. Only two of the Eleven disciples present in the garden, Peter and John, followed Jesus to Caiaphas' house. No proof, or indication, the Apostle Matthew, or Mark, the disciple, came later. (Luke's physical presence with the disciples of Jesus was years after this current timeline.)

Several scenes evolved in the courtyard below the High Priest Caiaphas' house while the Sanhedrin (aka ruling council) were meeting above to fulfill their plot for Jesus to be crucified. Over that span of time, Peter becomes the main Bible character through his verbal and consequential denials of Christ while inside the open-air ground level.

The reader of Scripture gleans insight into Peter's anxiety as it intensifies in the courtyard between his entry and exit timeline. Each of the four gospel writers acknowledges the apostle's lying through his three denials; some with additional insight into Peter's escalation of fear.

Peter is confronted in three verbal situations and denies knowing or having any association with Jesus, the Nazarene, from Galilee. The disciple's three denials happened before the rooster's pre dawn crow that morning. Jesus had predicted and warned Peter about the consequential timeline hours before it happened. (Matthew 26:34; Mark 14:30; Luke 22:34; John 13:38) This is what has been taught in the Church for centuries.

However, looking at apparent inconsistencies reveals the four writers are not in agreement. Why might a reader of Scripture be concerned if one becomes alert to a discrepancy? For whatever reason Christian leaders have ignored the fact that Mark's gospel has a slight difference in conveying not only the confrontations, but also how many times the rooster crowed. He is the only one of the four gospel writers who states the rooster crowed a second time as he provides information concerning the Lord's predictive conversation with Peter about the disciple's three denials in the future. (Mark 14:30) Why did Mark imply the rooster crowed twice? Did it? (More on this later.)

Whether it was once or twice… why would Jesus select a rooster as the announcing symbol? The Lord told Peter beforehand that this creature would set the implied boundary timeline.

Before looking at Peter's denials, it proves beneficial to look at and listen to the rooster. Strange that his crow is front and center. If he crowed twice… then the crows become symbolic bookends on the timeline. What would it represent?

A male rooster (cock) is a chicken. A near flightless bird with a confident attitude. One who makes excessive noise and struts. The rooster crows in the early morning hour after leaving the roost because it is the first out of the hen house. His internal intuitive clock followed by a crow warns all predators to scatter… projecting he guards his domain. The crow awakens the hens and they arise to leave for the outdoors to forge food.

When a rooster crows in the approaching pre dawn, it is his "wake up crow." He can crow in the evening; or any time of the day or night for various reasons. The vocal cords sound loud around 70-90 decibels (more or less) depending on his maturity; and interrupts silence as noisy as a neighbor's ever-barking dog a few feet away.

What role does Mark, as a disciple of Jesus, have as he writes about a rooster crowing a second time? In Scripture double, or twice, has a specific meaning. When something is doubled in "prophetic revelation" that means… it is fixed by God and will come to pass soon. (Genesis 41:32)

Looking at a small portion of the backstory from the Garden of Gethsemane helps to shed light. Many pastors and Bible teachers believe Mark was nearby around the precise time that the religious authorities arrested Jesus. Was Mark attempting to follow the arresting procession to Caiasphas' house? Two verses in his gospel, Mark14:51-52, tell of a young man resisting capture and running away. During Mark's hurried escape, in late evening, did he disturb a rooster, hearing its crow… the first one? Would this connect later to when the rooster crowed the second time? (Mark 14:72)

There is more to highlight. Both Matthew and Mark agree the "prophetic revelation" about Peter's soon-to-take-place denials came after the Last Supper, appearing to happen on the way to the Mount of Olives. Luke and John place it while the disciples were still at the supper table in the upper room. That complicates the timeline for the exact location related to when Jesus warned Peter.

References made above in those latter two gospels about Jesus' communications… covering comfort, teachings, and prayers are also in the mix on the chronology timeline. Taking place where? At the Last Supper or during the walk to Gethsemane?

Sometime after the Last Supper and before arriving at Gethsemane, did a rooster crow? Roosters can crow at anytime. Speculations allow for discrepancies to be dispelled.

Therefore on the way to the garden, did the band of Eleven disciples and Jesus through their movement and conversation disturb a rooster who sensed possible danger near the hen house? Poultry was raised outside the central city boundary.

Did the hearing of the rooster's evening crow prompt the Lord Jesus Christ's "prophetic revelation" of the future pre dawn crow to assure everyone and certify Peter's three denials were finalized? Then on the timeline... like symbolic bookends the crows tie together the imminent garden betrayal by Judas and Perter's final public denial according to Mark's writing when the rooster crowed the second time. (Mark 14:72; John 18:27)

Important Side Note: In the oldest of manuscripts from centuries ago they do not have this discrepancy in Mark that the rooster crowed the "second" time. However most readers of Scripture only have their personal copy of the Bible available for reference; and this difference brings forth unanswered questions as the careful reader discovers a potential discrepancy. Nevertheless it is notable that in the year 1604 A.D.; during the reign of King James1, he commissioned what became known as the King James Version of The Holy Bible (KJV). The first edition (printing) was in 1611 A.D. The subsequent printings have been used and read by generations for centuries.

Mark tells his readers (KJV) when the rooster crowed the first time; between a maidservant's first and her second confrontations with Peter. In the courtyard, the first as individuals were seated at the fire area; and her second time later after Peter had moved to the porch and while he was standing there. (Mark 14:68,72)

Verses referenced in this chapter follow the Bible translation, New International Version (NIV). The reason for digressing to another translation (KJV) concerning the rooster's crow becomes important for showing how throughout the generations the different printed versions of the Bible reveal potential discrepancies evolving through different translators and translations. Therefore a necessary and purposeful reason to be included here.

Overall when apparent discrepancies surface in the Bible it may have a detrimental attack on one's faith. This could happen to the Christian, or to the fallen away believer, or to the skeptic who does not believe in God because of whatever personal agenda they hold. The sovereign Lord knows the heart of the reader of Scripture. He is able to bring anyone back onto the path with sure-footing; if one is able to surrender doubts and reach out in faith for Jesus to affirm His truth, His power, and His presence.

When reviewing Peter's denials in the Bible they appear to unfold in rapid sequence. However considerable hours are logged throughout the total thirty verses written by the four gospel writers. This explains why those standing around recognize Peter's accent as being Galilean. Many people present knew Jesus was upstairs in Caiaphas' house; while their conversations flowed back and forth in the courtyard throughout the darkness of night prior to dawn.

Each writer references three confrontations and three denials. Often not the same ones. Nonetheless it leaves room for speculation. Who they mention as the confronter makes agreement problematic. Below a synopsis follows:

> Matthew: girl at the fire; another girl; those standing there (accent)
> Mark: girl at the fire; same girl again; those standing there (Galilean)
> Luke: girl at the fire; someone else (man); the assertive person (man)
> John: girl at the door; girl at the fire; a relative of Malchus (man)

As written, in the listings revealed above, calculating a precise list of confrontations exposes immediate complications. For centuries… the Church has only acknowledged a total of three confrontations and three denials. Of course, pastors and Bible teachers go by the Lord's "prophetic revelation" and numerical account of three. Why do they avoid the references supplied by the four writers?

Any attempt to prove 100% accuracy from the four gospel writer's composite information requires using biblical facts. Interpretation of inconsistencies could be considered when speculation prone. This chapter, as written, may not convey perfection in accuracy; regardless of the genuine attempt. Nevertheless the intended reasoning here is to cause the reader of Scripture to pay attention to what they are reading.

In referring to the confronters in the chronology format it appears to be: the girl at the door; the girl at the fire; the same girl again later; another girl; someone else (man); assertive person (man); and a relative of Malchus (man). The latter two might be the same man in Luke and John's references.

Also, in Mark's same girl again later, and in Matthew's another girl... a reader might consider them to be one and the same. In the courtyard, Matthew and Mark's someone in the standing groups could be combined as one person or remain separate as two people. Observation reveals a potential of three duplicates; plus the quad in references of the girl at the fire, resulting in a minimum of four different denial events.

In actuality there was at least six confronters and seven denials. Nearly impossible to align all thirty verses in 100% accuracy. Speculation does not offer guarantees. Nevertheless the reader of Scripture discovers a total of three females and three males are involved in the confrontations. One female confronts twice. Therefore a proven seven denials.

Peter's denials are infamous. When and where did they unfold? Throughout the multiple scenes inside the courtyard the reader of Scripture learns: Peter entered; then stood away from the center of the whole area prior to the kindled fire being started; he stood at the fire before sitting there; he left the seated area around the fire and stood for several hours among groups standing in the open porch area; and it appears he moved gradually closer and closer towards the available exit. These expose the reader to Peter's fear of man and his self-imposed trauma. Also gives insight to his being recognized as Galilean through his accent and dialect.

Does John have the three principle and important denials? Were they the girl at the door; the girl at the fire; and the male relative of Malchus who had been in the Garden of Gethsemane? The first denial immediate upon entering, the second centralized in the courtyard location, and the third just prior to exiting. As for John, it appears he wrote only about the three denials within his hearing range… his personal experience. This is important as the reader of Scripture might perceive and conclude that only John has the three genuine denials; thereby excluding the other three gospel writers validity.

John's gospel reveals a clear break. He seems to disappear from the courtyard as his writing steps from observation after Peter's first denial. Through a written interruption he references and expounds on Jesus being questioned by Caiaphas about His disciples and His teaching.(John 18:19-24) The apostle reenters as the second denial unfolds, then later hearing the third.

Where was John in his perceived absence from the courtyard during those other intense hours? Was he somewhere inside Caiaphas' house above the courtyard? Closer to the location of Jesus than one usually considers when reading the apostle's gospel? Or… was he in another section of the open covered porch?

To complicate matters… the four gospel writers often used words like door, gateway, and entryway, interchangeable words, for the same location. Also, when considering the confrontations and denials… Matthew, Mark, Luke, and John each write a generalized verbatim related through meaningful language for their initial reading audience on their A.D.; timeline.

A mental picture of the foundational structure might visualize Caiaphas' house where one enters through a massive heavy-weighted double door into the open courtyard surrounded by a recessed covered porch likely adorned by arched columned areas enhancing the architectural design. Above this area the house is located. In Scripture no stairways mentioned anywhere… neither outside, nor inside; only that the house is at a higher level.

The chronology of the unfolding courtyard scenes looks something like this:

Scene One / Peter and John / Apostles Enter

The two apostles, Peter and John, arrive at the courtyard… the former does not enter on the heels of John's timing though he followed, but at a farther distance. (Luke 22:54; John 18:15-16) John was known to the high priest, so the girl on duty allowed his admittance which unfolded with ease. Therefore upon arrival Peter was not granted permission to enter. Nonetheless John went back to the entry and spoke to the girl; Peter enters the courtyard.

Scene Two / Peter and John / First Denial

The girl on duty at the door immediately confronts Peter. His first denial follows upon entering. (John 18:17) No other gospel writer documents it.

Scene Three / Peter Standing

The outside temperature… cold. A kindle fire is started in the middle of the courtyard, but the servants and officials are standing away from it, possibly sheltered in an open porch. Peter is with them. (John 18:18) This reference implies: servants, guards, and the attendants who were the religious leaders frontline protectors. Finally the fire provides enough heat in the open area and some move to the center of the courtyard; first standing there, then are seated at the fire. (Matthew 26:58; Luke 22:55; John 18:18)

Scene Four / Peter Seated / Second Denial

In the middle of the courtyard, in the vicinity of the firelight, a servant girl of the high priest enters the evolving scene. She confronts Peter about his knowing Jesus. The second denial follows. However this being the first one, and the only one, the four gospel writers are in uniform agreement of an event happening. (Matthew 26:69-70; Mark 14:66-68; Luke 22:55-57; John 18:25) Nonetheless the heat intensified not only from the fire, but in Peter's concern about others seated around the perimeter.

Exposure in identity causes the apostle's self-retraction from the challenging situation as his internal fear dominates. In Peter's denial response… the servant girl identified as a woman in Luke 22:57.

Scene Five / Peter Standing

Following the fireside confrontation by the servant girl of the High Priest Caiaphas, Peter leaves that intimate area and moves to a location more accessible for an easier exit from the courtyard. (Matthew 26:71; Mark 14:68)

Scene Six / Peter Standing / Third Denial

After a little while, the same servant girl again confronts Peter and brings forth his third denial. (Mark 14:69-71) Those standing nearby recognize him as a Galilean man.

Scene Seven / Peter Standing / Fourth Denial

Another confrontation unfolds resulting in Peter's fourth denial. (Matthew26:72) The confronter is described in Scripture as another girl. (Matthew26:73) Further confirming Peter's geographical heritage because of his accent. The drama does not cease. Fearful anxiety escalates. (Matthew 26:74)

On the chronology timeline thus far three females have been the confronters. Scripture defines them as servants in general; there would be differences in age with their gender referenced as girl, maidservant, woman.

The pattern changes. Males become more aggressive for the remaining three confrontations. Gender implied because the word "man" spoken in each of Peter's last three denial responses. These final three denials take place in the area closer to the gateway location in the courtyard. People standing, gathered in groups, all possibly in close proximity.

Scene Eight / Peter Standing / Fifth Denial

A little later (Luke 22:58), Luke writes that someone else (man) confronts Peter, and his fifth denial comes forth. Those nearby affirm the confrontation because of Peter's accent.

The Sanhedrin (aka ruling council) has been meeting in Caiaphas' house this whole time; and with Jesus being disrespected, mistreated physically, and humiliated in various ways by the religious leaders. Also, on the timeline Peter has been standing for several hours.

Scene Nine / Peter Standing / Sixth and Seventh Denials

About an hour later (Luke 22:59), Luke identifies an assertive person (man) who confronts Peter… sixth denial ensues. However in this scene the two gospel writers, Luke and John, could be alluding to the same male confronter and confrontation timeline as they appear in close agreement… because of whom John names as a relative of Malchus, who had been in the olive grove when Jesus was arrested. He confronts Peter. This male knew Peter was the one who had cut off the right ear of Malchus. (John18:10) Identity confirmed. Truth exposed. The final two denials come forth in rapid succession. (Luke 22:59; John 18:25-26) The pressure on Peter intensified beyond measure!

On the chronology timeline… Peter, a disciple of Jesus, had stood near the entryway in the courtyard. While in this precarious place… he finds himself losing spiritual footing through fear induced lying and denying repeatedly at every twist and turn.

Scene Ten / The Rooster Crows

Fulfilled… "prophetic revelation" as the rooster crowed! (Matthew 26:74; Mark 14:72; Luke 22:60; John 18:27) This moment on the timeline is acknowledged where Mark's gospel states the rooster crowed the second time in the King James Version (KJV).

Scene Eleven / Jesus and Peter

Jesus turned and looked at Peter. (Luke 22:61) Extraordinary communication finalized. The rooster's crow jolted Peter into spiritual reality. Sounding the undeniable miraculous alert. The denials had taken place; Peter's disowning Christ forever sealed on the historical timeline.

Where was Jesus when He turned and looked at Peter? Jesus would have likely exited through the same entryway which He had entered several hours before. If so, this could align Him in close proximity to Peter. A near face-to-face encounter. Drama at its highest. Was the Lord being led from Caiaphas' house in the upper level and downward; then through the courtyard to the exit... on the way to being taken to the palace of Pilate, the governor?

Or... was the Lord in the upper level of Caiaphas' house and turning looked downward? Seeing His disciple, Peter, near the gateway. Nevertheless... the Bible is silent on the exact location of Jesus. However a gospel writer added further information about the unjust and evil religious leader's guards... their actions toward Jesus after Peter's departure. (Luke 22:63 -65) Therefore Jesus was probably still in the higher level.

Scene Twelve / Peter Exits

A sudden departure. Peter goes outside the courtyard and he wept bitterly. (Matthew 26:75; Mark 14:72; Luke 22:62) John's gospel makes no reference to this conclusion. Is this a deliberate lack of acknowledgement? Or... was John preoccupied elsewhere? Or... was he in his own mental tug-a-war through a tinge of guilt? If John had not secured Peter's entrance his denials would not have taken place in the courtyard. The confrontations in the secured religious area caused Peter to fear for his own life. He was vulnerable for arrest which added to his disowning Jesus.

Peter believed he was fearless. The former fisherman of strength and forthrightness lost sight of what it meant to be a true follower of Jesus Christ. His arrogance and impetuous self-sufficiency exposed. The apostle's fear of man reigned over his lack of reverence for godly consequences; opening the door for fear to sabotage his spiritual strength.

The number of denials... whether three or upwards to seven in count, matters only to emphasize how Peter entrapped himself. The four gospel writers had different audiences. Mark wrote first; Matthew and Luke drew from Mark's writing along with their own understanding of information available to them. John wrote, as the last of the four authors, referencing only the denials he heard.

Apparent inconsistencies do not invalidate the Omnipotence of God; nor the power of the Good News, the Gospel of Jesus, the Son of God / Son of Man. A reader of Scripture may struggle with the whole written dynamic concerning,... the number and the timing of the denials. Nevertheless the accounts warn Christians how vulnerable they can be in their daily spiritual walk. Non consistent wordage, causing possible discrepancies to emerge, should not prompt a falling away about belief in the Bible. However the reading of deliberate, consistent facts referenced could induce the reader to ponder the biblical truth by faith more readily. Producing an even greater trust and belief in the Lord Jesus Christ.

The Lord warned Peter he was vulnerable to an evil attack from the devil. (Matthew 26:34; Mark 14:30; Luke 22:34; John 13:38) Jesus told Peter, "Simon, Simon, Satan has asked to sift you as wheat. But I have prayed for you, Simon, that your faith may not fail. And when you have turned back, strengthen your brothers" (Luke 22:31-32). Therefore Jesus' earlier "prophetic revelation" of Peter's forthcoming three denials happened before the rooster crowed. Implied... stay alert; predators come at any time.

In closing... the Lord is always faithful to provide insightful intervention for a disciple... even if it involves a feathered fowl to signal that He knows all things. As for Christians throughout the centuries... Jesus through the power of the Holy Spirit provided ample opportunity to repent and recommit oneself to truth. In His faithfulness, He does the same today.

13
The Purple Robe

Looking at and sorting through various verses in the four gospels reveals an intriguing backstory which appears to expose an apparent discrepancy. Was there one robe; or a second one also worn by Jesus on the day of His civil trial?

This chapter, the second of four in this section, focuses on the purple robe. The importance of this subject should not be overlooked by the reader of Scripture.

Those everyday clothes Jesus had been wearing at the Last Supper in the upper room; and during His arrest in the Garden of Gethsemane, would come either in contact, or be replaced temporarily with one of two robes. Was it one after another; or both at the same time?

Following Jesus' footsteps after leaving Gethsemane at the base of the Mount of Olives finds the bound Lord being led… first to Annas, then to the High Priest Caiaphas' house. (Matthew 26:57; Luke 22:54; John 18:12-13) The Apostle John states he and Peter followed Jesus there and they entered the courtyard below. (John 18:15-16) The chronology timeline reveals Peter's denials, the Rooster's crow, and Peter's exit. While this was happening other scenes were unfolding above in Caiaphas' house.

The ongoing religious trial progressed as the Sanhedrin (aka ruling council) came into full session in the middle of the night. (Matthew 27:1; Mark 14:53; Luke 23:1) While Jesus was under the custody of these religious men… they spit on, struck with fists, and slapped the bound Lord. (Matthew 26:67) No mention of a robe. The title of king with indirect reference in questioning came through their derogatory referral to charges of blasphemy for His affirmative answer to being Christ, the Son of God; and with the Lord's own acknowledgement as His being seated at the right hand of God later and His future coming on the clouds of heaven. (Matthew 26:63-64; Mark 14:61-62; Luke 22:66-69) The spiritual authorities declared Him worthy of death. Nevertheless, before departing the location, the priest's officers of the temple guards mocked, beat, and blindfolded Jesus. (Luke 22:63-64) At daybreak Jesus is sent to the Roman governor with the expected intent to be sentenced to death by crucifixion. (John 18:28) The whole assembly led Jesus to Pilate. (Luke 23:1)

In John's gospel he provides a more definitive brake-down of the chronology related to Pilate's involvement. The apostle's focus centers on where the interactions between Pilate and Jesus takes place through providing a consistent reference point. The other three gospel writer's input interacts with John's timeline through providing either new or collaborating information; but Matthew, Mark, and Luke give minimal reference to the governor's proceedings. The passages in the Bible are: Matthew 27:11-27; Mark 14:72-15:4; Luke 23:4-25. The Scripture timeline presented here, in John's scenes have Pilate's location defined by whether he is inside or outside of the palace. (John 18:28-19:16) A synopsis of those verses follows:

John 18:28 / Pilate is inside

Jesus accompanied by the entourage of religious leaders of the Jewish people, along with their officers of the temple guards, arrive early morning at Pilate's palace. The Jews do not go inside in order to avoid ceremonial uncleanness because of the pending Passover celebratory meal. (Matthew 27:1; Mark 15:1; Luke 23:1)

John 18:29 / Pilate comes outside

Pilate wants to know what charge they are bringing against the man. The governor learns what the Jewish accusers want him to do for them; as they have no jurisdiction to kill Jesus. Pilate has the authority to fulfill their request; to implement a sentence of death.

John 18:30-32 / Sanhedrin accusations

False charges that Jesus is a criminal are part of their testimony. Pilate tells them to judge Jesus by their own law. Execution becomes a defining and divisive theme. A claim of being powerless to execute anyone becomes the reason the Jews have brought Jesus to Pilate.

John 18:33 / Pilate goes inside

Pilate summons Jesus. (More on John's chronology later.)

Important Note: In Luke 23:5-12, he intersects John's timeline with valuable information concerning King Herod Antipas and Pontius Pilate.

Through an off-handed statement the Jews claim Jesus had started in Galilee; and stirs up the people in Judea with His teaching. (Luke 23:5) Their reference alerts Pilate to a judicial problem. He learned Jesus is from another district. (Luke 23:5-7) Therefore the Lord's adopted Galilean residence (Capernaum) is under King Herod Antipas, the tetrarch's governmental jurisdiction. The Roman governor sends Jesus to Herod who happens to be in Jerusalem at the time of the Jewish Passover. (Luke 23:7) Herod's precise location is not given in Scripture.

Jesus being transferred to Herod's presence is the first time a robe is referenced on that day's timeline. Herod and his soldiers ridiculed and mocked Jesus by dressing Him in an "elegant" robe. (Luke 23:11) Apparently draped around the shoulders of Jesus as no mention of the everyday clothes having been stripped from Him. No color referenced. Only Luke gives any information about Jesus and a gorgeous robe while He stood before Herod. (Luke 23:8-12) Nothing about the robe being removed. While Jesus has been in Herod's presence the chief priests and teachers of the law were standing there. (Luke 23:10) Herod sends Jesus back to Pilate.

Mockery in motion. Jesus, while wearing a king's robe, when sent back to Pilate allows two things to justify the timely transference. First, Herod's unspoken, at least in Scripture, of thankfulness for having the exceptional opportunity to have Jesus of Nazareth in his presence. For a long time Herod had wanted to see Jesus and have Him perform a miracle. (Luke 23:8) In this current scene, void of any miracle, a desired appearance fulfilled through Pilate.

Second, it affirms and solidifies in the mockery that the Roman Empire's cohesiveness rules through… Caesar, Herod, Pilate. Therefore… impossible for Jesus to become a ruling Jewish king in the land of Israel. Herod's silent and self-protective, no charge semi approval now placed on the governor's futuristic final decision over the destiny of Jesus. Having been enemies, Herod and Pilate through this circumstantial timeline became friends. (Luke 23:12)

Palace Locations: Pilate and Herod each had a palace (residence) in Caesarea on the timeline. Nevertheless when court needed to be in session, for either one of them, they resided in Jerusalem. They were both in the city to keep order, thereby discouraging lawless deeds, during the Passover when the area swelled with the influx of celebrating Jews. The palaces in the Roman civil jurisdiction for Pilate and Herod were in close proximity; nearly the same area in exactness of location. This helps to understand the transfer process when Pilate sent Jesus to Herod. However clarity of precise palace identity unknown after Jerusalem fell to the Babylonian destruction in 70 A.D.

The size of the foundation structures were large; Herod's the largest of the two. The reference, Praetorium, is another word for Pilate's palace in Jerusalem. (Mark 15:16) Pillars were part of the exterior open-air common hall (Stone Pavement) where the judgment seat was located.

The religious entourage (Sanhedrin) had taken Jesus from Caiaphas' house first to Pilate… and then in convenience they followed Jesus to Herod… and followed again when the king sent Jesus back to the governor. (Luke 23:10)

(After Luke's inserted interruption included here, the timeline returns to the same previous place in John's gospel.)

John 18:33 / Pilate is inside

Jesus returns. This is the second time the Lord is before Pilate on the same day. However He has on a king's robe. Interrogation resumes. Pilate questions Jesus about being a king, a long discussion follows about His kingdom not of this world; and then the subject matter of what is truth. (John 18:34-37)

Also at this point, two gospel writers, Matthew and Mark, start detailed information related to the theme of Pilate's questions and the kingship of Jesus. An indication of their desire to cause awareness to the importance of this special moment in time.

John 18:38 / Pilate comes outside

The governor states he finds "no basis" for a charge. Pilate's motive revealed. Throughout the rest of the chronology timeline in John's gospel, Pilate remains intent on sparing the life of Jesus.

John 18:39 / Pilate's judicial custom

The release of one prisoner to the people during the Jewish festival was the Jew's custom which Pilate honored. (Mark 15:6; John 18:39) The Jews shouted they wanted Barabbus freed. He was a notorious prisoner, a murderer, known as an insurrectionist. (John 18:39-40) Chapter 18 concludes with this strange and alarming request.

John 19:1 / Pilate has Jesus flogged

Herod's purple robe and the everyday clothes of Jesus would have been removed prior to the flogging.

John 19:2 / Soldier's abusive treatment

The soldiers twisted a crown of thorns, then put it on the head of Jesus. (John 19:2) They struck Him on His head several times with a staff. Matthew and Mark emphasizes it was a whole company of soldiers. (Matthew 27:27-30; Mark 15:16) Then they clothed Him in a robe according to Mark and John. The color mentioned is purple. (Mark 15:16-19; John 19:2)

Also, here is where the potential discrepancy comes into the scene. Is this when a scarlet robe is placed on Jesus (Matthew 27:28) Applied out of necessity because of the head wounds bleeding profusely. Then is the purple placed second, over the first, the scarlet one?

Carrying a speculative theological thought further following this flogging… therefore the Lord is shouldering the weight of sinners and kingship on the natural timeline in a sacred moment. Happening before His actual crucifixion death… of taking the sins of worldwide humanity through the shedding of His blood while on the cross; along with fulfilling the Davidic kingly covenant that God, the Father, had given to King David centuries before Christ came to earth. (Isaiah 9:6-7; Mark 11:10) Later that afternoon, Jesus, the Son of God / Son of Man, was destined to die in obedience by crucifixion for the sins of the world and to reign as the King of kings for all eternity.

John19:3 / Soldier's mockery

Roman soldiers mockingly hail Jesus as the king of the Jews.

John 19:4 / Pilate comes outside

It becomes apparent Pilate was inside and near Jesus as the governor comes outside again. Once more Pilate said to the Jews he finds "no basis" for a charge.

John 19:5 / Jesus comes outside

Jesus is wearing the crown of thorns and a purple robe. Pilate tells the Jews, "Here is the man" (John 19:5).

John 19:6 / Jews see Jesus

The Jews continue with shouts to crucify Jesus. Again Pilate responds with you take Him; and reiterates for the third time "no basis" for a charge.

However the audible escalation by the determined accusers of Jesus, through their anger, rage, and fury in near uproar mode, sustained the provocative idea of a more violent scourging which preceded a crucifixion. The fixation from the Sanhedrin's religious trial and outcome only enhanced the political prospect of an unrelenting direction toward a more horrific and definitive result.

John 19:7 / Jews respond

Jewish law says He must die because He claimed to be the Son of God. The Sanhedrin considered the answer from Jesus to be blasphemy. (Matthew 26:63-66)

John 19:8 / Pilate goes inside // No reference that Jesus goes inside

Pilate more afraid when he heard Jesus is possibly the Son of God. The governor spends moments milling over consequences related to his own judicial involvement.

John 19:9-11 / Jesus and Pilate inside

Pilate tells Jesus he has the power to free Him. (John 19:10) Jesus responds, "You would have no power over me if it were not given to you from above" (John 19:11).

John 19:12 / Pilate comes outside

Pilate continues to try to set Jesus free. Has a conversation with the Jews about Jesus being their king. Their denial progresses still wanting the governor to crucify Jesus. They taunt Pilate with the words, "If you let this man go, you are no friend of Caesar" (John 19:12). The other three gospel writers acknowledge the Jews asked for Barabbus to be offered in exchange as they prefer his release, over Jesus being set free. (Matthew 27:20-21; Mark 15:8-11; Luke 23:18-19) Shouts to crucify Jesus prevail.

Important Note: Jesus is a Jew (Hebrew Israelite). He, the Messiah... the Anointed One... had come to His own people who rejected Him. (John 1:10-11; 7:5) Jesus was an outsider to the corrupt religious and political systems of His day. Intense friction and fracture prevailed between Him and them because of the Lord's wholeness teachings, supernatural power, and Godly authority. The Sanhedrin were envious due to the increasing admiration for Jesus from His followers... Jews and Gentiles alike. (Matthew 27:18; Mark 15:10) He had become a substantial threat. Could He possibly become the King of the Jews?

John 19:13 / Pilate brings Jesus outside

The judicial tide turns. Pilate sits down on the judge's seat; the place known as Stone Pavement (Gabbatha). (Matthew 27:19; John 19:13)

In Matthew's gospel around this timeline, the apostle informs his reader as the result of Pilate's wife's dream, she sent information to warn Pilate not to have anything to do with that innocent man… Jesus. (Matthew 27:19) Also revealed is the action of Pilate washing his hands and stating he would be innocent of the man's blood. (Matthew 27:24)

John 19:14 / Pilate addresses the Jews

Pilate's final conversation with the Jews affirmed truth as he told them, "Here is your king" (John 19:14). The timeline stated is around the sixth hour on the day of the Preparation of Passover week. Noon on the Gentile timeline.

Important Side Note: In the gospel of Mark he mentions at the third hour they crucified Him; and the extensive dialogue having finished with Pilate. (Mark 15:23) Christian tradition tends to follow this timeline. (Therefore later the penal flogging, walking to Golgotha, and nailing Jesus to the cross would have taken a substantial amount of time from after the third hour up to the sixth.) Jesus had been before Pilate since early morning; those hours within the first three of the daytime. While Jesus was nailed to the cross on Golgotha, darkness fell over the whole land for three hours. (Matthew 27:45; Mark 15:33) Noon to three on the Gentile timeline.

John 19:15 / Pilate succumbs to pressure

In John 19:15, Pilate asked a final question, "Shall I crucify your king?" The Jews are adamant they have no king but Caesar. Loud shouts prevailed. Pilate mentally sets in motion the penal torture to precede the crucifixion. (More on this later.)

John 19:16 / Pilate hands Jesus over to be crucified

On the timeline given by Matthew, Mark, and Luke, each states the release of Barabbus took place prior to Pilate handing Jesus over to be crucified. In Scripture, through the silent understanding of the Roman protocol, the scourging would transpire. (Matthew 27:26; Mark 15:15; Luke 23:25)

The soldiers remove the robe. A horrific scourging administered. Afterwards they put His everyday clothes back on Him. (Matthew 27:31; Mark 15:20) Pilate's soldiers had the final charge of transferring Jesus to Golgotha. (John 19:18) They led Jesus, the Son of God / Son of Man, to be crucified. (Matthew 27:31)

Jesus struggled physically while He walked the road to the crucifixion site. Simon of Cyrene, while on his way coming in from the country, is forced by the soldiers to carry the cross of Jesus the rest of the way to Golgotha. (Matthew 27:32; Mark 15:21; Luke 23:26) No robe is mentioned as being worn by Jesus.

Back to why a chronology focus on the robe becomes important. The reader of Scripture is alerted to an apparent discrepancy in the Apostle Matthew's color reference. Mark and John each confirm the color purple and each writer references that color twice. (Mark 15:17,20; John 19:2,5) Luke describes as elegant, no color given. (Luke 23:11) Matthew states scarlet. (Matthew 27:28 NIV) When making a theological attempt to justify the apparent inconsistency of cloth color... scarlet versus purple, does anything give validity to what Matthew's gospel signals about his choice of choosing scarlet?

Enter translation error... in the earliest manuscripts, including the Greek New Testament (Septuagint), only speculation could theorize why the translator chose to identify the robe color as scarlet in the gospel of Matthew (NIV). Even though the reader of Scripture is not likely to have a Greek text available to them, to eliminate including its wording here would be amiss. In Matthew 27:28, it actually has a purple cloak. Do translators tend to try and help out the Holy Spirit when translating the older writings into a new translation? Or do apparent discrepancies sometimes result from a simple misread?

Or… perhaps by the time the apostle observed the purple robe on Jesus in the natural outdoor lighting through shadows either on the Praetorium, or the Stone Pavement, it altered the color in the pre noon rays of sun cascading across the robe; revealing a shade or two color difference when reflected. Eyes and emotions can play tricks. Or… did Jesus, after the Resurrection, tell Matthew the scarlet robe was under the purple one?

If the robe was scarlet in color; then it belonged to Pilate because Jesus was under his judicial authority; therefore not wearing a king's purple robe. Rationale propagated. Scarlet is often related to sins and sinners. Scripture states, "Though your sins are like scarlet, they shall be as white as snow…" (Isaiah 1:18).

Blood Splatter Droppings… blood from an artery is bright red; from a vein dark red. It changes color when it mixes with air, and also with cloth. Then it becomes a darker red brown. Therefore all the massive amounts of blood coming from Jesus would bring spotted discoloration to an item of clothing.

Theological and political speculation falls conveniently on the timeline when evaluating Pilate's involvement. Pressure evolved in stages as the Sanhedrin applied unwavering insistence on the governor to order Jesus to be crucified.

John's references of Pilate's continual multiple statements (three) are that he finds "no basis" for a charge. Nothing deserving of death. (No rebellion against Roman authority. No evil committed by Him.) Creditable decision because the apostle tells his reader, "From then on, Pilate tried to set Jesus free, but the Jews kept shouting" (John 19:12). In the distance King Herod would be hearing this commotion.

No attempt is made here to excuse Pilate's political motives and judicial actions. He was responsible for authorizing the crucifixion of Jesus. Nevertheless important to be referenced because it gives authenticity to his own political agenda and personal mental anguish.

Pilate succumbs to his internal political tension rather than listening to his intellectual comprehension and personal conscience. He already knew Jesus was the king of the Jews; not earthly, but heavenly. (John 18:36-37) Later in the morning, Pilate is against changing the sign on the cross at the Jew's challenging request. His conversation with them gives credence to this theological perception.

Speculation neither affirms 100% accuracy; nor should it ignore apparent discrepancies. Insight and verse clarification can assist the reader of Scripture, during one's mediation time on the Word, in providing an awareness of a certain point on the chronology timeline. It is good to question, while becoming more attentive even when one only has their personal copy of a Bible translation (version).

A reader might also have two valid questions: Who had the original ownership of the purple robe Mark and John describe? How did the robe arrive at Golgotha?

Related are the three residential locations in Jerusalem, one each for Caiaphas, Herod, Pilate; and thoughts about a robe in each provides potential conclusive rationale. A mini review follows:

Obvious speculation… it could have been one of the chief priests sacred robes.
Maybe? Maybe not. In the Old Testament, God gave to Moses a seamless neck design for a priest's blue cloth robe woven top to bottom; and also a white linen undergarment. The latter not attached to the robe. (Exodus 28:31,42; 39:22-23) Sacrilegious would be the action if a priest's robe had been used in mockery. The Sanhedrin (aka ruling council) would never permit such a thing to happen. Color and design does not align with the Apostle John's description at the civil trial.

Obvious speculation… it could have been one of King Herod's elegant robes.
Maybe? Maybe not. A seamless robe with an attached undergarment placed around the shoulders of Jesus in the Roman king's presence; therefore the attached undergarment was between the everyday clothes on His back and the interior part of the robe. If yes, did Jesus exit Herod's presence wearing it? No mention of it having been removed.

If true... then the religious leaders followed behind Jesus who was wearing a king's robe when He left Herod.

Obvious speculation... it could have been one of Pilate's robes. Maybe? Maybe not. If true, Pilate's scarlet robe (NIV) contained massive amounts of blood and was not at the crucifixion.

Color purple represents royalty. A king's robe is symbolic of royal authority. Jesus was born a king and crucified as a king. (Matthew 2:2) In the civil trial Jesus confirms Pilate's kingship statement by answering, "You are right in saying I am a king. In fact, for this reason I came into the world to testify to the truth. Everyone on the side of truth listens to me" (John 18:37).

Important Side Note: What a phenomenal sight it would have been to have the presence of a king's robe at the foot of the crucifixion cross of the Lord Jesus Christ. Having a twofold purpose... used as a visual item for further mockery and validation of His criminal charge. A tangible trophy having been set aside earlier by the military participants because of the unique timeline and proximity of location; as Jesus had worn the robe back to Pilate's palace from Herod's residence.

Also an Important question to ask... does this tie into a reference later in John 19:24 where Jesus makes a statement about... and "my clothing"... as He possibly refers to the happenstance of a king's robe being there? If yes, then a twofold inference that a seamless undergarment (tunic) and a kingly robe are intwined as being spiritually joined in cohesive drama unfolding through a shocking moment related to destiny.

In a follow up reference to... and "my clothing"... in the Greek, the word, raiment, is used for clothing. Preceded by the word "and" indicating the action of two events occurring at the same point in time; therefore potentially along with the seamless undergarment while lots are being cast for it. In the scene, is Jesus also identifying with a king's robe as He looks down from the cross?

The word robe is used, in the place of other words for clothing, over and over in the English language throughout Scripture. Adding to language complications… generations of Christians have often loosely referred to what the four soldiers cast lots for as being a robe; after having divided up His other clothes.

Pilate's written sign stating the Lord's crime… Jesus Of Nazareth The King Of The Jews… was nailed on the cross above the head of Christ. (John 19:19-20) In an ironic attempt to state the criminal charge… it allowed all those at His crucifixion to read in three languages… Aramaic, Latin, Greek… the "sovereign" truth about the identity of the Lord's heavenly kingship.

Finally… was the centurion the robe carrier? Leaving Pilate's palace for Golgotha, did the Roman officer take responsibility for Herod's robe? Not far-fetched.

The same centurion… who after the death of Jesus proclaimed, "Surely he was the Son of God!" (Matthew 27:54). Again, this male who headed up the five person military presence at the Lord's crucifixion site… did he carry the robe of that "righteous" man? (Luke 23:47)

14
The Flogging Sequences

While tracking the inconsistency of cloth color for the previous chapter... it led to a necessary inquiry into the potential reality of two floggings in Chapter 19 of John's gospel. Of course, any rational attempt to insert this biblical and theological speculation upends Christian tradition; setting the original perspective ajar concerning the one flogging of Jesus prior to the crucifixion. When something appears amiss, or out of order, it requires returning to it for cautious evaluation. However careful reading provided the direction for looking deeper into the event-filled happenings at Pilate's palace. The reality of two floggings Jesus might have experienced does surface.

Before delving into the theme of this chapter, a brief visit to what happened "inside of Jesus" while He was in the Garden of Gethsemane; and taking a look at those three specific prayer times with His Father in heaven. (Matthew26:36-44) The pre crucifixion distress He experienced was described as, "sweat as drops of blood falling to the ground" (Luke 22:42). Also, an angel came and ministered to Him. (Luke 22:43)

Being acquainted with the civil knowledge of the Roman practice of their horrific flogging punishment, the Lord knew what torture was ahead. Those prayers caused the final laying down of His will, fears, and anything else inclusive which targeted His whole being... spirit, soul, body. The initial first part of His human struggle was in the garden as the Son of Man. (Matthew 26:36-44; Mark 14:32-33)

Beyond that human difficulty lies the spiritual reality of what He would actually endure on the cross as the Son of God during the darkest timeline of separation spiritually from His heavenly Father. He was taking the sins of worldwide humanity upon Himself. All of this terror and horror would unfold even though He was without sin... the sacrificial Lamb of God. A righteous and innocent man having done nothing deserving of death!

Moving on again... to the timeline and relevant flogging theme centered at Pilate's palace where the two floggings had potential to evolve. The related content covered here points to verses in John 19:1-6 and 19:13-16. Alluded to in the previous chapter, this one provides follow-up on specific civil flogging details.

Chapter verses 19:1 and 19:16, in John's gospel, reveals the starting of two different flogging timelines. In John19:1, it references an initial flogging... and later the "implied" more extended flogging Jesus experienced prior to the crucifixion. (John 19:16) This relevant awareness self-understood by John's initial readers.

Punishment in simple terms: If one's crime was less extensive in criminal activity they gave a lighter sentence related to being flogged. The use of a whip, void of intense beating. However if one was assigned a harsher judicial sentence, a more extensive flogging procedure happened prior to the crucifixion; then the final culminating punishment by death. (More on this later.)

In John's gospel, the apostle seems to imply that Pilate adhered to this plan. The governor appears to apply this option because of his initial involvement with the Jew's unrelenting loud crucify shouts. Their demand was unprecedented.

The governor allowed a lenient measure of flogging for a justified release before a more severe flogging (scourging) punishment happened later. Pilate offered to punish Jesus and release Him. (Luke 23:15-17)

John 19:1 / Pilate has Jesus flogged

John mentions the decision and action that a flogging takes place under Pilate's authority. Herod's purple robe and the everyday clothes Jesus wore would have been removed prior to the first flogging. It appears the governor was in the presence of Jesus during this time; possibly to control the company of soldiers' flogging action. Was one of Pilate's old scarlet robes placed on Jesus to absorb the flowing blood; before the actual replacement of the king's purple robe? Therefore as a result of this (possible) decision the robe of King Herod would be protected from damage.

John 19:2-6 / Roman soldiers mockery

Abusive actions intensify as the soldiers twist a crown of thorns and put it on the head of Jesus. They clothed Him in a purple robe. They mockingly hail Jesus as the king of the Jews. Pilate allows the mockery. (John 19:3) The military personnel knew He could never be a king in Roman-controlled Israel. Afterwards while Jesus is before Pilate and the out of control verbal shouting chaos coming from the Jewish crowd, the governor reiterates for the third time he finds "no basis" for a criminal charge during his crucial conversational attempts to set Jesus free. (John 18:38; 19:4,6)

An initial first flogging transpired before the judgement seat sequence happens later in the final confrontational scenes. The physician, Luke, also confirms what appears to be a first inquisitional flogging. (Luke 23:16) Notice on the chronology timeline there is no mention of Barabbus being released before the first flogging. However, later Luke appears to verify the penal flogging of handing Jesus over to be crucified... with the immediate release of Barabbus. (Luke 23:25)

Neither prior to, nor during the first flogging, no account of Jesus either denying or recanting any statements He had given to Pilate in the civil trial about His kingdom. No retraction of answers spoken in front of the Sanhedrin (aka ruling council) earlier at the religious trial in His affirmative response... to being Christ, the Son of God. (Matthew 26:63-64) In those conversations Jesus spoke truth.

How tempting the initial flogging must have been for the Lord Jesus Christ to be able to eliminate the second scourging by being offered a selective reduction in punishment. Christ had a last minute exiting temptation provided to avoid the public shame and disgrace of the crucifixion cross looming in His immediate future. He could forestall the will of His heavenly Father. Amazing how this moment on the chronology timeline is rarely considered by believers.

An explanation of the Roman two-stage flogging procedure follows:

In an inquisitional flogging... a milder form to extract a confession, afforded the criminal opportunity to be freed because of one's own confession to criminal actions and a personal verbalization of repentance which would be honored. Also allowed the accusers to grant mercy toward the one whom their accusations initially had brought the criminal before judicial authority. Therefore a deep inquiry for information to aid in the sorting of the facts to determine guilt or innocence. What does truth expose?

In a penal flogging... a horrific scourging evolved into a tortuous procedure. The Roman's flogging required a scourge instrument inflicting serious bodily injury. A leather or metal handle with twelve cords and multiple metal pieces attached to each. (There were other types available which differed in style with pieces made of various elements imbedded in the weapon.) Nonetheless the merciless whipping to the bare back on the criminal amounted to 39/40 lashes in Judaism authorization. Producing maximum tares in the flesh. Having a near deadly effect with massive bloodshed. The tearing of skin, through the Roman soldier's violent action, went beyond any comprehension of cruelty. Nevertheless the Roman protocol of unlimited lashes at the hands of the soldier's punishing actions could often bring death prior to a crucifixion.

John19:13-16 / Pilate's penal decision

The judicial tide turns once Pilate sits down on the judgment seat; the place known as Stone Pavement (Gabbatha). (John 19:13) The key transition point of no return will come with the release of Barabbas. The governor has a final conversation with the Jews. They knew the physical and mental agony the Lord Jesus Christ would endure; as the result of their overwhelming chanting to crucify Him that caused a near uproar. (Matthew 27:24) Their loud shouts prevailed. Pilate succumbs to their pressure and mentally sets in motion the penal torture to precede the crucifixion.

A more hostile flogging would be mandated, even though unspoken, at the judgement seat when Pilate delivers his eventful order… as he hands Jesus over to be crucified. (Matthew27:26; Mark 15:15; Luke 23:24; John 19:16) Therefore this probably validates and confirms the perception related to not just one, but a possible two floggings. Cruel military floggings would not be unusual. Given Roman practice when punishing criminals the extensive timeline where Pilate's continual action related to having Jesus released falls in line with the civil justification and protocol.

Nevertheless the initial onset must start with sanctioning the release of Barabbas. Matthew, Mark, and Luke, each state Barabbas' release took place just prior to Pilate handing Jesus over to be crucified. In Scripture, through the silent understanding of Roman military protocol the penal scourging would transpire. They removed the robe; plus any cloth coverings underneath. After the flogging they put His everyday clothes back on Him. (Matthew 27:31; Mark 15:20) Pilate's soldiers led Jesus to Golgotha. (Matthew 27:33) They nailed Him to the cross to be crucified. (John 19:17-18)

Nothing in the Bible about the crown being removed. If it had been, then more blood would come from the wounds. What happened to the crown of thorns immediately after the crucifixion?

Can the two floggings Jesus might have experienced be proven with 100% accuracy in the twenty-first century? No, not likely.

15

The Seamless Undergarment

The focus moves forward on the chronology timeline, related to the seamless undergarment, at the crucifixion site. Inconsistencies surface when the style is defined through various languages and translations. (More on this later.)

John is the only one of the four gospel writers who mentions specific detail associated with a seamless undergarment at Golgotha. The apostle was there! In John 19:23-24, he describes a timeline in the scene by writing, "When the soldiers crucified Jesus they took his clothes, dividing them into four shares, one for each of them, with the undergarment remaining. This garment was seamless, woven in one piece from top to bottom. Let's not tear it, they said to one another. Let's decided by lot who will get it. This happened that the Scripture might be fulfilled which says they divided my garments among themselves and cast lots for my clothing. So this is what the soldiers did." (The Old Testament Scripture referenced is Psalm 22:18)

Was this seamless undergarment something Jesus wore underneath His everyday clothes? This seems to be implied in John 19:23-24. If true, why would the Roman soldiers want to cast lots for His undergarment even if they deemed it valuable in design? The garment would have had traces of blood from the horrific penal flogging; having been underneath the outer everyday garments Jesus had worn to the crucifixion site.

Important Note: The style for the garment type is defined in various terms. In John 19:24, called... clothing in the New International Version (NIV); tunic and raiment in the Greek New Testament (Septuagint), coat in the King James Version (KJV). Also raiment and vesture, earlier when in other biblical descriptions; indicative of a kingly type robe, not a tunic. The descriptive classifications are too extensive and intertwined to elaborate on.

Therefore the seamless undergarment referenced above leaves unsettling viewpoints and interpretations filled with language difficulties. However... as for the social custom, males wore tunics just below the knee; wealthy men wore ankle length robes.

Somethings cannot be proven... emphasis on speculation only. On the one hand... sometimes the reader of Scripture must settle for... unknown... as an answer. On the other hand... it does not eliminate the possibility for asking multiple challenging questions. Inquisitive thoughts lend themselves to this type of theological and investigative journey. The intent within is to cause awareness to the difficulty of being assured a correct answer can be reached; if someone attempts to reconcile an apparent discrepancy.

Unanswered questions that might pop up can lead to substantial speculations. Four thoughts to ponder are:

First... what color and cloth type was the seamless undergarment referenced in John 19:23-24? Nothing mentioned. Was it white linen? If yes, then this would provide substantial insight and a thought provoking idea related to a priest's under garment which might surface. (Exodus 28:31, 42; 39:22-23, 27) Even though the blue robe mentioned in the Old Testament verses was seamless; the tunic (undergarment) was not designed in similar fashion.

Jesus became the sacrificial Lamb of God and the High Priest, through His shed blood, while on the cross. His atonement corresponds with this theological truth. The thematic subject of a high priest too detailed and complex to elaborate on here.

Second... how long did Jesus have possession of the seamless undergarment? The reader of Scripture is left without any knowledgeable answer.

Third... who made the seamless undergarment Jesus had been wearing? Nothing in Scripture gives any indication who the seamstress might have been. Was it purchased at a marketplace? Unlikely! Or... a gift bestowed on the Lord because someone had the revelation of the High Priest role which Jesus was about to enter. Names for obvious speculation are... maybe Salome, maybe Mary of Bethany, maybe Mary, the mother of Jesus? However this design, seamless, would be indicative that the resource person was wealthy.

Fourth... why might the soldiers cast lots for garments at a crucifixion? Especially for a valuable seamless undergarment. The latter available for their own use when wearing their personal clothing would be unique and discrete. Luxurious wear for a Roman soldier's ranking level. Nevertheless... missing on the circumstantial timeline is anything verbal the centurion might have said, before the death of Jesus, about what he observes taking place among the four soldiers.

In conclusion... the lucky one, an unnamed Roman soldier, walked away from the crucifixion site carrying the crucified man's prized seamless undergarment.

Section Four

Two Defining Statements

16
Today In Paradise

Looking at selective words on a timeline allows one to contemplate and organize a few random thoughts. Scripture is clear these are two of several statements Jesus said at His crucifixion. He told the criminal on the cross next to His cross, "I tell you the truth, today you will be with me in paradise" (Luke 23:43). Then seconds before the moment of the Lord's death, He called out saying, "Father into your hands I commit my spirit" (Luke 23:46). This chapter explores one of those factual defining sentences; and in the following chapter, the other referenced.

Questions asked here and expounded on; with free-range thoughts explored too. The reason for this spiritual rationale is to cause Christians to think; not just reread words they have read many times over. The biblical truth is in Jesus' statements.

At the crucifixion, on the cross, Jesus told the (repentant) thief he would be in Paradise today with Him. (Luke 23:43) Where is Paradise? Believers have differing views. Some are passionate in their belief it is upward in the heaven-lies somewhere. Others believe it was a safe protective compartment in Hades (hell). (This latter view discussed again in another chapter with the topic of Paradise explored further.)

Nevertheless, after the Lord's Resurrection, Paradise by name in Scripture, does not appear to exist as a specific place other than in Revelation 2:7; mentioned once by the elderly Apostle John when referencing the tree of life in the Paradise of God. However, on the timeline of the Fall from grace, the tree of life was in the garden of Eden where no harsh laborious tasks or bodily pain existed. (Genesis 2:8-9; 15-18)

For believers who die in Christ... after death is to be absent from the body, and to be present (in spirit) with the Lord in heaven. (2 Corinthians 5:6-8) Notice not Paradise.

Should questions be freely asked of biblical information? God desires that believers engage with Him in prayer. How else would they come to know, and to understand, and to trust Him more fully, as they walk with Him through the available presence and power of the Holy Spirit?

Christians are admonished to rightly divide the Bible's truth. The reference often quoted is in 2 Timothy 2:15, "Do your best to present yourself to God as one approved, a workman who does not need to be ashamed and who correctly handles the word of truth."

Therefore, implications might also be drawn; to better determine what, or what not, Jesus wants His faithful believers to know and understand. Some potential conclusions remain unanswered forever like any details for the reunion of God the Father and His Son in heaven on Resurrection Sunday. Jesus ascended to the Father, from the sepulcher area in the garden, after His appearance to Mary Magdalene. To be at peace with unknown spiritual facts becomes important too. Therefore, great significance given here to acknowledging... "It is the glory of God to conceal a matter..." (Proverbs 25:2).

17
The Father's Hands

A familiar and important biblical backstory becomes worthy of consideration. Therefore before launching into a theological and theoretical side trip centered on the conscious act of Jesus committing His Spirit into the Father's hands; another doctrine needs explored.

Backstory... Recorded in Luke 1:26-35, the reader learns, an angel of the Lord, Gabriel, appeared to Mary (the soon-to-be mother of Jesus). Mary's puzzlement of how this will happen is met with information that the Holy Spirit will overshadow her and she will conceive the Son of God / Son of Man. (Luke 1:33) Attention drawn to confirming prophecy from the Old Testament where a "virgin" will become God's selected vessel to conceive and birth God's only begotten Son (in the flesh); thereby providing salvation (redemption) for His people on earth. (Isaiah 7:14) Unexplainable fully; but accepted, and believed in faith, because of Scripture... The Holy Bible. Christians hold to this truth concerning the birth of Christ.

Jesus in His adult life told many, friend and foe alike, "Anyone who has seen me has seen the Father" (John 14:9). Not comprehendible for many of those listening. Nonetheless... Truth. As Bible believers, Christians know God is a Spirit; the Three in One... God the Father, Jesus the only begotten Son, and the Holy Spirit.

Explanation through the above backstory, leads forward to exploring the crucifixion and death of the Lord Jesus Christ on the cross. Taking up the statement referenced in Luke's gospel... Jesus said, "Father into your hands I commit my spirit" (Luke 23:46). Why the plural form of the word hand? Were the Father's hands cupped side-by-side together? Or were they separated with palms exposed; angled downward to receive the spirit of Jesus? God the Father, in spirit, received! How?

At the crucifixion, on the cross, Jesus commits His spirit into the Father's hands. Truth! A conscience act and statement on His part. What did it mean? For how long? Yes, of course, He died and was buried. Nevertheless, God the Father, raised Jesus from the dead... Resurrection. Jesus' spirit returned to earth. From what location? Heaven where God the Father is enthroned? Or from Hades (hell)? Remember Christ took upon Himself the sins of the world at the crucifixion. (2 Corinthians 5:21) Where did He have to descend? How far did He descend?

Moving further into the "what if" territory. While here on earth Jesus was still the Son of God. Incarnate as He took on flesh being the Son of Man... simultaneous in nature with God and spirit. (John 1:14) The crossing of boundaries... earth and heaven / mortal and immortal. Could the same happen while in Hades? The Lord was still the Son of God as He took on the sins of the world, thus becoming an embodied Lord of lords walking the chamber/chasm of Hades (hell). Complete and fulfilled redemption for sin. Again in spirit, the crossing of boundaries... Heaven, Earth, Hades... angelic, human, demonic.

Here comes theory... what if when Jesus died on the cross there was another unexplainable momentary separation of His Spirit once again after He committed it into the Father's hands? Something took place! Scripture at this juncture is revealing... but what? Readers of the Bible know there are three locations: the body in the grave, His spirit in heaven, and His descent into the heart of the earth. How does this become reconciled?

There was a heavenly, eternal separation to enable the overshadowing of the Holy Spirit in order for the conception of Jesus to happen and Him birthed in the flesh. Therefore, did something of a similar type happen for the Lord to descend and be in Hades (hell)?

Jesus was in "the heart of the earth three days and three nights." How could He be? Scripture is clear His buried mortal body was in the tomb until the appointed time. Resurrected in bodily appearance, His empty grave clothes remained behind in the tomb.

Visualize for a minute, those last moments of the crucifixion. His spirit moving upwards into the Father's hands. Received! Jesus died. Then His body buried in the tomb, His spirit still in the Father's hands. By spirit, from the Father, does He then descend into Hades (hell)? What really transpired has no explanation in Scripture. Hades is a place of spirits… demonic, wicked, and evil ones!

Back to the crucifixion scene… encompassing Christ while He hung on the cross, the overwhelming wicked horror of the spiritual reality of Satan's domain! Crucifixion was physical agony beyond measure. Nonetheless, nothing comparable to the extent of torment Jesus experience while dying through His blood sacrifice and taking on the sins of the world. (1 Peter 2:24) Complete and total separation from the presence of God, His Father; which Jesus had never experienced before in all of His eternal existence. (Matthew 27:46; Mark 15:34)

A horrific and totally different dynamic than what the two criminals hanging on the crosses on either side of Him on Golgotha were enduring. The people watching lacked any concept of reality unfolding during the crucifixion hours. Nevertheless, in the total darkness enveloping the scene, a centurion said, "Surely this man was the Son of God" (Mark 15:39).

Section Five

Distinct Locations

18
A Hidden Measure Of Time

A heavy-laden side-trip needs explored. At this juncture in telling the supernatural Resurrection event it requires a serious look into where Jesus was prior to any post Resurrection appearances. The inclusion of this chapter covers two prophetic statements of Jesus about Himself and the consequential circumstances of two stories He told.

During His earthly ministry, Jesus told the Twelve, other disciples, even Jewish authorities, that He would die and be in the heart of the earth for three days and three nights; and then rise from the dead. Timeline stated... Resurrection followed! Nonetheless, between the Lord's death and His Resurrection the interval of those days and nights lacks any major description in Scripture. Nothing!

No clear revelation of His spiritual and supernatural activity unfolding in that block of time. However, Jesus, through His teachings and before His crucifixion, gave snippets of insights to those willing to listen to His proclamation about the concealed location.

Time spans and teachings like the story of Jonah; and the story of Father Abraham, Lazarus the beggar, and the rich man; reveal valid information. This allows the reader of Scripture to draw some understanding and worthwhile conclusions of His "heart of the earth" proposed period of time.

What is the heart of the earth? Where is it? Are there extreme depths to that area? Yes, it appears to exist and with levels. However, what Jesus said about Jonah the prophet, who preached repentance for sin and forgiveness, needs to unfold first in this chapter.

In the Old Testament, in the book of Jonah, Chapters 1-2, it reveals what the prophet experienced as related to his not being obedient to the known will of God on that current timeline of his life. In brief, the story... he was commissioned to go to a city (Nineveh) and preach repentance for sins and available forgiveness from God so the people would avert God's judgement. Jonah declined by running away... far away... in the opposite direction. Long story short... in rebellion Jonah winds up on a ship, and then thrown overboard due to him bringing turmoil aboard.

By God's mercy a great fish comes along and swallows Jonah whole. The runaway prophet spends three days and three nights in the belly of the fish. At this point in his story details of his experience written in the second chapter of Jonah requires extra attention from the reader of Scripture.

Encased in the fish Jonah goes to the depths of the heart of the earth. He details the terror of the time sequence himself. Clearly he is describing depths of Hades (hell) as he understood it.

The prophet had a keen sense of death awaiting while going to the pit, at the base of a mountain, and being banished from the presence of God. In written phrases the reader learns through Jonah's details that "he knew that he knew" where he was... though protected by God's faithful resource (fish) during that complete span of time.

Remember Jonah has not physically died; and not being deceased he still has a chance for redemption through being "righteous by faith in God" according to Old Testament theology during his lifespan. Eventually he cries out to God for mercy, to spare his life, and a renewed chance to be obedient.

Why does Scripture convey those depths? Jonah's details provided insight from the Old Testament as to why the Lord Jesus Christ attempted to impart the truth to His disciples. As for the Twelve, they had not fully grasped that Jesus would die and be resurrected; the physical and spiritual thematic subjects appear to have gone over their heads... way over.

Moving on to another teaching, Jesus tells the story of three deceased males. Making a point, not a parable, because Father Abraham, was a deceased Jewish patriarch, Lazarus the destitute beggar, and the rich man were real examples. The latter in a different location after his death.

Here come those levels again. The reference by Jesus of a great chasm is central to the consequences of separate locations. (Luke 16:26) Father Abraham, and Lazarus (the beggar after having difficult and horrible circumstances in life) are now in a peaceful location and both worthy of it. The rich man, the third character in the story, finds himself in horror (fire) in the heart of the earth beyond belief of anything he could have imagined. His deeds had taken him to the depths of the earth. He wants a change to take place... it did not... and will not. (Luke 16:19-31) The spiritual center of the story is torment for the rich man. The word, rich, is a relevant term. He could have extravagant wealth, or be rich only compared to Lazarus' extreme lack of privilege. Bad or wicked deeds accompanied with a lack of mercy toward others are some key unrepentant sins which sealed the rich man's eternal destiny.

Why so horrific a judgment? The lifespan of a human's availability to accept Jesus as Savior and Lord does not go on endlessly. The story of Father Abraham, Lazarus, and the rich man is not about money per se. More about his "deeds" being the result of wealth that corrupts some people. Disobedience to the "known will of God" when it affects others seems clear in the Jonah story as another example of deeds. Withholding the knowledge of repentance for sins and opportunity for salvation from another person has clear consequences.

Deeds are seldom talked about in sermons. Christians are accountable for their actions. Judgement for bad or wicked deeds from their lifetime too. Any guilt for deeds through the sinful nature must be brought into the Light of Christ and His sacrificial blood covenant in repentance for redemption. However, Jesus being without sin, was known as a person powerful in word and deed. (Luke 24:19)

To skip over the "heart of the earth" sequence, within the story of the glorious Resurrection of the Lord Jesus Christ, ignores a spiritual reality Jesus experienced. Avoiding that portion of time immediately after His burial leaves out a missing link of His redemption through the crucifixion.

Jesus spent three days and three nights in the heart of the earth. What unfolded during those hours? The Godhead of the Trinity knows. Nevertheless an obvious note of caution is recognized here... "to not add to" Scripture (the meaning of eisegesis); however the possible gleaning of truth which Jesus was emphatic about concerned a certain span of time He wanted known. Therefore, with the careful "taking of truth from" Scripture (the meaning of exegesis) so valid questions and concepts can be explored while still acknowledging the unknown parts and information which remains in God's sovereign domain.

How does a reader of Scripture approach the concept of a spiritual or theological theory of levels in Hades? There appears to be a more silent insight that unfolded and requires exploration. Questions related to its theme and its consequence have little-to-no-answers in the natural. However the following chapter lets the reader question why another circumstance is often ignored which pertains to the Resurrection.

19
A Violent Earthquake

A violent earthquake happened! Those words, a violent earthquake, are only in the last chapter of Matthew's gospel. (Matthew 28:2) He seems to equate it with the angel descending from heaven, rolling back the stone, and sitting on it in the garden.

Matthew also told of an earthquake at the time of Jesus' death on the cross. Things happened... events unfolded... and people knew an earthquake had taken place. Earth, rocks split... (Matthew 27:51-54)

In Scripture these two earthquakes are like bookends on the timeline between the immediate death and pending Resurrection of the Lord Jesus Christ. Why does the gospel writer give special attention to the first; but remains silent about the second?

Does it not seem strange that only Matthew mentions a "violent" earthquake? One of those troubling scenarios... an earthquake that no one in Jerusalem felt or talked about afterward. No one... neither the women who were going to the tomb with burial spices, nor the fleeing guards who went to the chief priests.

Matthew's peers in writing their gospels ignore it too. No chaos, no disruption of stones, no pathways to-and-from Jerusalem being disturbed, as the result of a violent shaking? Not even a reference to a subdued tremor or rumble. Years later in the New Testament Church writings no one alludes to the happenstance which the Apostle chronicles on the timeline. It leaves the reader of Scripture with awareness; but lacking any wisdom-filled explanation.

Here are three scenarios to contemplate. Anyone of the three could be valid and might have unfolded. Or maybe not! Inquisitive searching does not always produce correct answers.

First... Mathew was present in the area, or en route, when the angel descended from heaven. Had the Apostle gone to the tomb to mourn? Was he near when the angelic visitor disrupts the sepulcher scene? Therefore, he finds himself in the midst of a supernatural timeline unfolding. Remember he is the gospel writer who focused on the guards along with the religious and political aspects for whom he wrote... to the Jews.

Second... Matthew had a vision of the whole earthquake event happening. Was it so violent in vision form that he did not feel released to describe it... fearful that no one would believe him. What if the earthquake involved Jesus and His descent into one of Hades' levels? The Apostle knew something he did not elaborate on.

Third... Matthew learned of the earthquake's sequential timing from Jesus during the post Resurrection appearances. Therefore, his informative knowledge came straight from the Lord. What if the earthquake is so deep in the depths of the earth that the ground upward absorbed the remnants of its grandeur. If so, then Jesus had to be the One who told of its existence.

Moving on... Had there been two simultaneous dynamics? Apart... way apart... from one another in location. Chronology difficult again because eternal and earthly events appear simultaneous. Nonetheless, important as how it was written in back-to-back sentences; the earthquake listed, followed by the angel's descent from heaven.

Was the atmospheric pressure a result of the heavenly guardian breaking through the boundaries of eternity and earth? Suddenly through the heaven-lies; first having left the third heaven, descending through the second and then the last, all with such unbelievable force and power. Was the angel, Michael the warrior Archangel, intent on reaching the guards at the tomb before any arrival of the women who came to attend to the deceased Christ with the burial spices? Nevertheless angels enter earth all the time without any grandstanding; whether in human clothing or with celestial angelic wings.

Back to the earthquake… What if the direction of the earthquake went downward from within the depths of the earth, rather than upward to its surface. The violent earthquake does not appear to have happened below earth's naturally explored geographic surfaces. Otherwise someone, somewhere, and somehow, would have corroborate with Matthew's reference centuries later.

Since most Bible readers are not geologists, a simple and brief conceptual process used here becomes a familiar base to work from in exploring the second earthquake written in Matthew. In the twenty-first century, a basic layman's knowledge can relate to an earthquake theme. There are perpendicular plates which can and do shift deep within… under the earth's surface. They are located between fault-lines and cause an earthquake's tremors to radiate upward to the ground level thus experienced and felt by people everywhere in the earthquake zone.

What about the opposite direction? Seismic disturbance through horizontal chasms, (similar to perpendicular plates on a fault-line) might be between the deepest levels below earth's unknown depths. Farfetched? Maybe? Maybe not? What if according to God's common usage of groups of threes, more than one chasm exists?

Jesus did not ascend, but descended to lead the captives free sometime after His death on the cross and His burial in the sepulcher. (1 Peter 3:18-19; Ephesians 4:7-10) What if the violent earthquake was the clash of the two diverse ranges of eternity… upper / lower, Heaven / Hades? Did the clash take place in Hades (hell) at the exact time of the arrival of Jesus? Or the precise time of the captives being set free? Or does the timing of the earthquake correspond with the moment Jesus is resurrected after the three days and three nights while in confinement in the heart of the earth?

The Lord's descent into the Hades domain did set those captives free... which were the unnumbered multitudes, including Abraham and Lazarus. Deceased individuals held in spiritual faith. Old Testament theology equated their godly righteousness as being by faith in God. Theirs had been a safe place of rest (sleep), free from punishment while waiting in grace for Jesus to reveal Himself to them as their promised Messiah, the King of kings from the lineage of King David. These were the spirit ones whom Jesus preached to in prison in the heart of the earth. (1 Peter 3:19)

The word Paradise becomes a likely conclusion for the paragraph above as the peaceful location described. Jesus told the thief on the cross during the crucifixion that he would be with Him in Paradise today. Not after the Resurrection... today. (Luke 23:43) Jesus had not died at that point; therefore in that moment of time referenced, the thief could not be saved... no blood covenant; but still a godly righteous confession of Old Testament faith.

Scripture is clear the rich man looked upward and saw Abraham and Lazarus who were far away. (Luke 16:23) Jesus was emphatic while telling the story there was a chasm in the scene. Does Paradise become a likely conclusion in location as being below a first horizontal chasm, but above the second? There definitely would be a first chasm, as a top-off-type ceiling, to a massive holding chamber where the righteous captives would be positioned. The ceiling chasm denying immediate spirit freedom until the initial descent of Jesus; and with a second chasm below them where the rich man was eternally.

If one believes there are levels of punishment in Hades, then below the chasm beneath the rich man there exists still another where the horribly violent, the wicked, and the evil ones are entombed in severity of eternal punishment. Jesus neither preached to the wicked in the second downward level who had sealed their destiny, nor to the tortured demons / fallen angels (third downward level) in the pit area.

Therefore, the violent earthquake becomes an initial glimpse into what the Apostle John describes in Revelation as the massive and lowest depth "to be" the final judgement and the lake of fire. Never-ending fire! (Revelation 20:14) If so, over two-thousand-plus years ago, the Lord Jesus Christ, and the Apostle John, each gave... a preliminary glimpse.

20
Three Gardens

The garden tied to the place of the Resurrection of Jesus was not a chance location. The miraculous Resurrection moment, set in a tomb in a garden, continues to weave the thread of intended redemption. Existing all the way back to the Garden of Eden where humanity became separated from God; this Garden of Resurrection raises the final curtain to finish the act of redeeming humankind. (The Garden of Resurrection, a creative title used here; but not stated as such in any New Testament verses.)

When looking at this thematic distinction, there are three gardens that set and validate three earthly scenes in the Bible. These gardens are: The Garden of Eden; The Garden of Gethsemane; The Garden of Resurrection. Nature becomes the environment setting. A focal point. Created beauty reigns in a garden, sometimes even among thorns and weeds.

The first man, Adam, through his willful disobedience to God his Creator, brought anarchy into the life of humanity in the Garden of Eden. His lack of obedience caused his fall from grace. Through one man, Adam, all tasted of sin and death. (Romans 5:12-21)

There was another garden, the link between the alpha and the omega of gardens. This middle or second of three, The Garden of Gethsemane, became the place where the battle of submitted obedience to God over human willful disobedience was won. (Matthew 26:36-44)

Spiritual victory regained for eternity. Through Jesus Christ grace and destiny triumphed there. Once for all humanity; but only if accepted by each individual person.

Eternal redemption from sin finished. Completed through the Lord Jesus Christ, Son of God / Son of Man. The Resurrection of Jesus no longer a prophetic prediction, but a promise fulfilled. (Hebrews 10:12)

21
The Riddle Of Galilee

In the New Testament, the spiritual heart of revelation becomes associated with Galilee; rather than the center of traditional religious worship in Jerusalem of Judea. Galilee is a region located from central Israel to its northern boundary. Well-known cities in a part of this region, but not all encompassing, are: Bethsaida, Cana, Capernaum, Magdala, Nain and Nazareth.

Within the central area of Israel, somewhat between the northern and the southern regions lies the domain of Samaria. The Jews and Samaritans detested one another. Resentment and hatred through hostile attitudes prevailed for centuries.Nevertheless Jesus did witness there. (John 4:39-42)

In the South, from the land of Egypt northward is the area of Judea. Again the major cities, but not all encompassing, are: Bethany, Bethlehem, Emmaus, Ephraim, Jericho and Jerusalem. The temple, the sanctuary of God, was in Jerusalem, the central location of Jewish worship where the seven Convocations were celebrated yearly. (Numerous synagogues were in the north and south throughout Israel where the Jews taught and worshiped weekly in their communities.)

Bethlehem (Judea) was the birthplace of the infant Jesus; however in a town called Nazareth, His childhood years were spent growing in favor with God and man. Therefore, the Son of God / Son of Man was not only known as Jesus of Nazareth, but also as Jesus of Galilee.

While on the topic of pointing out locations, it is also worth noting two names associated with the sea (aka lake) in the northern region. Identified most in Scripture references as the Sea of Galilee; especially at the northern half by Capernaum. Coastal villages were around the sea.

The Sea of Galilee was known to have other name tags recorded in Scripture. They were: Lake Gennesaret (Luke 5:1), and the Sea of Tiberias. (John 6:1; 21:1)

Gennesaret was a community on the upper west coast of Galilee. The water surrounding it referenced as being a lake located along the middle coastal area.

The more common and the one referenced most was the Sea of Tiberias flowing south in its exit into the Jordan River at the southern Galilean area; with a town also on the central west coast named Tiberias.

The Jordan River flowed south all the way to Jerusalem. The regional area known as Jordan on the eastern side, across from Jerusalem on the western side; with the river between which eventually ended in the Dead Sea.

At an approximate age of thirty (plus or minus) years, Jesus' public mission and passionate kingdom of God evangelistic message started in Galilee. Soon after His first miracle, with the changing of the water to wine at the wedding in Cana of Galilee (John 2:1-11); Jesus began to call specific persons to follow Him.

Peter and Andrew, James and John, headed the initial select list of Twelve (all later known as Apostles). Beyond these four there were seven more from Galilee; and Judas Iscariot who was the only one from Jerusalem of Judea. The total number of Twelve, traveled the regions of Judea and Galilee with Jesus.

Other male and female disciples from the hundreds / thousands who followed and listened to Jesus were challenged; by His compassionate love, His evangelistic message of the kingdom of God, His call to obedient discipleship, and His astonishing miracles. He moved back and forth across the land of Israel for nearly three years.

He proclaimed the coming kingdom of God to anyone who desired to listen. Overriding the religious practices and political systems of the day, His Light penetrated the mind and hearts of many disciples looking for truth, peace, and a promised Messiah.

Two gospel writers give indication Jesus spoke in a prophetic manner about His impending death, burial, and Resurrection from the dead; with these teachings taking place in Galilee and Jerusalem. (Matthew 17:22-23; Mark 9:30-33) However… much later on the timeline; and in the sequence of early on the morning of the Resurrection, angelic commands stipulated that Christ's followers meet Him in Galilee. Christ affirmed that proclamation the same day when Mary Magdalene encountered Him at the sepulcher. Repeated again… with the two unnamed female eyewitnesses. (Matthew 28:9-10)

Prophecy and revelation coexist in the spiritual realm. In a prophetic utterance, Christ said, "But after I have risen, I will go ahead of you into Galilee" (Matthew 26:32). Notice the phrase "go ahead." The Eleven apostles were there as He gave this futuristic direction while on the Mount of Olives, (in the Garden of Gethsemane), across the Kidron Valley.

Events need to be explored within this context of the riddle of Galilee. The Lord's focus on Galilee required the disciples to return there. Why did this geographical area hold such a future place of significance?

Before one can ascertain a few of the ramifications, preconceived notions especially about the location of the Great Commission should be reevaluated. There were Commissions and Ascensions and the one alluded to at this point must not be confused with the Second Coming of Christ. (The awesome and extraordinary powerful Second Coming of Christ, as the King of kings, highlighted in a later chapter.)

As for the Commissions combined with Ascensions, there was not just one, nor two or three, but four Commissions. If indeed this be true, what references can be brought to the forefront to unwrap the chronology pattern and to establish a concept of truth hidden away in the locations of the Commissions and Ascensions? (An in-depth look at Commissions and Ascensions unfolds later in another section.)

However it is important to acknowledge Jesus encountered His Ten disciples in Jerusalem on the Sunday evening after the completed early morning Resurrection. Few would have trouble considering this to be factual and biblical. Why then, the apparent contradiction to the statements earlier in the morning in the garden at the empty tomb? Does this not sound contrary to the command to meet Him in Galilee?

Add to the mix regional ramifications that were upper most in the mind of Christ. Did He want their focus to move from local, to regional, and beyond. The disciples had served with the man called Jesus of Galilee, rather than the more confined referral to Jesus of Nazareth. Significant borders and geographical areas were going to eventually change spiritually. Jesus had said, "...you will receive power when the Holy Spirit comes on you; and you will be my witnesses in Jerusalem, and in all Judea and Samaria, and to the ends of the earth" (Acts 1:8). That empowerment on the morning of Pentecost was several weeks away.

Why would Christ want to meet the disciples in Galilee? What if perhaps the promise was not for the immediate moment, but in the fullness of His timing; during those forty days after the Resurrection. Jesus, being omniscient, knew their doubts would continue concerning His Resurrection. (Matthew 28:17)

In conclusion, the Galilean landscape included rocky terrain along with various mountain ranges throughout the land. Mount Tabor, a high mountain, is believed to have been the location of the Transfiguration. Peter, James, and John were there with Jesus, along with Moses and Elijah. (Mark 9:2-4) Therefore, also a great probability... that Mount Tabor in Galilee was the Lord's concealed protective plan for where the Eleven were to meet with Him for a post Resurrection appearance together. (More on this later.)

Section Six

Angels Proclaim Christ Is Alive

22
First Angelophany - One Angel Sitting Outside
(Sepulcher - Scene One)

An unlikely opening for a first scene, a violent earthquake proclaimed the earthly announcement of the miraculous Resurrection. Action from eternity. Creative power provided by God, the Father, the Maker of heaven and earth.

This earthquake was the second since the Lord's crucifixion on the cross. A precise and valuable timeline. The first was at the moment of His death. This one at the time of Christ's Resurrection. God, who controls nature, used the earthquakes like bookends to signify and set apart the exact duration and time period of the Lord's death. Those were the hours He was deceased in the heart of the earth.

In perfection (if that word can be used), a cycle of three days and three nights timetable for Jesus being in the heart of the earth might look something like the following:

Christ died 3:00 p.m. on Wednesday (fourteenth). Actually for the Jewish timeline this is their twenty-first hour of the twenty-four hour cycle. A "day" timeline would not start until after a p.m. sunset.

First day/night cycle:

> Wednesday (fourteenth) p.m. sunset
>> to Thursday (fifteenth) p.m. sunset

Second day/night cycle:
Thursday (fifteenth) p.m. sunset
to Friday (sixteenth) p.m. sunset

Third day/night cycle:
Friday (sixteenth) p.m. sunset
to Saturday (seventeenth) p.m. sunset

(Saturday Weekly Sabbath is over)
Sunset: Sunday commences… Feast of Firstfruits

Nothing is tidy for a timeline. It appears that God the Father, used His own sovereign discretion for raising His Son in the glorious Resurrection. What time was the earthquake? Was it around 3:00 am… or earlier?

Two times graves opened. Earlier at the first earthquake, rocks split as the earth shook opening some sepulchers. People, holy people of God, experienced resurrection power. (Matthew 27:51-53) Raised to life; they too made a-type-of-post-resurrection appearance after the Resurrection of Jesus. These who numbered "many" even went into Jerusalem. Apparent physical / body recognition. Prior to the individual responses to this mighty eternal power, the temple curtain (spiritual or temporal or both) in the sanctuary of God was torn from top to bottom at the entrance that separated the Holy Place from the Most Holy Place. (Matthew 27:51)

Now a second earthquake. Just one tomb opened. Only the Holy One raised here. The power of God, the Father, raising His Son, the Son of God / Son of Man, from human death to eternal life.

Important Note: In a previous chapter, a theory was explored as a different type of scenario for this earthquake. Truth unknown; as to which possible theories has more relevancy.

It would be amiss to not bring additional focus on the specific earthquake scene in the garden. A general definition of an earthquake is the shaking of the earth's crust caused by some underground volcanic forces, or shifting of rock, or plates. This would be one source.

Another unknown type perhaps for their timeline, not an actual ground earthquake but what might be characterized as an atmospheric twenty-first century rumbling now typically classified as a sonic boom. However, there was not a clear understanding as such to the Israelites and writers on their early A.D.; timeline.

Scripture appears to equate the density of the earthquake with the descent of an angel of the Lord. Coming from heaven to earth. His garments white as snow give an appearance like lightning. Swift as a flash. Power propelled. This angelic being rolled back the stone. Used it for a seat of all things. Perched above the ground, the angel's appearance demanded a terrifying reaction from the humans present in the garden. Roman soldiers guarding the tomb were privy to the all-powerful and frightening appearance; perhaps that of Michael the Archangel, the Warrior angel.

A quiet scene? Not likely. The clanging of armor and swords provided noise which announced disruption. Watching the guards gives an unvarnished look into the scene. A stage filled with fear and terror, and more power than they had ever witnessed. (Matthew 28:4) Almighty God's Spirit and the presence of the angel of the Lord left no doubt who reigned with authority and control. If the men manage to keep their life while in the garden, their chance multiplies for death in Jerusalem because of their failure to carry out their military duty as soldiers.

These men shook and then became like dead men. Dead males usually lie horizontal, in this case on the ground. The guards were immobile. Their jurisdiction, authority and capability to carry out the task nullified. Involuntary, yet complete submission.

If it were not for Matthew's account, a reader of the four gospels would know little about the guard. Both the tomb burial setting in the garden and the soldiers terrifying experience at the Resurrection are deemed important to Matthew. This biblical insight becomes relevant for the followers of Jesus. However, Matthew does not set the guard issue aside totally even after the scene in the garden.

Do these five soldiers pass the women arriving at the sepulcher in the country outside of Jerusalem? (Matthew 28:11) Or do they attempt to hide out of fear somewhere in the garden? Or select a different road back to their command post in Jerusalem? The reader never has a clear revelation about the circumstances of their departure from the garden area. Nevertheless Matthew continues to inform the reader about these soldiers' lives intertwined later with the religious and political systems of the hour. (Matthew 28:11-15)

An earthquake, an angel of the Lord, and terrified soldiers on guard patrol invoke a captivating sequence in the garden. The first angelophany, and scene one comes to a close.

23
Second Angelophany - One Angel Sitting Outside
(Sepulcher - Scene Two)

In the garden, the soldiers had their encounter with an unexpected phenomenon. They move on, hurriedly. The reader loses sight of them for a couple hours.

Next, some of the women intent on a task to perform, reach their journey's end very early before "dawn" on Sunday the first day of the week. (Matthew 28:1) Way past 3:00 a.m. at this point on the timeline. Do they expect it to be quiet; uninhabited by any presence other than themselves?

The reader of Scripture has first-hand knowledge the Resurrection has taken place, but why did nothing cause suspicion for the females either before leaving home on their journey, or on the way there? Neither the women, nor the reader, catch a revealing glimpse of the timing, sounds, or natural reactions of the previous earthquake. Surely they should have felt the earth move or shaking even in a mild manner while at home before departing on their way to the garden. Awareness numbed by their grief? Trauma exposed. If so, would they have considered any earthquake to be associated with the Resurrection of Christ?

Days before, these weary, disillusioned, and grief-stricken women had witnessed Jesus crucified. Emotions of overwhelming sorrow clothed their hearts. Sorrow upon sorrow. Their teacher, the Rabbi, had died along with the hope of Him being the Messiah.

In the sequence of events, now taking place at the garden tomb, the generic term "women" will be used here to keep the scene less complicated. Clarification of "who" has been covered in a previous chapter and will be revisited later. Themes unfolding in the sepulcher scenes need to surface; thereby focusing on key essentials which transpired.

Suddenly all of life, natural and eternal changed. These female characters, as revealed by Matthew, upon reaching the garden will have a personal, private, and public part of history forever.

They look up. No stone covers the tomb entrance. Rolled away, it captivates the two women's attention. Not just because of its location, but they now see an angel sitting outside. Implied, but not stated: this is the same angel, Michael, the one the guards had seen earlier outside the tomb. Or is it a different one? Perhaps Gabriel, the messenger and proclamation Archangel. Maybe neither Michael, nor Gabriel? Confronted with the supernatural presence of an angel the women's immediate response became one of fear.

According to Matthew a brief oracle by the angel evolved after their initial stage of intense fright ceased. The angel invites the women to enter the tomb. A show-and-tell experience opens. This angel gives the first of three nearly identical proclamations concerning the Resurrection. He is not here. He has risen. The women learn and see the truth of Christ's prophecy realized in this place. An eternal visitation fulfilled through the power of God. Resurrection now a reality.

In the initial early moments of the Resurrection scene, angelic beings command the attention of those characters who were in the forefront of the drama. The sepulcher remains the primary location where the scenes continue to unfold.

24
Third Angelophany - Young Man (Angel)
Sitting Inside
(Sepulcher - Scene Three)

The storyline of the Resurrection takes another turn. In this third scene, as the supernatural event moves along, the women apparently stood inside wondering.

A brief scene unfolds. Referenced as a distinct location; inside and sitting on the right side, a young man (angel) wearing a white robe has appeared. The reader learns the women were alarmed. (Mark 16:5) This angelic visitor gives the second of the three proclamations about Christ being risen. The women appeared to pause in place; but ready to take off running.

The image of this third scene could almost be interpreted as evolving into the next; thereby being one and the same. However, the definitive location and posture of the one angel mentioned declares a defining difference.

Nevertheless, before the women depart, another dramatic and supernatural change is about to unfold inside the tomb... the fourth angelophany immediately follows the third.

25
Fourth Angelophany - Two Men (Angels)
Standing Inside
(Sepulcher - Scene Four)

Suddenly a distinct difference... two men (angels) in clothes that gleamed like lightning appeared beside them. Stood in close proximity to Jewish women? How intimidating. Totally out of character for the culture. Frightened, the women bowed down, way down, with their faces to the ground. A change from previous higher angelic anarchy almost establishes this as an entertained-angels-unaware scene. If so, Michael and Gabriel moved out and the next duo take a more common mode of appearance to signify an active change took place, but the hint of angels still reveals itself through their clothing. Angels (disguised as humans) always appear in the male gender looking form in Scripture.

Again, as before, the risen Christ proclamation becomes underscored. The third of the three proclamations now made by these two angels; and heard by the women happens in scene four as documented in Luke 24:6.

A recap... the vocal proclamations sounded three times, throughout the angels verbal appearances to the women at the empty tomb. He is risen... the intentional message. The first time, in scene two, with the angel sitting outside. (Matthew 28:2-6) The next, the second of the three, in scene three from the young man (angel) sitting inside on the right side of the tomb. (Mark 16:5) The final of the three, in scene four with the two men (angels) standing inside the tomb. (Luke 24:6)

Important Note: In stark contrast, the absence of those proclamations in three scenes; none in scene one with the guards and the angel. Absent again later in scene five with Peter and John while they were inside the tomb. Finally, missing also in scene six with Mary Magdalene outside the tomb and the two angels sitting inside the tomb; one at the head and the other at the foot area of the burial shelf.

Therefore in three scenes no angels speaking the revelation. In the seventh scene, Resurrection confirmed in reality! The risen and living proclamation… the Lord Jesus Christ… who stands behind Mary Magdalene in the final scene at the tomb.

Another important point comes forth. Luke tells his readers the women remembered Jesus' words about being crucified and raised to life again on the third day, as the angels reintroduce the pre crucifixion prophecy which Jesus had tried to comfort His followers with prior to His death. (Luke 24:8)

Having heard the Resurrection proclaimed at the tomb for a third time, they are possibly ready to hear a commission for the first time. They learn Jesus will go ahead of them into Galilee, because the angels give a verbal charge for the women to tell the disciples that Galilee will be a designated location. They are to tell His disciples, including Peter, that they will see Christ there in that place of meeting. (The Riddle of Galilee as a definite destination and rendezvous location has been covered in a previous chapter.)

Still alarmed and fearful, Mark states, the women fled the tomb. However, before moving on to the women as they carry out the angelic command, one further topic needs to be taken into consideration and explored.

Informed by Luke's gospel, the reader learns there was a vision of angels. (Luke 24:23) Notice the plural of angels. Could there be a valid reason Luke sets this revelation issue apart? Did he insert this side trip because he intended it to be a clarification of mood? Timing? Revelation? Maybe he deemed it necessary in order to present a distinction and to characterize the full drama which unfolded so quickly for the women present at the tomb.

A vision of angels in plural form needs further unfolding as referenced. Were they seeing angels all around the garden area and the immediate tomb location? Who were the angels there for? Why?

What about those "set apart" angels? They seem to multiply; even though only a few from the myriads of holy angelic beings. For sure, two. More likely seven. Sitting. Standing. Talking. Never seen walking by the women. Here, there, everywhere appearing to the women.

A referenced manifestation of an angel's visitation to a human more accurately called an Angelophany; versus, a vision of angels. The latter referred to in Scripture sometimes as a "host of angels" or angelic celestial beings. In the Resurrection scene was there a host of silent angels; supernatural in appearance as if suspended around the entire area of the tomb in the garden? Did celestial beings, unknown in number, form a protective encampment? Remember the birth of Jesus... the shepherds and the heavenly host of angels? (Luke 2:13)

However this time silent. Difficult to discern because there is an eternal timeframe that has "no timeline" as we know or understand it. Two-fold manifestation of tangible presence and spiritual presence.

What if the women were in denial; that a vision rather than an actual appearance gave sympathetic nurture to their thought process? In the first century, this was not an uncommon distinction. Angelic appearances promoted fear. A mental state almost unable to deal with and to convey to others as reality.

Visions... become a less threatening mode and terminology for seeing into the supernatural realm and more acceptable. Discernment, because of fear, could become clouded for the women. In justifiable denial, vision lessens the presence and intensity of power.

Remember the physician, Luke, wrote many years later after the angelic occurrence. Naysayers scoffing as related to the women, as a class, could have resulted in doubting they had any authentic encounter with living angels. Nevertheless, whether real, or vision, the gospel writer Luke deems it important enough to mention and set it apart.

This concept could be presented further as a chapter. However, because the basic theory written above cannot be proven in Scripture even though Luke in his two writings... the Gospel of Luke and the Acts of the Apostles... shows favor toward a thematic presentation of angels.

Section Seven

Obedient Proclaimers And Doubting Seekers

26
No Nonsense At The Tomb
(Obedient Interruption)

An interruption takes place in the scenes at the sepulcher. The angels had commanded the women to go quickly. A brief time-lapse unfolds as the group of females hurriedly leave the tomb to locate the Eleven disciples.

Startled, confused and probably disoriented, the women's detailed reports to the disciples afterward convey their moments as each experienced it. Mark describes them as trembling and bewildered. One can almost hear their talking all-at-once, with out-of-breath word enunciation. (Mark 16:8)

An attentive and sympathetic reader understands how fear and joy could reside in their hearts and minds. The gospel writers give the names of several women in an attempt to establish a record of who participated in the proclamation event.

One thing for sure, the women followed the instructions given by the angels. Immediate conversation in the presence of the disciples about the resurrected Christ took place. The grieving male disciples did not believe truth. Such an awesome story seemed as nonsense to them. (Luke 24:11) Nevertheless, Luke calls the disciples "apostles" for the first time after the Resurrection. His identification becomes a deliberate reference of not just a generic list of disciples, but the Eleven.

The reader presumes the Eleven, plus others, were in one place. Yet, perhaps, Mary Magdalene found John and Peter at Zebedee's Jerusalem residence since John's gospel isolates these three emphatically concerning the trio's cohesiveness in the hour of crisis now moving into chaotic change. (John 20:2)

Tradition and reality might silently declare other locations too. For example, some of the Eleven disciples could have been in Mary's residence, the mother of John Mark. Another destination, that of the upper room residence, where Jesus' last meal with the disciples took place prior to His arrest should not be excluded from possibility either. Therefore the women could have separated, going different purposeful ways. This is the celebration day of the Feast of Firstfuits and people are gathered together in various family residences.

After the women delivered the details about the scene at the tomb, the biblical account has taken the sequence of events up to the time before anyone else becomes visually aware that a glorious Resurrection has taken place. True supernatural angelic action and the storyline about the actual Resurrection are seen only in or near the tomb in the garden.

Characters come and go. Thus far, a few soldiers and a few women have experienced the supernatural realm of angels and the Resurrection.

27

Race To Believe
(Sepulcher - Scene Five)

Two additional characters, Peter and John, arrive at the empty tomb in the garden. Having heard the astounding claim from Mary Magdalene, these two male disciples had to see for themselves. John, having had first-hand experience, gives a more detailed written account than any other peer in ministry.

Peter and John in their unbelief have a neck-to-neck race part of the way to the tomb. Out of breath because of distance, their fear by now has drowned in sweat. John, the other disciple, having outrun Peter, reaches the tomb in their competitive race. (John 20:4)

Peter saw the remaining wrappings of linen fabric, strips lying there as well as the burial face cloth that had been around Jesus' head. Impetuous by nature, Peter steps inside the tomb without discerning that a miraculous event had taken place.

Strips of linen lying by themselves also had caught the attention of John. Bending over and looking in from outside the tomb, the reader relates to the disciple's posture of curiosity.

In John 20:7, he gives indication the burial cloth that was on the head of Jesus was different, referring to it by using the phrase "separate from the linen" without saying strips. On Resurrection morning, it lay folded up. This cloth becomes a focal point. Days earlier at the burial no mention is made of the mysterious cloth as a specific part of the burial procedure.

As can be inferred... past memories, collective experiences, and creative speculative ideas came rushing head-on as John chooses to enter the tomb. Denial in the midst of hopeful suspense must have fought to reign as he balanced his racing thoughts.

Peter is still inside the sepulcher. They do not exchange conversation, at least none documented. Competition on foot, nothing in speech. Recognizing something had happened Peter went away wondering to himself about the scene he had just encountered. (Luke 24:12)

Seeing the cloth and the manner folded, spiritually awakened John to the reality of a risen Christ. Could it be the natural and the supernatural became interwoven? What was it about how that cloth was folded? Could it signify... finished? Or, I will return?

An identifying, folding mannerism of Jesus that John had seen before. Perhaps at a meal's conclusion? Napkins at a meal conveyed the guest's intent. If they left the table with the indication they would return, or signifying they had no intention of returning; therefore a cultural understanding prevailed. Nevertheless, alerted by the cloth... it caused all doubt to diminish for John. He becomes the first believer, post Resurrection, without having seen the risen Christ. (John 20:8)

Up to this point on the timeline, the reader of Scripture never read any other description about the burial linens being seen after the Resurrection. Neither in the previous four scenes at the sepulcher; nor are they mentioned hereafter by the New Testament writers.

At the tomb, a silent scene, short in length and masculine. No tears, no fear, no voices. No indication given... that Peter or John touched the grave clothes! Absent from John's account... are reference to any angels, neither singular, nor in plural appearances. As for an angelophany, in general, males are less spiritually attune to supernatural beings in their immediate presence.

Silent action causes the reader to focus on the body language of Peter and John. Only the narrator's voice, that of John, five decades later conveys the images at the empty tomb. Amazing… that in writing his reflective thought under the inspiration of the Holy Spirit, he still makes no comment about conversation.

What a mystery. It was that silent? Perhaps the atmosphere resembled that of a holy place. Unseen angels radiate a holy presence. The intentional elimination of any words spoken alludes to the fact their holy presence may have dominated the scene both inside and outside.

Scripture indicates Peter and John each went to his home. (John 20:10) Plural residences; but did each head back to Galilee? Signifying John went separately to his residence in Capernaum of Galilee to tell Mary, the mother of Jesus. No. Not likely. Did John have a residence in Jerusalem like his parents? Regardless, John, Zebedee's youngest adult son, had custodial care of Mary, the mother of Jesus, since the crucifixion. Also, during the Spring festival season, extended families were in Jerusalem for the last of the three Convocation feasts.

Does Peter go to a place in Galilee; where Jesus appears later to His disciples collectively for the first time after the Resurrection? Not likely. However, a public appearance of Christ in Jerusalem in daylight would not be a practical verbal reference. For political purposes Galilee became a location of momentary diversion, at least verbally, for a few days. Christ does go to nearby Jerusalem the evening of the Resurrection… on Sunday. (John 20:19-20)

Recapping the previous scenes reveals the guards never entered the tomb. Women had. Peter and John do. Up to this point, the last and final person on the first day of the week to go inside was John. Only he, of the two males at the sepulcher site believed. No indication that earlier any of the soldiers believed.

Glorious angels, soldiers fleeing, dutiful women who arrived and left with the burial anointing task unfinished. Then, Peter and John arrive to see for themselves. Minutes behind, Mary Magdalene was bearing down on their heels. Of these three, only she remains afterward.

Section Eight

Angelophany And Christophany

28
Fifth Angelophany - Two Angels Sitting Inside
(Sepulcher - Scene Six)

The divine purpose in removing all other human characters from this scene is to give the entire stage to Mary Magdalene's sorrow. Peter and John have already seen the empty tomb and departed.

John's narration in his gospel becomes a vehicle for restoring faith and meaning to the divine and hopeful plan of the Resurrection. His account includes an angelophany, and a soon-to-be first post Resurrection appearance of the Lord Jesus Christ... a Christophany. (John 20:10-17)

In Scripture, in the Old Testament, a Theophany was a physical appearance of God. In the New Testament a physical manifestation of Christ is called a Christophany. This terminology means the real presence of Christ, not a vision of Him.

Standing outside the tomb Mary Magdalene gives no indication she desires to enter. Inside were two angels. clad in garments of bright white, the color signifying purity and glory. What a stark contrast this must have been compared to the gray of the tomb and the darkness of her sorrow and the early morning hour.

Though unknown, perhaps more angels were outside. Holy angelic spiritual beings may be discerned by some, but not an awareness by others. For Peter and John, apparently neither perceived, or had any connection to their presence. The spiritual world though not ordinarily witnessed by human eyes, remains valid throughout the Bible from cover-to-cover.

The appearance of angels is befitting to continue the affirmation of the holy and supernatural event... the Resurrection. The posture of these celestial beings in their precise location indicates their ease, as if at rest. These two are seated at either end of Jesus' burial shelf. (John 20:12) Could these two angels be Gabriel and Michael reappearing? The proclamation angel sitting at the head and likewise the warring angel at the foot position. Not likely, but a possible consideration. Also, an unanswered question looms: where are the linen strips and folded cloth in this present moment?

Their angelic appearance does not diminish Mary Magdalene's distress or anxiety over a missing Jesus. Fear seems to be omitted from her emotion. The irony of her situation causes the reader to have compassion for her.

Weeping, crying as a stated reference, acknowledged in the verses. Emotional darkness has become her companion and friend. Possessed by her fixed idea that the corpse of Jesus has been taken, Mary Magdalene does not appear alarmed or frightened with the angels addressing her. She has already seen angels in the earlier morning hours. Responding naturally to the angels as if she were simply talking to human beings. The relationship loss remains personal. Overpowered with her deep sense of grief, she seems almost frozen in time.

She did not expect to find Jesus alive, so it became quite natural for her to think upon finding the body missing, that it had been stolen. The term, "they" became tied to stolen, robbed, thieves, dreadful Jews. The irony was "life" had been the thief. Resurrection life. Even a higher distinction, eternal life.

However, in her invalid conclusion, grief overrides her conscious and physical discerning abilities. For she declares that upon the revealing of His location, she will carry the full weight of the body of a man away, possibly back to this very tomb. Agape love coupled with devotion knows no limit! Love would accomplish the impossible, as love so often does. Faith and hope had died. Love remained… still seeking. Love wants to do something, because love lives on.

Hours before, she initially had come to anoint the Lord for burial purposes. Now that seemed like such a minimal necessity in light of the disappearance of His body. Little did she realize how tragic it would have been had she initially found the corpse there in the tomb.

The two angels may have suggested by the direction of their look that Jesus was near at hand. Her conversation with them finishes abruptly. Not unusual, because angelic beings stay intent on focus, brief in conversation. Besides, the angels would have immediately yielded to the presence of the Lord Jesus Christ, pointing to Him through their silence.

29
First Christophany - Lord Jesus Christ Standing Outside (Sepulcher - Scene Seven)

Mark has told the reader this is the risen Lord's first appearance and Mary Magdalene is chosen as the recipient; but the details of the encounter are given by John. In all likelihood, John obtained his information directly from Mary of Magdala, herself. (Mark 16:9; John 20:14-17)

As the reader slips inside this scene, the gospel writer expounds through his method of show-and-tell. He established a temporal setting, the garden. Mystery and tension allows the reader to experience the Resurrection in the early morning hours. As always, throughout this and the coming post Resurrection appearances, Jesus will initiate His disclosure to the one nearby.

Voice becomes the dominant focus in the storyline. The passive action takes place through what the characters say: the angels, Mary Magdalene, and Christ. The dramatic irony of the event unfolds as Mary, playing the role of victim on stage, thinks evidence conveys that the corpse has been stolen, while the reader knows the Lord is risen.

She weeps for a dead Jesus, when in reality the living Messiah will be instantly in her presence. Grief crushing her heart of love obscured her spiritual vision. Unlike Mary of Bethany, Mary Magdalene had not grasped the idea of Resurrection life. The simplicity and vulnerability shown through her humanity in John's story gives the reader of Scripture an acute and accurate account.

Having seen and conversed with the angels she did not have a clue that something glorious, but disguised in commonality, was seconds away from being revealed. Distraught, Mary Magdalene encounters a person. She believes He is the gardener, but never calls Him so. Mary sensed the presence of a person behind her. One who was changed from what she had previously recognized as the Lord. Daylight and her posture played a significant role. (John 20:14-15) A Jewish female, encountering a male in a secluded place would demand extreme attentiveness on her part to remain respectable. Why would anyone be in the garden that early in the day, except the gardener?

Coupled with the outward appearance of His garment and the time of day, she makes a good intellectual guess which led her to a natural miscalculation and a spiritual mistake. Mere sight, by Mary, does not necessarily lead to understanding, nor faith. She saw Him, but seeing was not believing.

For the Jews, normally Sunday was a work day in the week. A gardener would have been on duty making preparation for the day's chores. However, this is no average week on the Jewish calendar. No ordinary person, either.

Mary had come to the tomb in darkness, and was progressing into the Light of Christ, but had not yet attained a firm position within this Light. One of John's themes in his gospel is leaving the darkness and moving into the Light. Soon it unfolds before the reader's eyes. In devoting space to this first Christophany, John records Mary Magdalene's failure to know and recognize Jesus immediately; followed by her sudden recognition as He speaks her name.

Throughout the gospels, the risen Lord is recognized with difficulty. Death and the Resurrection have wrought a change upon Him. He appeared in another or different form, a resurrected body. (Mark 16:12)

The first words of the risen Lord Jesus Christ are the initial words of the angels. An echo of the heavenly and eternal. The conjunction of celestial and eternal, human and temporal. He repeats their question, then adds one of His own. Jesus wanted to know who she was looking for. Really? (John 20:15) Generalized conversation does not awaken her spiritually to His presence. She continues to believe He is the gardener.

Then one word, the speaking of her name challenges her perception and pierced her being. The risen Christ simply says, "Mary." All doubt ended at the sound. That utterance was from the relational aspect of their fellowship; He as her deliverer, teacher, and friend. In a split second, in the twinkling of an eye, Mary connects. (John 20:16)

Then she responds with joy by calling out, "Rabboni." Another one word response; this name meaning Teacher, seals the old and new links between heaven and earth, between eternal and temporal, between imperishable and perishable.

Through her exclamation, John's narrative allows the reader to hear and see Mary Magdalene's spontaneous belief is imperfect; for she uses a mere human title for Christ. In the passage never quite perceiving Him as the Messiah. Sadly lacking. There is no recognition of the divinity of Jesus at this point in their encounter. She still does not understand the empty tomb, the Resurrection, or the future relationship of the risen Lord to His Apostles and all disciples.

Nevertheless, through John's verbal framing technique and the use of "Teacher" it helps lay the stepping stones from Resurrection morning to the eventual giving of the Holy Spirit fifty days later on Pentecost. He who will teach and guide all believers into truth from that day forward. (John 16:13)

The spontaneity of her response gives a glimpse of her priceless gratitude and joy, at seeing Him alive again. As sheep know the voice of their Good Shepherd when He calls them by name; she recognized His voice and responded joyfully to Him. (John 10:1-16; 20:16)

When the sound of the voice of Jesus goes forth, spiritual things happen. Those who hear His voice are part of the flock. In one spoken word she had the means of recognizing His presence, regardless of His appearance. The use of her name meant He knew her personally.

Through this communication in voice and recognition all doubt ceased.

Christ's appearance to Mary, followed by her natural attempt to approach Him is met with a verbal barrier... Do Not Hold. Jesus' return to the Father had begun, but was not yet completed. It was a process started at the moment of His death on the cross. He had committed His Spirit into His Father's hands. (Luke 23:46) There will be stages of completion because He had descended first into Hades (hell), and will ascend into heaven, soon.

The Resurrection has taken place, but the return to the Father must involve the completed cycle of leading... justice to victory. This indicates how soon after the Resurrection Mary encounters the Messiah in His fulfillment of redemption. Completed in Hades, then on earth, not yet in heaven. As bound on earth, soon to be bound in heaven.

Jesus repeats the same command; "Go, tell the disciples." In His evangelistic charge to Mary to tell the disciples, He had not said "our" Father. He carefully clarifies there still remains a distinction in relationship.

For God, who is Father of Christ and Creator of humanity, is so in different ways. Only by grace the Father belongs to humanity. The equality with Jesus between Him and His disciples reaches and touches only to a certain level. God is forever the Father of Christ according to the supernatural spiritual existence of the Godhead; but for believers according to grace, adoption and the covenant grafted-in relationship through which Jesus instituted. He is not on the same level as the disciples, as a man only. He is the begotten Son of God (the One and Only) in a unique sense, from eternity, for He is God. (John 3:16)

The reader hears another name for the disciples, that of brothers. Many relational names have been spoken before: children, slaves, servants, disciples, ministers, friends, apostles, and finally progressing to brothers. (Matthew 28:10) He comes closer relationally as His departure and ascent looms on the horizon.

There is no mention of Jesus leaving; nor for that matter of Mary Magdalene's departure either. All the reader is made aware of is the promptness of her obedience, this obedience of love. Her weeping and grief changed; she becomes the first eyewitness and bearer of the joyous Good News. An evangelistic commission direct from the Messiah. The last became first.

The place of the Resurrection in the garden becomes almost obsolete. The power of miracles detaches from locations. Miracles move into the heart, mind, and often into the body of the receiver and abide there to strengthen one's spirit and faith. The first post Resurrection appearance of Jesus Christ ends. The reader never returns to the empty tomb.

Section Nine

Earliest Appearances Of The Risen Christ

30
First Legal Witnesses

In the previous scene, Mary Magdalene saw the Lord and talked with Him. Alone, she leaves the empty tomb and garden area. The human messenger now en route to the disciples again. These apostles must hear the message about the risen Christ. He is alive!

Probably younger than the other women, Mary Magdalene has had a very active morning of foot-travel. To visualize her running slightly ahead of the older women after the first time at the tomb would not be unreasonable in theory. Back to the empty tomb a second time with Peter and John. Then off to proclaim the powerful Resurrection message has kept her in an activity mode that would exhaust anyone.

Where are the other women who had been to the tomb earlier? Did they stay together? Or split off into two, or three people groups, heading in different directions? Remember... the instructional angelic command said Jesus would meet them in Galilee. The tomb and the garden area are outside of Jerusalem in Judea. At least three of the six women were from the Galilean area. All of this coupled with the ongoing final stage of the three feasts in Jerusalem that week. Christ knew they could not immediately leave Jerusalem for Galilee.

Should the reader assume the Eleven disciples remained together? In the beginning, yes. By the time of the Resurrection, maybe not. Considering when the first revelation came forth from the women, even though the apostles did not believe; it is unlikely all those males were together at this hour of the morning. For sure, Peter and John had gone separate ways after leaving the tomb. (John 20:10)

Where is Christ in the immediate aftermath of His glorious Resurrection? Taking a side trip, one needs to reconcile two very different scenes.

The first concerns Mary Magdalene and Christ, where He says, "Do not hold on to me, for I have not yet returned to the Father" (John 20:17). The reader does not know He has not ascended (returned) to the Father when Mary encounters Him in the garden. In speech, He makes it known.

Often sermonized, the "do not hold" phrase, emphasized to mean Mary should get moving and tell the disciples. A valid exposition of Scripture? No. First, it is used to avoid dealing with the chronology of the Resurrection passages. Second, vitally important to another Christophany later somewhere beyond the garden location.

What if Mary saw the Messiah in the precise sequence between Hades and heaven yet on earth? A power not understood by humanity. This Resurrection power, still very much occupying His body. At this point, He would have already descended first into the depths of Hades; and returned to earth with the spiritual keys of death and Hades (hell). (Revelation 1:18) Then, and only then, a first ascending into the third heaven and the presence of God the Father. Did Mary leave the empty tomb area in the garden before that happens? A speculative guess would respond, yes.

Christ ascends into heaven and returns to earth with a heavenly body, in the twinkling of an eye, thus making His resurrected presence known for the next forty days. Touchable, He is. Therefore... in appearance, is there a difference between a resurrected body and a heavenly eternal body?

While Mary Magdalene is off locating whatever apostles she can find a second time, Jesus continues His post Resurrection appearances. How much time elapsed? The duration unknown. Whether brief or hours remains questionable and unanswered, between her having seen the Lord and two other unnamed women seeing Him?

Here is where reconciling the chronology of events takes an apparent unexplained turn. According to Matthew's account, after leaving the sepulcher two women now come face-to-face with the risen Christ. The chosen females (unnamed by the apostle) have a recognizable encounter with Christ. (Matthew 28:8-10) Where was the exact location?

They were headed somewhere. To Galilee? If so, Christ honored their obedience. Remember, Joanna, the wife of Cuza would be expected to head back to the vicinity of Herod's district where her husband worked. However, Herod, himself, had been in Jerusalem on the timeline of the arrest of Jesus and the Passover. (Luke 23:7)

In Matthew 28:8-9, the apostle tells the reader: First, these two women are greeted with a salutation from Jesus. He makes Himself known. Second, they approach Him, and He receives the touch of adoration and reverent deification from the women. In simple terminology… they clasped the feet of Christ and worshiped Him. Why them and not Mary Magdalene? Reason and her timeframe are already alluded to in this chapter.

In this second post Resurrection appearance of the risen Christ, He has a completed heaven-to-earth eternal body. That is all one knows. As quickly as He appears, He disappears from their sight.

These did not call Him Teacher. They did recognize Him for who He was, the Messiah. The women did only what they could. He assures them they have nothing to fear. In His awesome and eternal glory they are safe. Then they continue toward their destination.

Chronology, according to Matthew, offers this scene where the women, minus Mary Magdalene, are approached and greeted by the Lord as they are walking. Who were the women? Matthew does not name them. The reader can only draw a possible conclusion, because in his gospel earlier he names only Mary Magdalene and the "other Mary", and the mother of Zebedee's sons (Salome).

Speculation… in Matthew, this post Resurrection appearance of Jesus probably comes later, but still on the morning timeline of the Resurrection. A reasonable thought concerning placement, because the apostle having drawn from Mark's gospel written earlier, he does not appear to reveal the predictive lapse of time. In Mark 16:12-13, his gospel includes the word "afterward" and the location defined as in the country... meaning somewhere apart from the garden.

A twist thrown in here... what if Jesus moved from the otherwise assumed logical pathway? He easily could have. Matthew is writing to the Jews. Are the two Jewish women Mary of Bethany and her sister Martha? Had they come to the tomb after word had traveled to them of Jesus' Resurrection? Or, could the Lord now be southwest of Jerusalem, but moving closer east to Bethany. These women knew Him through being two of His disciples... and adored Him. Christ's fondness for their family of three, including Lazarus, gives a logical reason for His sudden appearance in this apparent happenstance scene.

Who the Lord appears to seems either unimportant to Matthew, or the apostle believed there would be no question about their identity for his immediate readers. Even though unnamed... how many in number surfaces as the primary fact needed.

In Matthew's gospel the writing of this information and chronology became exceedingly important. The two women, disciples of Jesus, were the first legal eyewitnesses of the resurrected Messiah. In Judaism, two or more witnesses were required to make the event or statement, one of truth. Without question, Jesus is alive!

These females, who served and supported Jesus in His spiritual mission and itinerant ministry, believed on that Sunday hours ahead of some of the male disciples who belonged to the band of Eleven apostles. Women were considered lowly on the scale of human beings. The supernatural revelation of Christ can and will be revealed to anyone He chooses. They were the first to worship the risen Messiah.

The two female eyewitnesses arrive at a residence where many are gathered. They precede the return of the two Emmaus traveler's which the reader will encounter soon through Luke's gospel. How might one know more about these women?

Matthew says when the women reported the truth of the Resurrection those present did not believe they had seen the resurrected

Christ. (Mark 16:12-13) The women arrived at the residence, possibly having walked from Bethany to the empty tomb near Jerusalem (two miles). Then back to a residence before Simon's arrival. The reader learns later that the group only believed the Emmaus traveler's report, that of Cleopas and his companion, upon their arrival because Simon, having seen Jesus, was already in the assembled gathering of the apostles and others. (Luke 24:33-34)

Another important calculation takes precedence in flashback. There are several known believers in Scripture at this juncture of the Resurrection storyline. Not all have seen the resurrected Christ, but faith abounds in the hearts of some.

Again, a women heads the list. Earlier in the gospels the reader learned Mary of Bethany had anointed the "feet" of Jesus for His burial six days before His crucifixion. (John 12:1-3) A truth which cannot be ignored. She had the earliest spiritual discernment, or revelation, to comprehend what lie ahead. His blood sacrifice. His Resurrection.

Later a second unnamed woman who was in Simon's house (the former leper) anointed the "head" of Jesus for His burial. (Mark 14:3) Some time in the final days prior to His impending trial and crucifixion... like Mary of Bethany had earlier. (This referenced scene should not be confused with the one in Simon's house (the Pharisee) having happened in the Lord's earlier ministry.)

Then the centurion at the crucifixion site in proclamation declares, Jesus is the Son of God. (Mark 15:39) John at the empty tomb believed, Mary Magdalene had a relational conversation with the Teacher, and now the two female witnesses had worshiped Him as Messiah. An unusual band of believers stand out as a somewhat random selection.

An important reference to witnesses... any two or three should be acknowledged and understood in relationship to the concept of verification as accurate testimony. Scripture neatly has parallels... like singular one on one... Mary Magdalene and Peter... for their visitations of the resurrected Lord. Collective two-person sightings will happen for required confirmation to honor Jewish law specifications. (Matthew18:16; Hebrews 10:28) Therefore, these two unnamed female

175

witnesses and the (supposedly) two male Emmaus Road travelers... confirm on Resurrection Day the factual affirmation of the risen Lord Jesus Christ. Female and male counterparts show forth intentional documentation. The female first, not the male, in both classification and encounters.

A new precedent is taking place. One which will not be accepted easily in the early Church, nor later by example. Nevertheless, a foundation for revelation and the ways it unfolds is being laid.

While this is happening, Matthew takes the storyline back to the guards. Informing the reader of the soldiers travel to Jerusalem and reporting the event as it unfolded before their eyes. First, to the chief priests, who then meet with the elders of the people. Schemes and reams of stories, entangled with money, become the conversational deception as it continued through the religious and political entities. (Matthew 28:11-15) A cleverly constructed story that the body of Jesus had been stolen became universally accepted; circulating among the Jewish communities. Deception, bought and told, reigned because falsehood often becomes easier to believe than truth.

31
No House Guest Tonight

Jesus, the Eternal One, appears on the Emmaus Road as He catches up with two commoners. Fully engaged in grief and mourning, these disciples download their miscalculated perceptions to the third person now in their midst. No ordinary traveler meeting this duo. No small-talk conversation, either.

In the Bible, one verse mentioned in Mark 16:12-13, appears out of context about the event, and gives minimal information. Often interpreted to mean the Emmaus Road travelers, but probably meant to be a brief mention of the unnamed two female eyewitnesses already described. Therefore these latter two become the male counterparts of the two female witnesses from hours before.

Luke provides the only Emmaus documentation in fulness. His hearing about the encounter on Resurrection Sunday made an impression on the beloved physician. He preserved the spiritual and historical facts and the reader of Scripture has the privilege of walking on the road with the trio. (Luke 24:13-35)

On Sunday, possibly early afternoon, two with downcast faces and heavy hearts were walking toward Emmaus about seven to eight miles northwest of Jerusalem. Significant attention drawn to the location, Emmaus... and classification, a village, the suggestion made that the community is small. The site is difficult to identify; of four possible locations, only two were in existence in Jesus' day.

These two distraught and weary travelers who seem to appear obscure and unimportant become the center of attention. The underlying message points out the importance of all in the sight of God and the willingness of Christ to manifest Himself to anyone; independent of their personality, position, power, or prestige. He, the Savior of humanity and the most influential and powerful One, has chosen to walk in their midst.

The reader learns Cleopas, along with a companion, have engaged in conversation. A companion? Who is it? Could be Mary, the wife of Cleopas, mother of Joseph and Joses. If so, why would she not be named?

Luke, the physician, who favors women both in writing and social position would have named Cleopas's wife had it been her. Or, at least named one of his sons, Joseph or Joses. Did Luke leave it unconfirmed for a family reason? Or perhaps Joseph and Joses could be confused with the commonality of others with the same names. However, there is a more pressing question to ask. Once in Emmaus, why do they happen to be in Cleopas' house without any family members named?

Joseph of Arimathea, (who lived north of Emmaus) or any one of a host of disciples from Jesus' ministry, could have been the companion. These Emmaus travelers make reference to Peter and John, as companions who had visited the empty tomb. So does it mean only apostles? Of course not. The mystique of identity, name, and gender, leaves the reader speculating about the unnamed companion.

Also, unlikely that Luke was the second of the two. He refers to himself in his writing in Acts 16:11, in the first person plural "we." The preface in his first book implies he himself was not an eyewitness of the risen Christ. (Luke 1:1-4)

Travelers hooked-up for safety on roads between cities and villages in Israel. The footsteps and appearance of One looking more like a friend, than a foe, happens along. This duo becomes a trio. Earlier Luke refers to Jesus in another form. Jesus' physical appearance again remains unrecognizable. The initial two travelers welcome the friendly stranger into their midst and their dialogue. They reiterate their views about the events of the previous few days, unmasking their confusion and discouragement.

Jesus of Nazareth, a distinguished prophet, because His word and deed matched, becomes the central topic and figure discussed. The moments of that day, and those previous, had brought confusion about the hoped-for-redeemer of Israel. Christ had been seen as the one to provide national redemption. Actually, the reverse had taken place. Jesus came to liberate humanity as a redeemer from sin, not to save one nation from another. They were looking for the wrong type of kingship and the wrong kingdom too. Nevertheless the Messianic hope was fulfilled through God's sovereign plan.

Unexpectedly walking at their side, Jesus elicited a response now totally different in their body language. These talking individuals, stood still. Motion ceased, painting a vivid picture. Their journey interrupted. Does their countenance change along with their stance? A stunning, shocking astonishment camouflaged their previous disposition which had been sad, moody and pessimistic. Cleopas, and his companion, rehash the current morning details of the Resurrection briefly with this third person. A verbal scolding in gentleness unfolds in their speech pattern. How could this road traveler probably from Jerusalem, not be aware?

Admonishment springs forth verbally from the stranger walking in their midst. The scolding of minutes before becomes a boomerang. Words verbalized are, "how foolish you are," "how slow of heart to believe," targets the unbelief. (Luke 24:25) Strong words. With the focus drawn to an empty tomb and the absence of a body, can these two traveling companions grasp what the stranger wants to reveal? Will spiritual dullness overrule? Or will faith and spiritual perception be rekindled?

Next, expounded by Jesus are the all-important Scriptures. A reminder of the pre crucifixion prophecy pinpoints the one-sided discussion. The expository explanation of the Hebrew Old Testament from Moses through the Prophets must have been like no other they had ever heard. Jesus enlightened them with generational, patriarchal and prophetic figures from Israel's history.

Luke's fondness for the word "all" does not mean "all prophetic quotes" from the Prophets concerning the Messiah were elaborated in detail by Christ. He unwound the skein and unveiled the seams of a timeline. Suffering and its purpose was not a part of the plan anyone previously grasped in fullness. Once shrouded from them, Scriptural recall and recognition opens eyes wide and gently touches their hearts, leaving them burning within.

The risen Lord Jesus Christ, then and always, is the life-changing key to opening the Scriptures. His evangelistic intent? To personally start the proclamation of the Good News far and wide by example. Earlier in command, it started in the garden at the empty tomb, Now Jesus singles out and justifies the importance of evangelism. His stamp of confirmation upon the angelic proclamations to the various women who visited the empty tomb also shows in this Emmaus visitation. Spread the message far and wide, Jesus' presence and action implied; from Jerusalem, to Judea, to Samaria, and the outer most parts.

Time passes and arrival at the outskirts of Emmaus is imminent. Their gesture of hospitality with much persuasion and common practice in the culture finds the welcomed stranger eventually dining in Cleopas' home. In this case, as in the past, once again Jesus lets meal time, food, and hospitality, pave the way for a relationship to extend beyond a previous level. If no hospitality had been offered, no revelation.

Luke brings suspense and surprise. A non-recognition and then recognition structure unfolds in his narrative. Initially the disciples were kept from perceiving who this stranger was. God, Himself, is the actual author of this action. Restraint in an unusual seesaw manner. Moreover, the last thing they had really expected was to see Jesus.

The breaking of bread changes everything. The scene has been set. In the unusual turn of event Jesus acted as host rather than guest. He changed roles right in the middle through a simple tradition by giving thanks and distributing the bread. Did He lift His eyes heavenward?

Or the bread upward? Possibly another of those unique mannerisms pertaining only to Christ; or the exposure of the nail scarred hands. Then… when they truly saw Him, suddenly He ceased to be seen.

Interesting to note… the cup did not follow. Christ kept His promise from the Last Supper. (Mark 14:25) No fruit of the vine partaken until in His kingdom.

After having walked through an open door with Cleopas and his companion, a short time later Christ disappears from the presence of the Emmaus travelers through a different mode of exit. Their recognition of the Messiah led to His immediate departure and the climax of Luke's narrative. No house guest here tonight.

32
Nine, But Only One

Jesus had places to go and people to see. Appearances of the risen Christ continue to increase apart from the tomb location. During the forty days, Jesus will appear and disappear in the midst of humanity on earth.

In His glorified state being transported provided no limitation. Neither did time. Nor locations and rooms with closed doors. The risen Jesus Christ will appear again, but when and where?

Before Christ arrives in Jerusalem and appears behind locked doors with the Ten disciples as a group on the evening of the Resurrection, He selects one individual, a male, for an isolated appearance to make His Resurrection known. A counterpart to the solo female appearance to Mary Magdalene hours before. Jesus in this particular moment and fourth Christophany has chosen Simon.

Without a large portion of Scripture giving any details about this appearance to Simon, the reader learns the information along with the Emmaus travelers upon their return to Jerusalem. Luke's documentation seems written and validated almost as an afterthought. Why so quiet and allusive in appearance? Does Luke believe there would be no question who Simon was? (Luke 24:34)

Who is Simon? Which Simon? There are nine in the New Testament. Some fit into this sequence of events, others do not. Mini biographies follow:

Simon, known as Simon Peter, or Peter, one of the Twelve disciples (Apostles) who walked with Jesus in His inner circle of three

Simon, the Zealot, also one of the Twelve disciples (Apostles)

Simon, the Pharisee, in whose home Jesus dined and where He was anointed on the feet by a female sinner

Simon, the step-brother of the Lord Jesus Christ, referred to only in genealogy lists

Simon, of Cyrene, know by the location where he lived; and who by Roman military force, became the carrier of Jesus' crucifixion cross

Simon, the former leper, (possibly living east of Jerusalem in Bethany beyond the Jordan) in whose home Jesus was anointed on the head for burial by the unnamed woman

Simon, the father of Judas Iscariot, whose son betrayed Christ

Simon, the sorcerer, who desired the power of the Holy Spirit, after the birth of the Church recorded in the book of Acts, because he believed it was magical and financially profitable

Simon, the tanner, who opened his home in Joppa to Peter after the birth of the Church recorded in the book of Acts

Looking at each of these Simons requires a search through one's mental data base; plus recall from the whole counsel of the New Testament to assist in sifting through the possibilities. A systematic elimination proves no easy task, neither does it guarantee an accurate perception or a full-proof conclusion from error in selection.

Some readers might concur at once it was Simon Peter. Maybe yes, maybe no. He would tend to be the favored biblical choice. Often sermonized as the selected person because of his famous denial trilogy in the courtyard of the high priest during the religious trial of Jesus.

Before a hasty conclusion is made, perhaps for a moment Simon Peter should be ruled out. Had an appearance of the risen Christ with Peter taken place on the afternoon of Resurrection Sunday before nightfall, it is unlikely a one-to-one lengthy encounter would have been necessary later at the shoreline near the Sea of Tiberias in Galilee. (John 21:15-19) Therefore supporting spiritual evidence can point to Peter not being singled out. Suppose the Lord believed it necessary for Peter in this timeframe and moment to simply become one of the group.

He had already doubted and dismissed the women's truth as nonsense. Peter had been to the very place of the Resurrection. The empty sepulcher with burial linens in place, gave him a second opportunity to believe. At the tomb, he left wondering. Seeing for him was not believing. Neither had been hearing the confirming testimony from Mary Magdalene later as she told him, Jesus is alive.

The experience of isolating his place of prestige for a season, humbling as it felt in the moment, might come to benefit the kingdom work later-on through Peter having learned compassionate understanding. In the very next appearance, Peter is included with the Ten when Luke refers to them collectively as a group. Insight into spiritual dullness, experienced and learned now, would meet challenging times better with more significance in ministry and in his own life. Grace experienced becomes grace more freely imparted to others.

The fact that Peter led other disciples back to fishing, a profession and laborious occupation rather than their vocational call of apostleship lessens credence to the belief Simon had the honor of this early solo encounter with the Savior. (John 21:1-3) On the other hand, it might be argued that the name, Simon, used here rather than, Simon Peter, refers to Peter's return to walking in the natural. Wallowing and wading in the anguish of his soul. Perhaps guilt permeating his being, limited self-forgiveness for what he had spoken in the courtyard at the religious trial of Jesus. (John 18:15-18; 18:25-27) Did a continuous echo of the rooster's crow reverberate in his head?

Simon, the Zealot, lived in Cana of Galilee. A man zealous for freedom and liberty, he followed Jesus because the Lord offered an alternative for national interference of the Roman government's political regimes and the Jewish legalistic religious stigmatization. A Jewish patriot, yet one who craved the spiritual emancipation Christ offered. Jesus' kingship in Israel would be an added enhancer from Simon's perception. Especially as an apostolic follower of the Lord.

Acknowledged and surrendered zeal remains commendable because Christ did choose him as one of the original Twelve. There does not appear to be any reason Christ would select Simon, the Zealot, over any of the other disciples for a personal Christophany. The Canaanite male, remained a valid part of the Twelve disciples, but outside the inner circle. Consequently, he moves into a place nearer the bottom of the list of Simons for this chapter.

Simon, the Pharisee, hosted a banquet for his distinguished visitor, Jesus of Nazareth. When the woman, a sinner and outcast in society, enters and washes the feet of Jesus with her tears, Simon is appalled. (Luke 7:36-50)

A humble female along with words of rebuke directed toward Simon from Jesus opened the way for a dramatic and valuable lesson in the moment. The humility of a sinner overflows to a humiliated self-righteous Pharisee. The effect caused Simon to be humbled along with his peers. This male and the others present become first-hand recipients of three principles being taught: forgiveness, love, and grace. The immediate all-important life-learning lesson had been experienced. No need or dominate reason for a select one-to-one appearance from the risen Christ on Resurrection Sunday in the afternoon.

Simon, the step-brother of the Lord Jesus Christ, falls into the category of unknowns. Little comes to light about this man, a step-sibling of Jesus. Being one of four step-brothers, he has no known place of prominence or need for being singled out among the siblings. Matthew 13:55 and Mark 6:3 are the only two times Simon has a place of mention and only in the naming of the step-kin of Jesus of Nazareth. Documentation gives little reason or purpose for a visitation from Christ on the all-important Resurrection day.

Simon, of Cyrene, gains entitlement on the list for consideration next. He, the innocent man who happened along, was deployed into the processional headed for Golgotha. The cross, burdening the bleeding Jesus, ends up on the shoulders of one forced to intervene. Simon does so willingly; of course, clearly encouraged by the Roman soldiers. Fear prevailed.

Following Simon beyond his pre crucifixion timeline, a current Christophany scene could open post Resurrection. The debtor, Simon, now redeemed by the resurrected Christ. He may have received a singled-out post Resurrection appearance. What if the compassionate Savior gave the gift of a personally delivered thank you, from Himself to Simon of Cyrene, for assistance in His hour of catastrophic need.

Elsewhere in Scripture Matthew and Mark inform the reader this Simon, a Cyrenian, was the father of Alexander and Rufus. Later in the history of the early Church, the Apostle Paul mentions a Rufus and his mother. Simon's sons, at least Rufus, is believed to have moved to Rome and became instrumental in the growing Christian church in that country. The historical documentation of this family's religious progress could give credence to the outstanding effect of what might have been one of the unpredictable, but long term productive Christophany to one individual outside the Eleven.

Simon, the former leper, lived in Bethany; the one northeast of Jerusalem; probable location is in the Bethany beyond the Jordan. In his home an anointing took place. An unnamed woman, with an alabaster jar of very expensive perfume, becomes singled out and forever memorialized. The intentional act of pouring the oil on the head of Jesus happened because of her spiritual awareness of the impending crucifixion.

A leper healed early in Jesus' itinerant ministry, Simon once had been an outcast. Now, completely restored, he lived among society. To consider this Simon as being selected has little validation. He had heard, if not learned, a life-changing lesson about meeting the needs of the poor. The outcasts and those less fortunate have residence in the population always. There is a time, however, when for a select moment financial benevolence has the purpose of blessing among the less challenged.

Simon, the father of Judas Iscariot, appears as a viable character when reflection centers on his circumstances. Word had spread that his son betrayed Christ. The impending shame and reproach upon the family opened the way for a devastating long term effect. Then as a link to that incident, Judas Iscariot completed suicide. A father filled with shame, remorse, and mourning for his own son might have few options in the spiritual renewal about to spread throughout the Jewish jurisdictions.

Also, this male figure has familiarity with the remaining Eleven because of his son's daily involvement for three years with the intimate band of disciples. What better way to teach the disciples another example about forgiveness in earthly relationships. Would not Simon be ecstatic to report to the disciples who were in hiding that Jesus had risen and He wanted the disciples to know. Somehow this could make a small amends for his own son's unspeakable behavior and evil betrayal.

On the other hand, Judas Iscariot's father could have been elsewhere. Thereby eliminating him in the mind of the reader. Nevertheless, if Christ chose this Simon, He deemed the patriarch of the family worthy of comfort only the betrayed One could provide.

Simon, the sorcerer, and Simon, the tanner, do not fit the timeline, nor the sequence of events surrounding the Resurrection. Though both have roles which surface in the book of Acts, they should be ruled out as experiencing any eyewitness post Resurrection appearance from Christ.

Other disciples were with the Ten (minus Thomas) when Jesus entered the room, on the evening of Resurrection Sunday, through locked doors. Any one of the first seven Simons, or combination thereof on the list, could have been present.

The two most likely to be chosen ... Simon of Cyrene and Simon, the father of Judas Iscariot. The former because of gratitude, the latter to dispense forgiveness and the necessity to dispel guilt.

The outline and summation in this chapter, though provocative in theory, demands speculative thought. To just decide it was Simon Peter reads into (eisegesis) Luke's passage and timeframe preconceived thoughts; without taking from the rest of Scripture (exegesis) to contemplate whether accuracy prevails.

One truth stands. Does anyone on this side of eternity know for sure which Simon of those listed had the awesome solo privilege of experiencing a Christophany?

Section Ten

Sudden Appearances Inside Houses

33

Closed Doors, No Barrier

The urgency to continue appearing and encountering His disciples on Resurrection Sunday remains prevalent. Only the personal appearance of Christ seemed to convince anyone that He was alive. Hesitation to believe hidden behind a veil of doubt challenged His appearances first hand. This happened within two categories, the disciples in general and the Eleven apostles.

Revelation moves into another stage. Luke and John take the reader inside the scene. Jesus' first appearance in the presence of more than two people at the same time startles and frightens those in attendance. (Luke 24:36-49; John 20:19-23)

Sunday progressed hour by hour. A timeline suggests sunset. Traveling in semi-darkness makes for a dangerous journey. The Emmaus travelers do not seem to have received any special command; to go, tell. Nonetheless, their emotional and spiritual jubilation carried them back to Jerusalem. Cleopas and companion returned from whence they originally came having traveled a round trip of approximately sixteen miles. (Luke 24:33)

They entered where the Ten apostles were assembled. Overwhelmed with excitement they were eager to tell them the news. They had seen Jesus. Their faithfulness in delivering the message, even though Simon had already reported seeing Him, afforded them the privilege of seeing Jesus a second time.

Jesus would now appear to all gathered in this different location inside the city of Jerusalem. The doors, not just closed, but locked, were meant to keep everyone out. (John 20:19) What might those Pharisees and Romans do next? The Eleven, and the other disciples in general, were still living in terror from having the horrible knowledge of the crucifixion of Jesus happening three days before.

The stories had stunned them concerning the empty tomb and the missing Jesus. So far Mary Magdalene boldly proclaims she has seen the Lord. John believed at the tomb without a post Resurrection appearance, but remained silent. Two unnamed female eyewitnesses have relayed seeing Jesus. Simon (Peter) received a visitation from the risen Christ. Also, the two ecstatic Emmaus Road travelers confirm… Jesus is alive.

Suddenly Jesus appears in the room. Not having used the preferred choice of entrance, the door. The disciples learn first-hand about the resurrected transformation. First, Jesus' presence in another form. Second, His body aligns with reality.

Christ reiterates the importance of understanding the Scriptures including the Psalms this time. As with the Emmaus travelers earlier, He now opened the minds of those in the house to the truth. He confirmed they were witnesses and attempts to dispel any doubt that remained within their hearts and minds.

He stated He would send the Holy Spirit directly to them in Jerusalem. They must wait for His arrival. This will ensure that through their obedient action they will be clothed with power from on high.

The Trinity will function in this process. The Father promised; Jesus will send; and the Holy Spirit will give unleashed power for guiding believers into all truth. In essence, what Christ had redeemed they will have, experience, and pass on to others. To tarry would bring a new level of spiritual reward.

John's gospel goes further to enlighten the reader that the physical played a larger part in His identity. Luke states, Christ showed them his hands and feet. John includes the Lord's side where the sword had pierced Him. The marks of crucifixion caused an added dimension of verification and released the emotion of being overjoyed. Jesus, per His request, even eats broiled fish offered to Him. (Luke 24: 39-43) No ghost here.

The bestowing of peace stands out twice: first in salutation, then in relationship to their commission. Immediately He breathed on them saying receive the Holy Spirit. Simple enough. Right? Except what followed would change the course of a believer's life.

A message of repentance and forgiveness of sins challenges the apostles and disciples to embark on a new path. Christ places forgiveness in the hands of the offended. On the one hand, God only forgives because of a sinner's repentant heart attitude. On the other hand, Christ said the Father's forgiveness is declared by the believers. If they forgive, and only if they forgive, will the offender's sins be forgiven on an interpersonal level. This awesome power, authority and responsibility is transferred in the supernatural. No dramatic, overwhelming, or lengthy preaching by Jesus to convey the truth. Subject closed.

However, the full revelation of the Holy Spirit had not been given prior to the Resurrection because Jesus had not yet been glorified. (John 7:39) The Son of Man on earth had power to forgive sins just as easily as any act which provided healing. The Lord pardons. (Luke 5:24) The gift of wholeness imparted to the redeemed. Truly the practice was not new. Even Moses had this symbolic relational level with God and stood in the gap for the Israelites in an earlier stage in the Old Testament.

Important and valid, repentance and forgiveness would be preached in spirit and truth; and would begin in Jerusalem. (Luke 24:47) As for Jesus, quite possibly the Romans and Pharisees were uppermost in His thoughts as He gave instruction where to begin. Also as a beginning location this might be a good place for spiritual healing to be experienced by the Apostles.

Through John's documentation of the unplanned encounter with the risen Christ, the reader discovers Thomas misses this strategic time with the band of disciples. Later, Thomas takes center stage and the reader learns his response about the outlandish story he hears from the disciples. John reports on Thomas' response to his peers, almost as much as he does about the previous initial conversation having taken place between Jesus and those in the room. (John 20:24-29)

34
Adrift In Doubt

As the chronology of events unfolds the disciples discover the depth of Thomas' doubt. The reader does too.

Labeled the "doubting Thomas" for centuries by believers, one can often forget he was giving a personal and distinct voice to what many were thinking and feeling, but not expressing on that first day of the Resurrection. No second-hand storytelling would satisfy his personal need to validate this supernatural and holy mystery himself. Thomas had precise requirements. He let it be known to the other disciples that He would accept nothing less.

Thomas (Didymus) not only wanted to see and hear, but actually feel the authentic living Messiah's body. Being very specific, he desired to see the nail marks and feel them with his finger. Going even further he required a somewhat offensive physical procedure of placing his hand in the side of the risen One. A week later, on Sunday, in the same house with the doors locked, Thomas had an unexpected opportunity. The timeline here is extremely important and documented by John, himself, because he was present. (John 20:26)

First, where had Jesus been? There is little documentation about the Lord's travels, procedures, and visitations during this time lapse of one week. Also, the disciples do not see Jesus during these days either. John states this is the second time.

What is the backstory on these days? Was Jesus in the second and third heavens? He had a body that knew no limitations. Or even spending some time with those multitudes that had arose too? (Matthew 27:51-53)

Secondly, it gave Thomas time to debrief from the controlled chaos of the previous days of the Resurrection itself and to process the possibility the Resurrection was true. Combined with the first opportunity missed, the desire anew could begin to dilute the doubt because he had missed out on the previous small group experience. To wait with semi-patience, doubt, and unbelief, in an otherwise semi-forced solitude afforded an opportunity for the coming together of circumstances.

Perhaps there is a higher plan and not just for Thomas. Waiting... taught in preparation for Pentecost. They have already surrendered one week, could they have patience to faithfully wait six more? The return of Christ to this same room, as before, validates not just His Resurrection, but the fulfillment of His promise now and for later.

Thomas' request was honored. The experience opened not just his eyes, but his heart also. Chided by the Lord Jesus Christ for his unbelief, Jesus said, "Stop doubting and believe" (John 20:27). Those four words changed Thomas' life. The humbled man proclaimed a confession of faith on a level he had never experienced the last three years. Then Christ pronounced a blessing upon all others who believe without seeing. (John 20:29)

John concludes his twentieth chapter as if he was not going to write anything else related to the Resurrection appearances. He states Jesus did many other miraculous signs. Was this during the time of the post Resurrection appearances? The disciple also alludes to them not being recorded in this gospel. In addition he writes what the reader of Scripture knows as Chapter 21 which concludes his intended information.

The Apostle John's reason for writing? His desire was for others to believe as he himself had done. Therefore, the Resurrection stories written by the four gospel writers, under the inspiration of the Holy Spirit, provide and ensure every opportunity for the reader to believe the Lord Jesus Christ is the Son of God.

Section Eleven

Shoreline At The Sea Of Tiberias

35
Good Food, Good Will

The next two scenes at the edge of the Sea of Tiberias (in southern Galilee) takes the Lord back to a familiar environment where He first extended a call to some of His disciples to follow Him. Four of those disciples, James and John, Peter and Andrew, two sets of brothers, drew their livelihood from the sea.

One of these, the Apostle John, documents the early morning sequence of action. Seven disciples, after a tiresome and fruitless night of fishing, with their net wet, dirty, and empty; hear a voice coming a certain distance from the water's edge. At this early morning hour a distinct sound from a man cooking fish. One who then gives precise direction to these seasoned fishermen on how to fish. The men were: Peter, James, John, Nathanael, Thomas (Didymus) and two unnamed others.

These confused and disheartened seven men in a boat watch as the early morning mist camouflages the presence of this mysterious man on shore who calls to them. John invites the reader into the scene as he tells the conversation that emerged. (John 21:1-14)

By now in the sequence of appearances after the Resurrection, there should be any number of the males in the boat who know the voice of the One calling to them. Even Thomas, possibly a non fisherman, becomes a person of interest in this scene.

The terminology "friends" used to identify, moves fellowship with the Lord to another dynamic. Reinforced here… it tends to place the relationship with the disciples on a higher level after the Resurrection. This goes beyond the title of apostle and their working leadership designation, to an intimate very personal connection of Lordship.

Intimacy moves from servant, to brother, to friend. Jesus makes his plans known. Servants… obey blindly in a servile mindset. Brothers.. obey in a cooperating kinship mindset. Friends… obey in a motivational love mindset. These three levels are distinct and independent, yet interdependent. Progressive, while constant. A disciple never leaves any one level entirely.

John takes specific care to note this is the third time the manifested presence of the risen Lord made an attempt to assure the disciples. From previous documentation, the reader knows Christ has appeared more than three times. Does John, seeing himself as a key player in the life of Christ, confidently consider this as only the third appearance because he was in attendance? John knew the importance of eyewitness in Jewish culture; therefore he remains explicit about only those appearances he has seen.

These weary fishermen want to call it quits from their fishing excursion. They encounter the voice from a rather obscure person who beckons them to continue fishing. Hearing specific instructions to continue the task they had already concluded in defeat must have been irritating… a level of edgy frustration.

They follow the command to continue and cast their net on the right side of the boat. Direction important in Scripture, as right produces the pleasing results intended. Left, being off-side, or in many instances evil, brings less than desired results. Right, equated with Christ's righteousness brings fruitfulness which lasts.

The wrong way yields little in productiveness. When these fishermen listened and did as instructed they not only followed the voice and command of the Lord, but found themselves in a position of being taught again by the resurrected Messiah, the Eternal One.

Peter had led them back to the natural. To the secure profession that several in the boat knew. An unproven apostolic leader, he had taken followers away from the will of God; a pattern to be avoided by both leaders and followers. A difficult lesson for all to learn.

Jesus set the scene to teach them how productive and precise His vocational call would be. Distinct in number leading towards the salvation of humankind. A purposeful mission brings in a net complete each time. This time 153. (John 21:11) A precious and personal number not difficult for the sovereign Lord to predict at any moment.

A meal awaits the exhausted fishermen. Fish already cooked takes the edge off of their hunger; but accompanied with the requirement that they contribute also. They brought some of the newly caught fish. This was going to be a duration of time spent together. Christ had plans they had not conceived as they approached Him on shore.

Meals deserve attention again at this juncture in the Resurrection appearances. This being the third since the morning of the Resurrection. First, the breaking of bread with the two traveling companions after their arrival in Emmaus. Second, eating broiled fish on the eve of the Resurrection having taken place with His disciples in a locked room (minus Thomas). That appearance of the Lord had obviously come at the near conclusion of the evening meal because people did not leave cooked fish laying around in a residence. A third meal, now outdoors at the shore, will be the final one. Scripture does not give precedence hereafter to mealtime with anyone else prior to the final Ascension.

Food plays a role in fellowship. Always did, always will. Food was part of the fall recorded in Genesis where Adam and Eve ate the forbidden fruit from the tree of the knowledge of good and evil in the Garden of Eden. (Genesis 2:9; 3:6,11) Their disobedience brought devastating eternal consequences. Having held the highest available place of fellowship with God, they foolishly chose to follow their own discourse. Their disobedient character led to corresponding sinful and dysfunctional behavior.

Jesus, the Son of God / Son of Man, came to do the will of the Father. Nothing more, nothing less. "My food," said Jesus, "is to do the will of him who sent me and to finish his work" (John 4:34). With this, He enlightened and instructed the disciples when pressed about eating earthly food at one point during His ministry.

Each of the meals provides a glimpse into Christ's purpose. Open revelation was a result of the Emmaus traveler's evening meal... in the breaking of bread. Christ revealed His new state of physical existence when He ate the broiled fish in a second meal on Resurrection Sunday and with the Ten disciples. Tied to revelation is doing the will of God, which the seven disciples experienced through His teaching in the seashore breakfast. Three important times of eating and fellowship documented in the Bible after His Resurrection.

The depth of understanding has only begun. Hauling the remaining catch of the 153 fish home would be preceded by more than cleaning those fish. The joy of a lesson learned, leads into a new challenging time of fellowship like none previous. A rather unusual and unexpected one-to-one encounter with one of the disciples was on the horizon along with the sunrise.

36

Reinstated Among Peers

Simon Peter and six other companions had enjoyed fellowship with the Lord while they sampled fish and bread from the only available menu. Encircled at the camp scene they reap the social benefit as the fire gives heat to ward-off any early morning chill. Rugged males in a picture-perfect bonding scene. In transition, one might expect breakfast to end rather naturally. Not so.

When the resurrected Christ decides to extend the dialogue He abruptly singles out Simon Peter (aka the son of John). The topic of conversation would be less than ordinary. Intent focused through electrifying content. Peter would hear words he probably thought would never come from Jesus. (John 21:15-23)

The Sea of Tiberias (aka Sea of Galilee) will forever be etched like the rooster's crow in the mind of Peter. Not just because it happened to be a place of pleasure, labor and business, but for the life-changing three-fold verbal confrontation. The dialogue was brief in duration. Confrontation at its best comes from Christ.

A question, then an answer, followed by a command. Not once, but three times. Jesus outlines the ministry of Peter with shepherding specifics. The mission will expand the soon-to-be-birthed Church; having capacity to nurture and strengthen all levels of individuals involved in the unknown future. Peter seems to understand and accepts the teaching.

The deep emotional and challenging encounter would have been difficult enough for a strong personality like Peter if it had been solely in the presence of Christ. Six peers were there to witness the exchange as the intensity increased. What must they all be thinking? Would they be next?

John, though present, does not document anything other than the conversation between Peter and the Messiah. However, John becomes a focal point near the end of the twosome's exchange. (John 21:20-22)

Peter took additional responsibility which Christ immediately rejected and defined as unacceptable. John, also an apostle, was not the focus of Peter's mission. The competitiveness seen earlier in the run to the tomb would not be sanctioned in ministry.

37
Sequence Of Post Resurrection Appearances

This chapter introduces an outline and recap for concluding this section. A listing for telling the known story and the references for each of Christ's post Resurrection appearances... a Christophany. Starting with the Resurrection revelation at the sepulcher, it goes up to the time of the final Ascension, thus covering those all important forty days.

The precise moment of the Resurrection is not recorded in Scripture. No indication if Christ was alone, or if angels accompanied the power that raised Christ from the dead. Belief in Jesus' own words of the three days and three nights in the heart of the earth, could place the Resurrection sometime between 3:00 a.m.- 5:00 a.m. on Sunday on the Gentile timeline.

Jesus' First Appearance
Location - At the Sepulcher
Timeline - Sunday morning
Scriptures - Mark 16:9; John 20:11-17
Characters - Jesus and Mary Magdalene
Specifics - Go, tell the disciples. Mark affirms Jesus appeared first to Mary Magdalene; John places her with Jesus in the garden scene. Jesus said, "Do not hold on to me, for I have not yet returned to the Father" (John 20:17). Christ, the Son, then ascends to God His Father, as He returns with the keys

of death and Hades (hell). Following this first Ascension, Christ returns to earth for forty days continuing the post Resurrection appearances.

Jesus' Second Appearance
Location - Unknown (on a country road)
Timeline - Sunday morning
Scriptures - Matthew 28:8-10; Mark 16:12
Characters - Unnamed women (Appears to imply Mary Magdalene with the "other Mary" in this scene, but unlikely these two.) More likely Salome and Joanna, or those other two unnamed women (servants?) in Luke's account. They tell others gathered that Jesus is alive; but they are not believed. (Speculation offers up a potential thought… Mary of Bethany and her sister Martha cannot be eliminated.)
Specifics - Clasped the Messiah's feet in worship. (Matthew 28:9)

Jesus' Third Appearance
Location - Emmaus Road
Timeline - Sunday afternoon
Scriptures - Luke 24:13-32
Characters - Two travelers, Cleopas and his companion.
Specifics - Jesus' emphasis on Old Testament prophesies; also His being made known in the breaking of the bread, followed by His sudden departure.

Jesus' Fourth Appearance
Location - Unknown
Timeline - Sunday afternoon
Scriptures - Luke 24:34
Character - Simon
Specifics - Simon, (tradition points to Simon Peter); but two others: Simon of Cyrene or Simon Iscariot could rank high on the list.

(Emmaus travelers return to Jerusalem, Cleopas and his companion. Upon arriving they are informed Jesus had appeared to Simon also. The sequence of the third and the fourth appearances might be reversed, but Scripture gives no clue to a precise timeline or location where Jesus appeared to Simon.)

Jesus' Fifth Appearance

Location - In a residence
Timeline - Sunday evening, the day of the Resurrection
Scriptures - Mark 16:14-18; Luke 24:36-49; John 20:19-23
Characters - Ten disciples (Thomas absent / Judas Iscariot deceased)
Specifics - Evening first day, behind locked doors, eating broiled fish. Jesus' first appearance with Ten disciples in a collective group; states signs will follow, revealing power evangelism. Also, definite instructions from Christ to those present on the subject of forgiveness of sins.

Between the fifth and sixth appearances... there is a missing week. Where was Jesus?

Jesus' Sixth Appearance

Location - In a residence (the same one as the previous Sunday)
Timeline - Sunday, one week after Resurrection Sunday
Scriptures - John 20:26-29
Characters - Eleven disciples (includes Thomas)
Specifics - Appearance to Eleven disciples in a group, though not stated as such; John mentally catalogues and counts this as the second of Jesus' appearances apparently because he was present both Sundays.

Jesus' Seventh Appearance

Location - Sea of Tiberias (aka Sea of Galilee)

Timeline - A work day (catching 153 fish)

Scriptures - John 21:1-23

Characters - Simon Peter, Thomas (called Didymus), Nathanael, James and John, plus two unnamed disciples

Specifics - Seven disciples in a group. John counts this as the third time Jesus appeared to His disciples, an apparent reference to the disciples collectively and only when it includes John himself. (John 21:14) (The eating of fish in two of the three that John counted.)

A detailed face-to-face encounter between Peter and Jesus concerning Peter's love for the Good Shepherd and his future apostolic ministry happens in this scene through a three-tiered call. No additional post Resurrection appearance singled out here concerning Peter because the timeframe and location are all the same. However, by this time, Peter has been in the presence of the risen Lord at least four times since His Resurrection.

In the sequential listing above, the post Resurrection appearances follow the chronology timeline in the Bible from the tomb through the Apostle John's fishing scene near the shoreline.

However... there are three remaining post Resurrection appearances. These have been deliberately set apart because of their own sequence related to Commissions. They would be the 8th, 9th, and 10th post Resurrection appearances in numbers. Each having their own place tucked into the chronology timeline somewhere within the 40 days after the Resurrection of Christ. They will appear in greater detail as the Commissions and Ascensions in the next section.

Section Twelve

Commissions And Ascensions

38
Sequence Of Commissions And Ascensions

The post Resurrection appearances are complete except for the final one, the Ascension. However, the conclusion is not that simple. What if there are four Ascensions in the gospels? The outline below reveals a specific verbal Commission, each time, from the Lord before His Ascension:

First Commission, First Ascension

Related Event: Evangelistic Commission
Characters: Jesus and Mary Magdalene
Key Action: Go, tell His disciples
Scripture: John 20:10-18
Location: At the empty tomb
Purpose: Proclaim He is risen
Related Reason: Evangelism
Specifics: Voice recognition (John 20:16)

Second Commission, Second Ascension

Related Event: Great Commission

Characters: Jesus and the Eleven disciples

Key Action: Go, make disciples

Scripture: Matthew 28:16-20

Location: On an unnamed mountain in Galilee

Purpose: Traditional Discipleship - Teach to obey

Related Reason: Develop character - Fruit of the Spirit

Specifics: Some doubted (Matthew 28:17)

Third Commission, Third Ascension

Related Event: Transfer Commission

Characters: Jesus with Eleven (two angels plus others / 120)

Key Action: Go, wait for power

Scripture: Luke 24:50-53; Acts1:8-11

Location: The Mount of Olives

Purpose: Spiritual instructions to wait in Jerusalem

Related Reason: Holy Spirit of the Trinity leads to truth

Specifics: Visible cloud in the Ascension (Acts 1:9)

Fourth Commission, Fourth Ascension

Related Event: Power Commission

Characters: Jesus and the Eleven Disciples

Key Action: Go, with signs accompanying

Scripture: Mark 16:15-18

Location: Outside of Jerusalem

Purpose: Christ's spiritual power transferred from heaven to earth

Related Reason: Outpouring of supernatural power - Gifts of the Spirit

Specifics: Jesus sat at the right hand of God (Mark 16:19)

39
First Commission, First Ascension
(Go, Tell His Disciples)

The first Ascension follows the initial evangelism Commission given to Mary Magdalene at the empty tomb in the garden. In the moment, Mary thought little or nothing of this responsibility as a perceived Commission. She was more intent on sharing the overwhelming and astonishing news with others that their Teacher was alive; rather than any intentional evangelistic proclamation. Referred to in Christian circles… to proclaim the "Good News" of the Gospel of Jesus Christ. He is alive!

Jesus commissions Mary, the first person to have seen Him resurrected and alive, to "go and tell" the disciples He will meet them in Galilee. During this brief encounter, Jesus acknowledges He has not yet ascended (returned) to His Father in heaven. (John 20:17)

How does the reader of Scripture know this Ascension happened then and there? First, the tomb scene ends in a very abrupt manner. Second, details lack for either departure, His or hers.

Later on the timeline, after the first Ascension, but still early morning, the Lord encounters two female eyewitnesses together outdoors, but possibly a long distance away from the tomb area. (Matthew 28:8-10) In this scene the overall general appearance of Christ is more recognized by these women. Also, He does not admonish them to remain disconnected as they worship Him. They fall at His feet. The Lord is more open to acceptance of any happenstance, spontaneous, or planned physical contact through their worship.

Notice the message the Lord gives to the two women. The "go and tell" theme remained, along with whom to tell. The futuristic location, Galilee, continues too.

Some of these basic thematic threads were touched on in previous chapters. Nonetheless, necessary to reaffirm here for the continuity of the chronology format.

40
Second Commission, Second Ascension (Go, Make Disciples)

In order to move forward with the Ascension theme, the best starting place probably would be what is taught in churches from the pulpit and in Bible studies. A neat package is usually presented for Chapter 28 of Matthew's documentation of the Great Commission, and supposedly the one and only glorious Ascension. The specific location Matthew mentioned is often overlooked in those teachings. This is a glaring discrepancy shouting to be acknowledged and confronted.

Neither simple, nor without challenging possibilities, the Great Commission as a subject invokes dialogue. Throughout the centuries, sometimes heated debate concerning the traditional and the supernatural Commissions arises in conversation with theologians and church leadership. In the content here and in the context of the post Resurrection appearances of Christ, the need for reflection on this theme cannot be ignored.

Mathew's documented Commission and the scene's location needs brought into focus on the Ascension timeline. This supernatural event with Jesus and the Eleven, sealed the group's relationship to Him which concerned leadership.

Most Christians have little difficulty with Matthew's gospel, Chapter 28:16-20; where the Great Commission has been made clear in the last five verses. Mark's gospel written to the Gentiles leads down a different path; from Matthew's commission which had nothing supernatural; no miracles, no wonders, no signs and no healing power.

Some theologians tend to scrutinize all the verses of Mark 16:9-20, concerning the timeline. To avoid mentioning this as a theological controversy would be amiss. However, it is not problematic. Inclusion in the canon of Scripture decrees that the Holy Spirit's affirmative validation rests on all these verses for a purpose. Simplistic? Maybe. Nevertheless, Christians read their Bible for both devotional and teaching purposes. Therefore the issue here for the reader surrounds Commissions only, not the possible dateline of Mark's additional verses.

To take a look at all the distinct and separate Commissions proves beneficial. First, the evangelistic Commission from the angels and Christ, Himself... go, tell... Jesus is alive. Second, the discipleship Commission, Jesus defines His own discipling example... go, make... disciples. Teach the truth of discipleship. This whole traditional practice unfolds in the verses referenced in Matthew 28:16-20.

A threefold, clear Commission from this passage consists of: 1) baptizing in the name of the Father, and of the Son, and of the Holy Spirit; 2) teaching obedience to Christ's commands; and 3) making disciples. The dominate ongoing message in the teaching moment is the full Commission.

Often used as the basic teaching for discipleship, Christian church leadership, past and present, adhere to this philosophy with high regard. The call to the personhood of Jesus, becoming "little Christ" is promoted with intent today as in the early Church... "The disciples were called Christians first at Antioch" (Acts 11:26). The message remains central to the gospel. As the Father sent Christ, so Christ sends His disciples too.

The Commission evolves beyond salvation for the repentance and forgiveness of sins. A walk with Jesus in obedience through faith by following His commands goes steps further than salvation by leading a novice believer toward the importance of the Lordship of Christ and walking as a mature Christian believer. Only genuine heart obedience and love can bring one into this second level of commitment with Jesus.

During the Lord's time on the earth and on many occasions in various locations, Jesus went off to a mountain to pray by Himself. In Galilee, on a specific "high" mountain, the Transfiguration of Christ took place during His ministry. (Matthew 17:1; Mark 9:2) In Luke 9:28, Luke does not mentioned height. (Centuries of speculation focuses on Mount Tabor.) The synoptic gospel writers do not name the mountain. John does not write about the Transfiguration even though he was present; however he does mention having seen the Lord's glory. (John 1:14)

Did another private event unfold on a high mountain in Galilee? (Matthew 28:16) One that Jesus had apparently identified as a future location; which Peter, James and John would know. Again Mount Tabor stands forefront. (Even the angels at the tomb did not reference a location by name.) Jesus' reference in His "go ahead" of the disciples seems to be two code words used (repeated) after the Resurrection to enable understanding with regard to a preferred location. Of course, Jesus knew because of the Feast of Firstfruits the disciples would not leave Jerusalem on Sunday.

Nevertheless in Judea, the Mount of Olives was dominate and across the Kidron Valley outside of Jerusalem. However, this was not the location of this second Commission.

41
Third Commission, Third Ascension
(Go, Wait For Power)

In the previous chapter, the reader learned how Matthew gently, but gradually brings his gospel to a close with Jesus returning to God, His Father, from a mountain in Galilee. He kept the Commission and Ascension matter more private with a numbered count limited to the Eleven disciples; thus exposure to only Jesus' apostolic leadership team.

Important Note: The Apostle John remained almost mute on any factual statement or reference in his gospel about any Ascension he had not seen. Only his documentation about the first Commission given to Mary Magdalene; and the information she provided to John about Jesus not having ascended yet to His Father before His talking with her near His empty tomb. As the apostle's practice, he is careful in dealing with these two events as he was not there.

Of course, the first Commission and Ascension mid-morning on Resurrection Sunday in the garden was both supernatural and spiritual. The Ascension was solely between Jesus and His Father. Unlikely Mary Magdalene saw the revelation. Neither she, nor anyone else for that matter, could have fathomed an additional dramatic event in the immediate timeframe following the Resurrection. Comprehension overload... emotional, spiritual, and intellectual. This helps to understand the necessary sightings of Jesus in Jerusalem before any took place in Galilee.

Unfolding in this chapter... The important dynamics of the third and very different Commission and Ascension happens. Many attended the premier public departure of Christ at this Ascension probably not knowing the magnitude of what they watched unfolding. An amazing and awesome sight. For the first-hand observers, the Eleven apostles and other disciples of Jesus, little could compare to this moment of Christ's Ascension outside of Jerusalem. A grand spiritual conclusion to all the preceding events and post Resurrection happenings.

The Commission and Ascension in Luke's writing is a public event. (Luke 24:50-53) However, the physician keeps his explanation simple in documentation. On the other hand, it would be amiss to ignore Luke's second and later writing. The physician focuses in the opening of the book of Acts by striking a greater emphasis on detail than in his earlier writing.

In Chapter 1:1-11 of Acts, Luke recaps the mission of Jesus, alludes to various post Resurrection appearances, and then aptly writes about the third Ascension. The latter portion of these first eleven verses alert the reader to the spiritual reality of the "one cloud" that hid the Lord Jesus Christ.

An Ascension, in definition for the Christian Church, implies the taking up into heaven of a living person. The risen Christ had been in heaven before. However the visual exposure as seen by others in this particular divine event is different. Only in this scene after the post Resurrection appearances do the observers experience the presence of a cloud surrounding His body as a covering in the Ascension. Therefore the dramatic subject clamors for further exploration.

Normal clouds are formed of moisture or tiny water droplets. However this cloud was anything but common. It did not have a concentration of water inside, but that of the power of the Holy Spirit. Twofold reality. The cloud both reveals and conceals the Lord's presence. The Trinity of God, a threefold revelation of divine presence through vehicle, veil, and victory displayed for all to see. The vehicle...

the cloud, the Father. The veil... concealed the Holy Spirit's power. The victory... the risen Christ. Ascensions link earth with heaven.

This cloud appears different, more captivating in visual intensity. Diameter, circumference, height... hid the Lord Jesus Christ. Was it filled with angelic celestial beings? A brightness indescribable. (Acts 1:9) A completed work in the moment, the Son of God / Son of Man with all earthly restrictions removed.

Ascensions confirmed Jesus belonged to a higher realm. Victory was not only in the Resurrection, but coupled with Christ's ability to return to His Father. The cloud becomes a manifestation of God's presence, not unlike in the earlier Transfiguration scene recorded in the Bible by the gospel writers. The voice of the Father was in that cloud. (Matthew 17:5; Mark 9:7) Jesus had been transfigured in the presence of three disciples... Peter, James and John, from the inner circle of the Twelve. A prelude to what they now witness with their eyes at this Ascension. These three disciples able to attest to the similarity of the previous Transfiguration and this immediate Ascension. For the first time their silence surrounding the Transfiguration now available to be broken! (Matthew 17:9; Mark 9:9; Luke 9:36)

Backstory again... Early in the Israelite's exodus from Egypt, the twelve tribes of Israel in the Old Testament experienced the guidance of God through this miraculous phenomenon too. A cloud initially went before them on their difficult journey toward and across the Red Sea. In the form of a pillar, the cloud guided them by day. It was the manifestation of God's presence. (Exodus 13:21)

Power realized in fulness became a prerequisite to the Ascension. The eternal power was with Christ on earth, in word and deed. Also, in the post Resurrection appearances. Power came from the Father in heaven, dwelt with Jesus, raised Him from the dead. Following the Resurrection, He returns to eternity; but the power descends thereafter in another form, the Holy Spirit. Christ makes it clear that this "same" power will reside with the disciples thereafter. (Mark 9:1; John 14:16-17)

As if the third Ascension needs anything more dramatic, here are those two angels again; speaking mysteries beyond the viewer's grasp. Looking at the cloud, the Ascension brings a euphoria of amazement from the spectators. Their curious intellectual questioning brought a response from the angelic beings standing nearby.

Were these two angels also the ones appearing in like manner at the empty tomb? The angel's message of comfort brings pause and reason to pursue additional thoughts.

First, those observing the Ascension were addressed as men of Galilee of the Gentiles. Of special interest to note since they were outside of Jerusalem of Judea. These Eleven apostles were Jewish Galileans. Second, Jesus will return again, guaranteed. (Luke 21:27; Acts 1:10-11)

Luke's all-important hour reached earthly and eternal fulfillment. All the stages of Christ's earthly ministry completed in the Father's timing with this third Ascension? Or were they?

Had the post Resurrection appearances ceased with this third Ascension? Was it the Father's way of confirming what Jesus had said. The completion prior to the eventual (and centuries later to be) Second Coming in the clouds of heaven. Would Jesus' next appearance seen by the Eleven be the Second Coming of Christ? What if there still remained another Ascension first?

The disciples believe a final curtain comes down on the Ascension scene while the polar opposite is happening. They know they must tarry as a people gathered together in an upper room. Waiting for the Holy Spirit that is promised. Unbeknownst to them in the moment, the dramatic event of Pentecost would be on the immanent horizon ten days later.

The reader of Scripture understands and finds the early Christian Church waiting in expectation of the Lord's second coming. Surely He would come soon. However, in reality what is soon? (Revelation 22:7,12, 20) The Church on earth still awaits the glorious Second Coming of Christ!

In the mean time, Luke's writing in Acts moves into the immediate happenings following the Ascension and Pentecost. Christ was not finished. Dramatic events were on the horizon with the about-to-be-birthed Church. Nothing like the disciples had ever witnessed before in their relationship and walk with Christ. Since the future is unknown, the unexpected happenings become pieces to a new spiritual puzzle.

The Ascensions, and especially the fourth one on the timeline before Pentecost, becomes the major connector from post Resurrection to post Ascension revelations of Christ in Scripture.

42

Fourth Commission, Fourth Ascension (Go, With Signs Accompanying)

Important to notice for clarification, the New International Version does not have any subheading in the Bible, beyond the initial heading of "The Resurrection" above verse one of Mark 16:15-20. Should the reader consider... and deem the expected Commission results to definitely be included in Resurrection power?

One might believe from reading verse 15 that this "Commission" could even have taken place on Resurrection Sunday in the room behind closed and locked doors. (John 20:19-23) Did it? If it had, would those in attendance have fully comprehended the eventuality of a supernatural commission for themselves? Did Mark hold off adding the truth, verses 15-20, until experienced manyfold through the disciples in the early Church? Probably yes.

Continuing to read, verse 19 appears to have the place of Christ's Ascension outside Jerusalem once again. By verse 20, the disciples are already experiencing the supernatural power. A sample portion of His unbelievable full measure now in the servants of the Lord Jesus Christ, as seen in His own ministry before His crucifixion and death.

Moments before Christ's death on the cross He committed His Spirit into the hands of His Father. After the Resurrection, this same supernatural power, from God the Father, raised Him from the dead; and thereafter His Ascensions into the heavenly realm. The Holy

Spirit returned to earth for the transformation and empowerment of all believers in the Church.

One thing for certain. The reader of Scripture knows the supernatural power of Christ descended after His third Ascension. He promised power if they waited in Jerusalem. The Holy Spirit was and is power. Indeed they waited and the promise was fulfilled on the day of Pentecost, fifty days after the Resurrection; but only ten days after the third Ascension of Jesus Christ told in Luke's gospel.

Why these two distinct and somewhat contradictory Commissions? The second, personalized, which affords the setting apart of individuals for eternal life. The fourth, a corporate purpose, intended to unleash believers to function with an inter-dependability on each other for ministry in both the Church and the world. The gifts of the Holy Spirit would anoint, giving the propensity to set-in-order a functioning Church in fullness.

The traditional Commission exemplifies the fruit of the Spirit, the character of Christ. Without these basics in depth, power becomes a dangerous mode. The supernatural Commission exemplifies the gifts of the Spirit, the power of Christ. Without the Holy Spirit's presence the Church can become stagnate like a cistern. With the Commissions and Ascensions recorded in the gospels, the disciples and the reader of Scripture has extraordinary insightful nuggets into an eternal plan. When reflecting on the post Resurrection appearances and the four Ascensions, a precedent has been set by Christ. He is here, there, anywhere, on any timeline.

The post Ascension appearances in the Bible, when connected, display the need and importance of Christ's supernatural power being released to flow freely for the Church's empowerment.

This revelation affirmed over and over in the New Testament as a valid spiritual component of the new covenant. The Gospel comes not only with words, simple words; but also with deeds through which character... and powerful miracles, wonders, and signs can be revealed.

The connecting ground work has been laid. For what? The telling of the futuristic post Ascension revelations of Christ. His appearance (Christophany), evident without visual Ascensions following; but still referenced in emphasis throughout the New Testament writings.

Section Thirteen

The Promised Power

43
Tarry For Whom? And What?

After the completed third Ascension, the reader of Scripture learns from Luke in Acts 1:10, that two men (angels in white) appeared and acknowledged the Apostles, as men of Galilee, a distinction to set them apart. They are named as such so no confusion exists; they are not men of Judea. Yet somehow there are another 109... of the total 120 who were in the upper room on Pentecost morning ten days later. Also, those apostles, affirmed as leaders by the celestial beings, appear to have chosen the others to be attendees

Some of the others listed in those 109 believers... were Mary, the mother of Jesus, and His brothers. Classification meaning those as being in the faith. Also possible... step-brothers They headed to the upper room in Jerusalem, a Sabbath's day walk from the Mount of Olives... 2 miles. (Acts 1:10-12)

An important question to ask: Why Jerusalem? On the timeline of only forty days after the Resurrection, the city and its religious and political leaders would not be kind toward any disciples of Jesus, and most of all the Eleven. Jerusalem seems the most unlikely of place where they wanted to wait. Obedience is key in the Lord's plan.

The Jewish feasts become a symbol of the death of Jesus and His Resurrection. The Lord's Passover, the Feast of Unleavened Bread, and the Feast of Firstfruits... three Convocations were honored and everyone was back into their daily routine. These were people with responsibilities including business and family. However, soon to follow on the 50th day... Pentecost, was the next feast on the calendar (of the seven Convocations) honored by the Jewish people each year. Pentecost means fifty, therefore always celebrated as many days after the Feast of Firstfruits.

The Lord Jesus Christ continues His eternal plan. Jerusalem must witness the transfer of power from Him, through the Holy Spirit, to His disciples. This large group of people (120) would experience the miraculous phenomenon in a location where others would be witnesses that it was fulfilled. Nothing in secret. This happens in a bustling city; in an upper room open to the street below with those in proximity of hearing.

Next two questions on their minds must have been... For Whom? And What? They had a basic knowledge explained through Jesus' teaching about the Holy Spirit being the Comforter. An even better revelation of seeing the power without measure (limit) in Christ revealed unto them throughout their earlier travels while being at the Lord's side. (John 3:34)

Those (120) being obedient, believe in faith, and cling to the fulfillment of the Lord's words, "Do not leave Jerusalem, but wait for the gift my Father promised, which you have heard me speak about" (Acts 1:4). The Apostles and other disciples had little-to-nothing in comprehension as to what voids or experiences might be encountered in the daily hours ahead. Of course, their imaginations must have embarked on speculative mental journeys.

44

They Wait... And Wait... And Wait

In diligent obedience the Eleven (120) headed off by foot travel to Jerusalem to tarry in semi-seclusion. Patience along with obedience would be tested. Food and water must be provided along with other necessities. No simple task or circumstance. Breathing people have needs.

The daily noises, of day and night, drifted upward and united with their apprehension and expectation. They counted off the days... 1, 2, 3, 4, 5. Still little changed. What was happening? Nothing?

Which action, or reaction, or mood dominated? Prayer. Quietness. Isolation. Faith. Conversation. Disturbances. Boredom. Sleep. Unbelief. Fear. Could it have been fear that the religious and political leaders might invade their premises? Is there a betrayer in their midst?

They tarried. Would faithfulness continue to reign? Readers of Scripture, have a foreknowledge of the circumstance and the awesome blessing which would be imparted. The participants, on the other hand, did not. Not the day. Not the hour. Just waiting!

A natural void exposed. As usual Peter could be counted on to fill it with his words and impetuous behavior. Using self-sufficient conventional wisdom he declares and undertakes responsibility to fill the vacated seat among the Twelve left by the deceased Judas Iscariot, the betrayer. The lot is cast and a disciple of upstanding is chosen. No apparent dissension arose from the group gathered. Now they are back in their comfort zone. Whole once again.Twelve. Nothing else is recorded about the chosen Mathias and his future endeavors including his personal life and spiritual works in the remainder of the New Testament. However, the disciples have not heard the last from Peter in this upper room.

More days counted off... 6, 7, 8, 9, one after another. Hope, faith, trust, courage, appears to sustain them. Was there love and unity of purpose?

Backstory again... In the Mosaic law they were instructed to count off, after bringing the first sheaf on the Sabbath, seven full weeks, from the Feast of Firstfruits. This Feast of Weeks, as it was called then; became known as Pentecost on the 50th day. (Leviticus 23:15-16)

Present day... forty-nine days passed, since the glorious Resurrection. Tomorrow on the Jewish calendar is the conclusion of the God-ordained Feast of Weeks. Celebrated for centuries by the Jews in obedience to the Mosaic law. The celebration this time would be like none ever experienced before on Pentecost.

45
Pentecost Morning

Time: 8:45 a.m. on the tenth day after the fourth Ascension. Would this day be any different? Yes... at 9:00 a.m. The waiting ended on the divine timeline because... "Suddenly a sound like the blowing of a violent wind came from heaven and filled the whole house where they were sitting. They saw what seemed to be tongues of fire that separated and came to rest on each of them. All of them were filled with the Holy Spirit and began to speak in other tongues as the Spirit enabled them" (Acts 2:2-4).

Awestruck people. Released in joyful emotion, physical stance, and spiritual jubilation. What would happen next? How long did they remain in the upper room in the house? Where did each person go afterward? Did they spill out into the street? Heading for the Temple to tell others about the awesome outpouring of the Holy Spirit.

Had some previously been to the temple during these nine days for prayers? Is this one of the reasons it took ten days? To begin their withdrawal from religious legalism.

Important Note: In Scripture, the 120 were told to go to Jerusalem and wait. They were not instructed to stay "only" in the upper room the whole time. Someone, or perhaps a group, had to purchase food and other necessities throughout the waiting time. Resources, like blankets, among other things, would have been needed for 120. Also...

surely at least a few of these people had children who would require assigned caretakers to step-in and protect them.

If they left the upper room on occasion, for whatever reason… then Jerusalem was aware of these Jews traveling back and forth from the pre designated location. Did it cause suspense to arise. Could a group this size remain unnoticed in their radical commitment? Unlikely! Remember… an extra population of people, including their family, friends, and even other believers they knew, were in Jerusalem to celebrate a festival. The Feast of Weeks was the culmination of seven Sabbaths after the Feast of Firstfruits.

Everything changed for those in attendance on Pentecost. They, and their world, would never be the same from that hour forward. The immediate scene told an unexpected and unprecedented story; but still never giving a futuristic clue for the metamorphosis about to unfold. Radical transformation… revolutionary upheaval.

In a moment, God's power from eternity descended transferring His anointed resource to earth… to human beings. Those below on the city street who heard, affirmed the supernatural had happened. They were hearing the wonders of God proclaimed in their own languages. God-fearing Jews from many nations (70), near and far, who were there for the Jewish festival witnessed the outpouring of the Holy Spirit not just in their national language but also in other languages. (Acts 2:5-12)

Who is this Holy Spirit, the Third Person of the Trinity? What would He and His power be like? First and foremost, He would be a believer's life-long companion.

Jesus had said another Comforter will come in power. (John 14:16-17) The promises of the Lord always fulfilled. What would it mean? Cause? Effect? Important because the Holy Spirit testifies of Jesus and confirms Him as… " the way, and the truth, and the life" (John 14:6). Affirms the Lord's teachings too. Better because originally Jesus had been bound by the limitations of His human flesh as the Son of Man... even though He was also fully the Son of God.

The Holy Spirit guides, teaches, prays, comforts, empowers, speaks to the believers in the Church, soon to be known as the body of Christ. They would not only have the outer presence surrounding them but the indwelling of His presence and His power.

At this point they have no personal first-hand knowledge of the gifts and fruit of the Holy Spirit; nor the effectual results of prayer in the Spirit. This nucleus of people had observed a first glimpse of the wonder-working power of the Third Person of the Trinity. Time and days would guide them as they learn how the Spirit's faithfulness leads while they bring historical change forevermore.

Before the seekers in the room leave, another event unfolds, with a dramatic conclusion. Those tongues of fire not only purify speech, but anoints words too. Change comes to the city of Jerusalem and beyond through evangelism.

46
Anointed Evangelism Message

The leadership of Peter changes. He moves from his self-sufficient conventional wisdom into the supernatural experience of discovering and realizing the release of the Holy Spirit's anointing. This becomes the first evangelistic sermon preached through Peter with a God-given authority.

Observe the body language of the apostle. Peter stands. Intention forthrightly determined. Remember Jesus told Peter He had prayed for him that he would lead and strengthen his brothers in faith after he turned back (converted), in a spiritual maturity level. (Luke 22:32) Unfolding started on the day of Pentecost.

A reference which cannot be overlooked. When Peter stood up, then the Eleven did also. In the sight of the 120, what a powerful show of apostolic team unity. (Acts 2:14) Then immediately the reinstated apostle took the lead by raising his voice. He addressed the crowd assembled outside who were within hearing range with the same enthusiasm that the Lord had placed in love upon him at the Tiberias shoreline. (John 21:15-19)

The Holy Spirit must have quickened Peter's spirit that this was the hour. For Peter it is a new day. Empowered to effect change in the lives of people. Stepping from his past impetuous behavior, to walk in the Spirit, seeking the wisdom of God, and to lean not on his own understanding. In the immediate present, Peter experiences the truth of these potent words from the Old Testament, "...Not by might nor by power, but by my Spirit, says the Lord Almighty" (Zechariah 4:6). When accomplished rightfully, powerful changes unfold.

In Acts, Chapter 2:14-41, Peter addresses the bewildered crowd; those who had heard the Holy Spirit's commotion and foreign languages spoken from those 120 gathered. He affirms the Lord by stating, "... Jesus of Nazareth was a man accredited by God to you by miracles, wonders and signs which God did among you through him, as you yourselves know" (Acts 2:22). Peter goes on at length declaring the Crucifixion, the Resurrection, and the Ascension. The apostle warns, pleads, admonishes, and proclaims, to the hearers... Jesus and the power of the Holy Spirit.

The last verse concludes with, "Those who accepted his message were baptized, and about three thousand were added to their number that day" (Acts 2:41). From 9:00 a.m. on the day of Pentecost, nothing successfully halted the growth of the Church through the power of the Holy Spirit because numbers of believers continued to be added and recorded throughout the entire New Testament and centuries beyond.

Worth noting, they were baptized. Really? This meant a spontaneous onward walk to the pool near the temple, or going farther to the Jordan River. The reader of Scripture knows not where, only that water was involved. Water baptized... following the Holy Spirit baptism. (Acts 2:41)

Immediately after the day of Pentecost, in the book of Acts, the physician continues to inform the reader how the unprecedented unleashing of the power of God was not only on the Apostles; but others too. Influencing their deeds, words and evangelistic ministry.

Section Fourteen

Evangelism Pillars

47
A Measure Of Faith

Christians walk in a simple truth... they believe... in God the Father, in His Son the Lord Jesus Christ, and in the presence and power of the Holy Spirit. Each person started on their God-given spiritual journey with an innate capacity to believe in the Lord Jesus Christ. They could accomplish this because God has given everyone a measure of faith to believe. (Romans 12:3)

Seekers have an awareness provided by the work of the Holy Spirit to use that measure of faith in their life for the realized need of forgiveness for their sin and for salvation through the redemptive work of the Lord Jesus Christ. Then that life-changing moment in time should move from there into the desire to seek a deeper knowledge of Him. This faith increases by being rooted in the Word of God... The Holy Bible. A joy-filled life is knowing and living in a victorious faith.

In the New Testament, Romans 10:17, informs the reader, "...faith comes by hearing the message, and the message is heard through the word of Christ." Scripture states, "... without faith it is impossible to please God, because anyone who comes to him must believe that he exists and that he rewards those who earnestly seek him" Hebrews 11:6). Jesus, who is the Alpha and the Omega, is also the author and perfecter of a Christian's faith. (Hebrews 12:2-3)

Christians have the responsibility to exercise and develop their faith in God. Challenges come and go that causes one to reach outside of oneself and to trust the Creator of the Universe. In doing so, as a potential overcomer they must challenge fear and doubt which are robbers of faith.

In one of the Apostle John's small epistles, 1 John 4:18, the reader learns of perfect love; God's love within a believer casts out all fear. His Light and truth disperses the darkness. Nevertheless, Christians must choose to walk without fear as they experience God's love.

As faith increases, a Christian learns to walk in different levels of faith. This expanded Scriptural theme not explained here; but worthy of learning about and discovering while walking on one's spiritual journey.

Leaders in the early New Testament Church placed their faith in God, and increased in the God-kind of faith. They developed the measure of faith given to them. Each initially had the same, but exercised it at various levels in their own lifetime. The apostles and other disciples had to be faithful in order to be fruitful in ministry; otherwise doubt and unbelief becomes a major hindrance to miracles, wonders and signs, not being fulfilled in the lives of the needy they encountered. All faith is possible by God's grace (unmerited favor) and anointing on His people. Through faith they pleased God. Only then could the promises of the Lord Jesus Christ be revealed and rewarded because they diligently sought Him.

They feared God and walked with Him in His righteousness which exemplified how they laid the foundation of Christ, His works, and His love. In their ability to trust the Lord Jesus Christ, those initial Eleven, and other eyewitnesses of Him, grew in their trust and increasing knowledge by the Holy Spirit. These disciples did not have the written New Testament. They became the human examples; living it for those who came after them.

It is worth noting that the early Christians worked and ministered as individuals, as groups, and as house churches. Some chapters in the Bible actually followed their day-by-day and action-by-action living experiences. Maturity came with obedience exercised through the simple threefold process… Ask, Seek, Knock. (Matthew 7:7-12)

They became outstanding living examples of their firm belief and overwhelming trust in following God's will. Classic and faithful obedience revealed in their good deeds too.

Revelation given, received, and followed by faith, became the necessary pathway how the early infant Church had to learn. How challenging it must have been. The subject of faith in the Bible is simple, yet complex.

48
Resurrection Light

People who do evil also shun light in its various forms because it exposes their sin and wicked deeds. Truthful words exposes lies. Light invades darkness… swallows it up every time. A lamp in a room does the same. Even the moonlight invades the blackest nighttime on earth.

One of the four gospel writers, the Apostle John, wrote more about this issue of Light than his three peers. Focused on Jesus Christ being the "Light of the world" is one of several themes he conveys. Being a witness and a disciple of that Light for three years, John saw the many confrontations Christ had with so-called spiritual men who did evil deeds as religious leaders and authorities in Israel.

Evil deeds hide inside darkness. (Romans 13:12-13) These completed actions sheltered their excessive upholding for the Mosaic traditions, spiritual legalism devoid of mercy and love, flagrant hypocrisy, outspoken lies, and overt suppression. In Jerusalem, the Pharisees staunchly opposed… any spoken truth, compassionate actions, and blessings of godly righteous deeds… from being able to set someone free. Oppression was the wicked plan.

Jesus, constant in His bold approach against evil in all forms, proclaimed without shame or shyness that His Light was the all-consuming Light for humanity. Therefore His earthly presence as the Son of God / Son of Man became equated with Light… not just in the eternal realm, but for the world too. (John 9:5) There is a supernatural connection between Light and life. Those who follow Him walk in the Light and the eternal life He provides and promises; for He is a Light of revelation to the Jews and Gentiles alike. (Luke 2:32)

There was a different type of darkness which overwhelmed the disciples of the Lord Jesus Christ after His crucifixion. Doubt prevailed as they mourned and wept for the Messiah they thought had come to be their national King. Fear and lack of understanding on their part allowed this overpowering emotional and spiritual darkness which forced them into seclusion... until belief and faith in His Resurrection became a reality to them. Nonetheless, the cloud of doubt encompassed the disciples on-and-off during those forty days after the Resurrection. Thomas was the prime example, but other disciples were not exempt or void of it. (Matthew 28:17)

Even in the twenty-first century doubt (versus faith) attempts to invade the life of Christians. However believers of the Lord Jesus Christ today have no excuse for doubting He is Truth. The Old Testament and the New Testament each confirm over-and-over the truth, purpose, and reason Jesus humbled himself as the Son of God and came to dwell in the flesh as the Son of Man; being the example of the truth and grace of God.

Jesus brings eternal life and in that life is Light. (John 1:4) All that anyone will ever need. His Light came at all times and in all situations; but especially in His glorious Resurrection. God, the Father, raised Jesus from the dead. Thereby freeing Him from the agony and darkness of death; and then able to walk forever in Resurrection life.

Also, what was it like when the Light of Jesus permeated the darkness of Hades (hell) in the Resurrection sequence? His descending event experienced by those entrapped through the result of their own evil deeds and experiencing excruciating suffering must have been even more terrified in that place of horror.

On the earthly side, believers are to walk in the Light, as Jesus provides the ultimate way of escape by lighting the pathways for all who desire to be an overcomer. His Light is promised to the obedient and upright; to the faithful Christians who purpose daily to seek His righteousness.

However, on the eternal side, beyond this current world, the glory of God, the Trinity, gives Light forever. The new Jerusalem awaiting the believers will be filled with Light; no sun or moon to give eternal viewing, only the presence and glory of God radiating throughout eternity. The Apostle John penned this truth in Revelation 21:23, "... for the glory of God gives it light, and the Lamb is its lamp."

What is the difference, if any, about the Light of Christ pre crucifixion and post Resurrection? Prior to the former He was the Light of the world. In the Light of His Resurrection... He overcomes the deeds of darkness and wickedness... sin, corruption, and crime. Therefore as the true Light, He provides eternal life in a believer's resurrection because Light is life. In Jesus Christ, in His eternal personhood... the full and complete presence as the Son of God / Son of Man, redemption prevails forever.

Validation comes both in the living Word, Jesus Himself; and the written Word, the Holy Bible. Fulfillment of the Old Testament prophecies of His coming in the flesh; and also about His life, and the birth of the Church in the New Testament should inspire and challenge all doubt beyond measure.

Without the Lord's Resurrection there is no Christianity! Jesus, the Overcomer of all sin and its consequences of eternal damnation, truly becomes the gate and door into enjoying resurrection life with the Godhead, the Trinity, for eternity. (John 10:7; Revelation 4:1)

Jesus said, "I am the light of the world" (John 8:12). His Light spiritually guides and leads His disciples through the indwelling power of the Holy Spirit!

49
Levels Of Divine Revelation

Jesus always initiates His disclosure. One can prayerfully ask to see His will, but a surprise one-to-one physical encounter happens only in His divine providence. Authentic revelation from the Lord usually unfolds through a combination of three basic things: His written will; His verbal will; His community will.

Dominate in importance, these three openings provide practical spiritual guidance; and especially in major decisions in life. In general, specifics look and happen like this: 1) revelation comes through written direction from the Holy Bible, His Word; 2) the indwelling leading presence of the Holy Spirit's still small voice speaks or prompts one in their spirit, especially during prayer; 3) the outward verification of direction often revealed by guiding through current circumstances.

In the early Church, the Christians were walking in the Spirit as they honed the basics of a consistent life of obedience to His will. The power of God, accompanied by the divine supernatural revelation of the gifts of the Holy Spirit given at the outpouring of power at Pentecost, guided them in various ways. The believers were learning day-by-day how to make adjustments for communication with Christ through the Holy Spirit and how to become the body of Christ for His glory.

Whether moving forward or backward in the New Testament one encounters many instances of divine revelation. Nothing more, or less given; just what was needed and adequate in the impending circumstances. As Christians... their experiences, current needs, and futuristic perceptions, required different levels of revelation. Various incidents were personalized according to His timing. The reader of Scripture becomes confident of this truth through the event-filled narrative accounts in the New Testament portion of the Bible by watching the characters on the stage of life.

There are many ways revelation is imparted. In the Bible, a number of verses give glimpses centered on voice, vision, dream, circumstance, prophecy, angelophany, Christophany, transported, spiritual gifts, and temporal things. (For the early believers it was only the written Hebrew Torah for reference, the five books of Moses, plus the Prophets and the Psalms read from scrolls).

Along with having heard first-hand the teaching, preaching, and healing messages of Jesus Christ, they now live their future in spiritual experiences alive through God-given zeal. Written documents would come later. The larger Septuagint of both the Old Testament and the New Testament in Greek translation would eventually become available centuries later.

A brief outline follows of the ways revelation was and still is imparted:

Voice... To build faith and trust, communication initiated by Christ came in voice on several occasions. Especially the calling of one's name in singular such as "Mary" at the empty tomb or the double emphasis as in "Saul, Saul," at the dramatic conversion of Paul. The persecutor of the Church did not see the physical bodily presence of the Lord, but he did see a bright Light more intent than the sun and heard the audible voice of Christ calling and talking to him. (Acts 9:3-4)

In order for communion and fellowship to take place there must be the ability to discern and hear the voice of the Lord. It is a prerequisite. Jesus taught about the Good Shepherd's voice. He not only anticipated, but expected His followers to hear and recognize His voice. The still, small voice in the spirit of a believer. (John 10:3)

Vision… What is a vision? A spiritual reality not seen with the natural eye, but a real means of important communication. All visions should be tested against the Word of God… the Bible.

A person can receive a vision at anytime of day. Seeing the invisible, like Stephen the deacon who was in the most trying of circumstance… between life and death. (Acts 7:54-56) Alone high on a roof, the Apostle Peter had a trance-like vision before him of a sheet let down by its four corners from heaven. (Acts10:11) The greatest of all… was the part vision (and revelation) in the Bible; the Revelation of Jesus Christ given to the Apostle John on the Island of Patmos. (Revelation 1:1-22:21)

Dream… In sleep or light slumber, dreams are night visions given for various reasons. God-given dreams are susceptible only to divine interpretation. Supernaturally received; a supernatural interpretation defines their truth, given by the Holy Spirit.

An evangelistic vision (in a dream) to preach in Macedonia altered the Apostle Paul's life. (Acts 16:6-10) The uprooting of his heart's desire to bring Christ's salvation message to the Jews; the Lord Jesus planted him far from Israel as the Apostle to the Gentiles. As a result… his evangelistic missionary trips bring major insights through his epistles (letters) included in the New Testament.

Circumstances… A keen awareness to the supernatural presence of the Lord through the ordering of circumstances or the unfolding of specific events. A spiritual world exists and God is Spirit. He has command of the world as well as revelation. The believers were learning that He is the same yesterday, today, and forevermore. (Hebrews 13:8)

Prophecy… Specific words given to believers in the Church for edification is prophecy. This can come as inspiration, direction, or guidance. Also as admonishments and protective warnings. A powerful convincing work of the Holy Spirit. It brings hidden things to light and uncovers the secrets of heaven; which could not have been known beforehand. Revelation, the entire book in the Bible, reveals a stunning and awesome example of prophecy given. Jesus is the Spirit of Prophecy. (Revelation 19:10)

Angelophany… Angels intervene as messengers or ministering spirits coming either seen or unseen. An angel came to strengthen Jesus in the Garden of Gethsemane. (Luke 22:43) There is the entertaining-of-angels-unaware where recognition and understanding unfolds after the event. An angelophany can be an angel dressed as a human being; or be quite holy in appearance with celestial wings and a radiance beyond expectation as revealed at the empty tomb at the time of the Resurrection. The physical manifestation always appears as a male gender type, never female.

Christophany… Consistent physical manifested revelations of Christ are infrequent in real time, other than immediately after the Resurrection in His attempt to dispel any doubt that He had risen from the dead. After His final Ascension recorded in Scripture, revelations of Him (Christophany) in real-time down through the centuries remained uncommon… or at least seldom revealed by the recipient as occurring.

Transported… Christ was transported so the probability was modeled by Him. A dramatic, transporting-event might happen for a human being like what Philip, the Deacon, experienced. (Acts 8:39) The unplanned transporting from one location to another for evangelistic purpose was rare indeed, but shows limitations are left to the Lord's discretion. The Apostle Paul, transported, in vision, into the third heaven. (2 Corinthians 12:1-4) Also, the Apostle John to the third heaven. (Revelation 4:1-2).

Spiritual Gifts… The nine gifts of the Holy Spirit rely on power. Given and manifested through the whole body of Christ in the New Testament. The list of the gifts are: message of wisdom, message of knowledge, faith, gifts of healing, miraculous powers, prophecy, distinguishing between spirits, speaking in different kinds of tongues, interpretation of tongues" 1 Corinthians 12:7-11. The fivefold leadership, vocational calls given by the Holly Spirit for ministry involves... Apostles, Prophets, Evangelists, Pastors, and Teachers. (Ephesians 4:11) Also, there are other leadership gifts in the New Testament, but not listed here.

Temporal Things... Items gain respect such as the folded burial cloth in the empty tomb. (John 20:6-8) Though less likely, but in real time mannerisms can be used as a means of revelation as in the breaking of bread in the Emmaus story. (Luke 24: 30-31) One of the greater examples and exceptions was Peter's shadow whereby the people were healed. (Acts 5:15) The handkerchiefs and aprons of Paul transferred anointed healing power by faith. (Acts 19:11-12)

As observed in the listings above, supernatural revelation can be revealed to anyone. The purpose... for any number of reasons. Comfort being provided, or even a preliminary warning of something evil about to attack a person's life. The more common form comes through a vision by day, or a dream at night.

Jesus gave the Twelve a taste of spiritual power before they totally believed! Authority to drive out evil spirits and to heal every disease and sickness. (Matthew 10:1-10) He sent them out two-by-two to preach and to have authority to drive out demons. (Mark 6:7) Later, Jesus sent out seventy-two others two-by-two; He became a sounding board of correction and encouragement after they returned. (Luke 10:1,17-20)

In the Old Testament there are many examples of supernatural revelation, but not pertinent for reference in this chapter. The Lord Jesus Christ had the Spirit without measure (limit) in His body as the Son of God / Son of Man. The same Holy Spirit that guided and comforted the early Church... and has for centuries... does also today!

50
Mission, Truth, Reality

The disciples had seen and witnessed Jesus in His earthly ministry. The high points... dramatic healings and His compassionate lifestyle stand out. The Lord's never-ending teaching opportunities resulted in conversions which clearly gave witnesses a first-hand view of a model of unconditional love.

On the other side, there were problematic challenges too. They had seen confrontational encounters with the Pharisees, along with self-denial, and the daily hardships of traveling in the land of Israel. Of course, the ultimate sacrificial giving of His life through crucifixion and death was beyond expectation. To mention the Resurrection and the Ascensions as awesome would be an understatement. With the Church endued with power this period closes; but moves forward into what will become an unbelievable Bible history. The future unfolds.

A new progression in ministry for the disciples would begin through a drastic turn of events. With a commencement on the horizon, they find themselves in the start of a spiritual phenomenon about to reach heights and depths they never would have believed to have gone beyond Israel's borders and worldwide.

Section fifteen of this book assists the reader to rediscover how the Church begins to advance toward a higher level of maturity. Experiencing and feeling the power of the Godhead, they could not have perceived how they were still in a toddler level of learning ministry leadership. With the post Resurrection appearances completed, believers and leadership alike will experience a new phenomenon, the post Ascension appearances of Christ. The word, appearance, takes on a new meaning.

The anointing had descended upon them as the power was released within. Apostles, prophets, evangelists, pastors, teachers, elders, deacons, and disciples alike were making valiant progress in fulfilling the four Commissions given at the Ascensions. The advancing of the Church through evangelism... shown in the obvious gains of converted souls for Christ, accomplished through the teaching, preaching, and healing ministries.

The Holy Spirit's leading takes a turn in theological perception and direction. Church leadership would begin to experience another change. These observations unfold and lead them into the "school of continuance" by seeing the Lord's physical presence (Christology) manifested differently. A valid theology begins to unfold. These kindergarten graduates move into a level of personal faith and trust through new avenues of supernatural power and spiritual revelation.

This happens abruptly, with a godly deacon in the Church taking a stand for the truth as he proclaims the message of the Lord Jesus Christ. What the apostles were about to learn eventually was this would be no one-time persecution and death event. They would all have to move into a level of commitment beyond their comprehension at this juncture of their apostolic journey.

It would take time, actually years before the first century Church lived up to the reality of becoming known as "little Christ" as they were first called Christians in the city of Antioch. (Acts 11:26) They only had the first sour taste of persecution... leading to death and being remembered as a martyr. As devoted followers of the Lord Jesus Christ, they would learn anew what the spiritual commitment truly encompassed.

The power had been with them all along through healings and other miracles. However, the revelation of the personhood of Christ began to be manifested unexpectedly in another manner.

Some conceptual thoughts explored in these last few chapters become insightful preparation for leading into the next section where the Lord's post Ascension appearances unfold.

Section Fifteen

Post Ascension Appearances Bring Change

51
Sequence of Post Ascension Appearances

A list of Christians which the Apostle Paul mentions in 1 Corinthians 15:5-7 can contribute to a conflicting claim. For the reader of Scripture, it poses thought-provoking questions needing potential answers related to the Lord's appearances on the chronology timeline. Referenced here, those Paul named were: "...Peter, and then to the Twelve. After that he appeared to more than five hundred of the brothers at the same time, most of whom are still living, though some have fallen asleep.Then he appeared to James, then to all the apostles, and last of all he appeared to me also..." as Paul, ends the list. In his conclusion referring to himself as the one abnormally born; referencing his spiritual birth.

A reader of Scripture might question why Paul would write them only as post Resurrection appearances which had been known and preached previously when he was initially with them in Corinth. Even more perplexing, perhaps the referential list can be attributed to or even divided between two chronology timelines.

This name-filled list which the apostle has written to the believers at the Church in Corinth can be perceived and believed as distinct references; which many pastors and students of the Bible attribute them as being post Resurrection appearances. They are dauntless in their intentional and persuasive debate. Nevertheless... why would Paul have himself on that post Resurrection list because the Christophany he experienced was definitely a post Ascension appearance.

Without question Paul preached Christ raised from the dead. Spoken from his personal and spiritual heartbeat; delivered through his pointed and passionate evangelism message which he shared with everyone... Jew and Gentile alike.

In Paul's letter he was attempting to prove the bodily Resurrection of Christ. Was the apostle's rationale for naming those individuals and groups that the revelation of Christ was real; validated on both timelines. Therefore including his own experience on a post Ascension timeline. In those verses, Paul does not name any of the locations where the appearances occurred... which hinders problem-solving!

Or... is there a camouflaged answer, to the seesaw speculation and theory of the appearances? Possibly centuries ago the list was included by a manuscript translator while writing; thus it becomes a translation error. Therefore inserted in the Corinthian passage by mistake; or even misplaced when it should have been added elsewhere. Maybe? Maybe not?

Important Note: There is a list of six appearances, individuals or groups, given by Paul. He finalizes the list with his own Messianic encounter which refers to a post Ascension appearance. (Of course he does not name the Apostle John's post Ascension revelation of Christ at the end of his list; as he, Paul, was deceased before that glorious Christophany as witnessed by John.) Also, notice at the beginning of the list no mention of Stephen, the deacon, which is used in an attempt by some to validate the references were post Resurrection appearances. More on this later.

A theoretical side trip... in a potential rearrangement of the post Ascension appearances one also might place Paul's experience in a different numerical position on a chronology timeline. To include that premise would require changing the original order of Paul's listing of six; therefore the consideration was not undertaken.

Nevertheless... the placement of the categorial information from 1 Corinthians 15:5-7 included in "this chapter and others following in this section" proposes they are more likely post Ascension appearances. Biblical fact... there are Bible passages with details that Jesus did appear in "various ways" to His disciples post Ascension.

A brief categorical listing below staying true within the named sequence of Paul's six... now includes Stephen and John like added bookends related to post Ascension appearances. This was chosen as a purposeful setup. Therefore the middle section, Paul's sequential list of six, remains in tact.

Of course, one is not expected to agree line-by-line about the potential timelines included. Missing information makes it difficult to place them on a precise chronology because Paul never mentioned locations. Accurate dates or years often unknown in history. Conflicting beliefs hedge also because of the unknown actual dates for the year of the Crucifixion and Resurrection of the Lord Jesus Christ.

The concept being presented explores how the presence and power of Christ was manifest in the nurturing and maturing of the Church. His appearances gave an anointed and spiritual dynamic for the future of Christianity. More thoughts and perspectives included in additional chapters in this section.

First Post Ascension Appearance

Location - Sanhedrin (aka ruling council) in Jerusalem
Timeline - 36 A.D. (Actual date unknown)
Scriptures - Acts 7:54-56
Characters - Stephen, a Grecian Deacon
Specifics - Stephen, the deacon, while being martyred by an enraged mob, looked up to heaven and saw the glory of God and the Son of Man standing at the right hand of God. (Acts 7:56)

Second Post Ascension Appearance

Location - Joppa
Timeline - 36 A.D. (Actual date unknown)
Scriptures - Acts 10:9-16; 1 Corinthians 15:5
Characters - Peter, an Apostle
Specifics - In a trance-like vision, while on the roof at Simon, the tanner's residence; Peter saw a sheet let down from heaven by its four corners (three times); filled with unclean animals; and heard the voice of the Lord.

Third Post Ascension Appearance

Location - Jerusalem (Actual location unknown)
Timeline - 35 A.D. (Actual date unknown)
Scriptures - Acts 1:20-26; 1 Corinthians 15:5
Characters - Twelve, Jesus' apostolic band of disciples
Specifics - Almost nothing is known about this appearance. Based on the number Twelve it comes after experiencing the authentic supernatural power of Pentecost. Mathias appears to be included in the number, as having been chosen by lot to replace Judas Iscariot, the betrayer.)

Fourth Post Ascension Appearance

Location - Galilee or Jerusalem (Actual location unknown)
Timeline - 36 A.D. (Actual date unknown)
Scriptures - 1 Corinthians 15:6
Characters - More than Five Hundred at the same time
Specifics - Appears this was not one of the post Resurrection appearances of Jesus. If it takes place during the second post Resurrection appearance at Mount Tabor in Galilee when the Twelve apostles were there receiving the command to "go make disciples" and Jesus was high above the five hundred. They would have heard the commission given to the Twelve. (Matthew 28:16-17) (Or... at the glorious third post Ascension?)

Fifth Post Ascension Appearance

Location - Jerusalem (Actual location unknown)

Timeline - 44 A.D. (Actual date unknown)

Scriptures - 1 Corinthians 15:7

Characters - James, an Apostle

Specifics - First apostle martyred, James, (the brother of John), murdered with the sword by King Herod Antipas.

Sixth Post Ascension Appearance

Location - Jerusalem (Actual location unknown)

Timeline - 45 A.D. (Actual date unknown)

Scriptures - 1 Corinthians 15:7

Characters - All the Apostles

Specifics - Appears to be the Lord's final collective opportunity with the chosen apostles as a group on earth to encourage those remaining apostles after the death of James.

Seventh Post Ascension Appearance

Location - Road to Damascus

Timeline - 38 A.D. (Actual date unknown)

Scriptures - Acts 9:1-9; 1 Corinthians 15:8

Characters - The Messiah, and Saul of Tarsus, and the other unnamed ones in attendance

Specifics - Only the soon to be Apostle (Paul), was keenly aware of the presence of the Lord Jesus Christ by a bright white light and by voice. Those others saw the light, but did not hear the voice of the Lord Jesus Christ.

Eighth Post Ascension Appearance

Location - Island of Patmos

Timeline - 85 A.D. (Actual date unknown)

Scriptures - Revelation: Chapters 1-22

Characters - Jesus, the King of kings, and the Apostle John

Specifics - John, while in exile on the Island of Patmos, received the Revelation of Jesus Christ; documented as the book of Revelation in the New Testament.

52
First Deacon Martyr

In the New Testament, in the life of the fledgling Church, apostolic leadership established a vocational two-level organization structure with elders and deacons for ministry order and implementation. However... the Lord Jesus Christ reveals there is no hierarchy used when applied to Christians for receiving His open revelation.

Just as the reader learned that Christ chose a woman to be His first eyewitness of His Resurrection and the human proclaimer of the message... He is alive; they learn that on the dominate male leadership scale, elders and deacons held a place of authority. Nevertheless... supernatural power and revelation could overrule a leadership boundary.

A deacon, named Stephen, surfaces as more than an articulate and servant-minded person. According to Luke, the people selected Stephen as a deacon because he was, "...a man full of faith and of the Holy Spirit" (Acts 6:5). He had already accomplished great wonders and performed miraculous signs through the power and grace of God. Chosen as one of seven from among the Grecian Jews; Stephen was known to be full of wisdom. (Acts 6:3)

Elders had responsibility for prayer and the ministry of the Word, but a deacon's service was assigned to waiting on tables. In other words, the deacons in their locale gave their attention to needy widows in their daily necessities starting with the provision and distribution of food. These men were not only task workers but spiritual leaders.

Nevertheless, during this timeline the apostles (elders) sanctioned this cluster of seven men known as deacons. As a result, the Good News of the life, ministry, and Resurrection of the Lord Jesus Christ spread. A rapid increase in disciples happened. Two leadership distinctions, elder and deacon, brought a duo complement furthering the evangelistic outreach of Christian ministry arising after the Resurrection and Ascension of Christ. Centuries later the apostolic call became known at times in church denominations… as Bishops.

Details about Stephen's life and church ministry are mentioned in Luke's account in the book of Acts. What does stand out and which Luke deems most important to convey becomes the increased opposition toward Stephen from the Jews of his location. Argumentative attitudes increased, projected toward him, holding Stephen responsible for division. Stephen, now a first-hand activist in the revelation movement through the power of the Holy Spirit, became a threat to the older religious system soaked in traditionalism and legalism. Revelation exposes stoic, stagnate and stifling procedures. Stephen's leadership and wisdom alienated many. (Acts 6:8-15)

When all else fails, an evil attempt ensues to dilute godly power and supernatural revelation. Charges of blasphemy rears its ugly head. Motivated through envy and jealousy, this pseudo charge seeks and finds a place to roost. Say the word "blasphemy" in either Old Testament times or during the years of the birthing of the New Testament Church and people became easily stirred up. The adversaries' subtle, vicious, and threatening stance, were exposed with fervor and passion as undercurrents surfaced. Enter those from the Sanhedrin (aka ruling council), combined with their plotting and persuading false witnesses, and the scene sounds and looks like an instant replay of events leading toward the darkest hours in Christ's life.

Looking a little deeper, into Acts 7:1-53, the reader learns:

First… During Stephen's speech to the Sanhedrin, he elaborated on the historical events recorded in the first five books of the Hebrew Torah (Pentateuch), covering Abraham, other Patriarchs, and Moses, while detailing the working of God in the life of the Hebrews known as the Israelites.

Second… This sermon resounded like a megaphone because of his boldness and authority, as part of the revival proceedings. Stephen went on and on how one Jew, Jesus Christ, had come unto His own, the Jewish people of God, to lead them out of their disobedience and complacency and into the Light through Him being the way, and the truth, and the life. The glorious example of Godly righteousness.

Third… To say the onlookers were displeased at what they were hearing diminishes the intense language which the Bible states as their response. They were furious! (Acts 7:54) Covering their ears, they reverted to mob tactics. They charged after Stephen, dragged him out of the city, and eventually stoned him to death. (Acts 7:57-60) The fear and dread of Stephen's authority drove those full of violence to commit corrupt acts before God and humanity.

Fourth… Scripture alludes to a dramatic change in the countenance of Stephen; for the accusers, "…saw that his face was like the face of an angel" (Acts 6:15). The power and revelation of God would be manifest in a way seemingly above or beyond the previous post Resurrection experiences.

Prior to the accusers rushing at Stephen, he "…looked up to heaven and saw the glory of God, and Jesus standing at the right hand of God" (Acts 7:55). Stephen saw heaven open, and Jesus about to receive his spirit forever into the eternal realm.

A most unusual manifestation of the eternal Christ revealed. This revelation, whether in real time or vision, becomes a primary teaching moment for building faith and trust in the onlookers who had hearts willing to receive. Scripture does not indicate how many disciples were in the vicinity of the scoffers and stoners. Luke does inform his readers that godly men not only buried Stephen, but they mourned his death.

Nevertheless... in some references... Hebrews 1:3; 8:1; 10:12; 12:2... these make known that Jesus as the high priest was seated at the right hand of God Many times, sermons down through the centuries have made the valid and important distinction between Christ seated or standing at the right hand of the Father. The Lord standing at this moment when Stephen saw Him, many believe, signifies the importance of Jesus welcoming Stephen, the first martyr from Church leadership, into eternity.

Important Note: In Paul's list, 1 Corinthians 15:5-7 the reference to Stephen, the deacon, is not listed. Nevertheless... It needs to be included in this section because Saul of Tarsus (the future Apostle) was present during the stoning of Stephen. (Acts 7:58; 8:1)

For the related purpose used here, the post Ascension appearance of Christ remains dominate, not His posture. Prestige, power, or position of a believer has nothing to do with the ability to receive the revelation of God. The power of God continues to touch even the simplest life. Any disciple who takes a stand for truth, and verbalizes a profession of faith, who walks both in humility and obedience, doing the will of God out of a personal love for Christ, has the distinct possibility of being singled-out. Opportunities may open through a vision to touch even the eternal realm. If a believer can reach the throne of God through prayer because Jesus as the believer's intercessor is seated at the right hand of God; why not otherwise?

53

No One Declared Unclean

The Apostle Paul starts his list in 1 Corinthians 15:5-7, first by naming Peter as to whom the Lord appeared. Any reader of Scripture knows that both Mark and John, without exception, and even Matthew and Luke give a same indication that Mary Magdalene was the first one Jesus appeared to on Resurrection morning.

Why would Paul, who was not among the Twelve at the time of Jesus' itinerant ministry, signify Peter as holding this place of distinction? Could it be that Paul was not talking about a post Resurrection appearance, but a post Ascension appearance after Stephen's? This appearance through a vision unfolds for the apostle early-on in the infancy of the Church. Luke's account in Acts 10:1-48, places it a short time after Stephen being stoned to death.

A previous chapter, in Section 9, details who the Simon (Peter) was that received an appearance from Jesus on Resurrection Sunday. Therefore, the reader of Scripture might question whether Paul's possible timeline of his letter (epistle) offers potential flexibility as it could point to either a post Resurrection or post Ascension appearance.

Back to Peter's experience…the unusual and uncharacteristic change-of-course happened in a simple daily event of apostolic ministry. Peter, a devout Galilean Jew by birth, and as a follower of Christ, adhered to many Hebrew traditions including the Seven Feasts of the Lord. However, Peter had legalistically programed into his mind that salvation through Christ belonged to the Jews only. Even though he saw many non Jewish followers of Jesus during His earthly ministry, for whatever reason Peter could not accept the possibility that Gentiles would become a genuine and grafted-in part of the kingdom of God. His rationale had come from having been told and sent by Jesus along with the other Eleven disciples only to the house of Israel as documented in Matthew 10:5-8. Peter needed to learn what the Lord directs one time may not prevail later, or long term.

In Luke's account the reader learns two individuals each receive a vision from the Lord. (Acts 10:1-23) The first came to Cornelius; the second, to the Apostle Peter. The latter's vision and story covered later in this chapter, but first the reader of Scripture learns of the essential part a devote man played in the life of Peter.

Cornelius, a God-fearing centurion in Caesarea, stands out as an extraordinary person for his time and place. Paganism should have reigned in his life, but it appears to not have been a dominate attraction for him. He evidently turned toward God at least intellectually at some point in his life. God's apparent spiritual grace was on Cornelius. The centurion was prayerful and benevolent. His generous spirit towards the poor touched the heart of God. Jesus signaled him out to receive a vision.

In the vision, an angel spoke to him; and Cornelius was to heed the direction given in order to meet the spiritual need for himself and his extended household. Immediately the Apostle Peter was sent for and brought to his doorstep. The hand of God linked two unlikely people together through His spirit, power, and revelation.

Peter, the Jew, was in the midst of his own struggle to believe in his mind that Gentiles could possibly be set apart by the Lord Jesus Christ for His kingdom work. He finds himself in the presence of Cornelius. Obedient to the vision, Cornelius' action to fulfill the Lord's direction placed him in a position to become the first Gentile convert in the region on the post Ascension timeline.

The Gentile leads because of his being open and available through his obedience and disciplined personal nature. One cannot overlook the fact that Cornelius was not a Christian prior to the vision.

Therefore on the simultaneous timeline with Cornelius, Peter received his detailed life-changing vision to overcome his own prejudice. According to Jewish kosher eating precepts, principles and practices, Peter would never defile himself by breaking a stringent eating pattern. This dogmatic thinking would be forever changed through a vision of a sheet let down by its four corners from heaven, filled with unclean animals. Not once, or twice, but a third time. The sight of this unusual visionary scene, accompanied by the "voice" of the Lord, changes not just the apostle's life and direction of ministry, but also ministry worldwide.

The importance of taking the Gospel and being witnesses to the Gentiles, followed on the heels of Peter receiving a bold and specific command concerning Gentiles...the so-called heathen. Later, not just the Apostles, but other disciples, proclaimed the Gospel to many nations not of Jewish origin. Pagan people, no longer second class citizens in the eyes of the Twelve, would hear the Gospel and have an opportunity to be exposed to the reality of a risen Christ who through grace provides their salvation.

Confirmation brought a change from the initial evangelism course. Through these two separate visions, that of Cornelius and Peter, the reader of Scripture becomes attuned to how the Lord Jesus Christ, along with the power and presence of the Holy Spirit, establishes anew that spiritual revelations unfold for the benefit of humans worldwide; then, now, and forever.

54
Twelve Together

The title, Twelve, became an important reference point. The early Christian Church referred to the original Twelve in their gospel writings who continued on as the Apostles; those selected, called, and known by Christ.

In 1 Corinthians 15:5, Paul writes "and then" giving his immediate focus to the "Twelve" as he seems to revert back to Sunday, the day of the Resurrection. Could this be the only possible opportunity where Christ appears to the Twelve as a collective unit? Actually, neither were Twelve in that locked room on that glorious day. Ten was the number of apostles. Even one week later when Thomas happened to join them their apostolic total was Eleven. (Judas Iscariot, the betrayer, deceased before the crucifixion, was not there either time.) Does Paul use Twelve as a group classification rather than an actual count?

When the reader looks at Paul's reference in 1 Corinthians 15:5, and places it after the Ascension there would have been a specific reason for Christ to appear to them collectively on the post Ascension timeline for the Church.

Remember Matthias? The person chosen to take the place of Judas Iscariot. The key ruling factor for church leadership (apostolic), on the timeline determined whether the person to be an apostle had been an eye witness of Jesus' ministry… and the post Resurrection appearance. (Acts 1:22)

There are those students of the Bible who believe Matthias' call, falling by lot, in Acts 1:12-26, somehow became invalid or nullified. This theological perception gains momentum because of the dominate apostolic call of Paul later. Some pastors believe a lack of historical documentation (information), both inside and outside of the Bible, minimizes validation of Matthias' ministry after the post Ascension appearances of Jesus Christ. Therefore, they dismiss a possible divine affirmation of Matthias being chosen.

When Matthias becomes categorized in this manner, should the reader of Scripture then have to believe the Twelve dwindled down to three or four? Little information is conveyed about the many in the band of Twelve. In the initial core of the disciples appointed as apostles, other than Peter, James, and John in the inner circle of three... confirmation about the apostolic call of several others goes virtually undocumented in the New Testament. Should this nullify those experiences?

Now that Matthias has been covered in theory, another reference needs to be considered and explored. Remember those four Commission scenes and the spectacular third Ascension event? What if sometime later, and that being after Peter and the infamous sheet let down from heaven, Christ made a post Ascension appearance to the Twelve together. Unofficially, or officially, a collective Twelve according to Paul.

Is it possible the gospel writers... each have it correct concerning Ascensions? Mark wrote first. Were not miracles a predominate part of the Lord Jesus Christ's ministry? Mark's entire writing carries an air of immediacy and especially power, not just in the moments surrounding the fourth Ascension.

Categorically where one places the timeline of Peter's vision; then the message given to the disciples "move in power" which they had been experiencing according to Mark's later verses, now moves far and wide by going to all nations (70). The New Testament bears witness that these disciples followed the command in obedience.

Note: In the backstory of Jesus' itinerant ministry He had given a portion of His authority and power (related to gifts of the Spirit) to the seventy He sent out two by two. (Luke 10:1-24)

The command of making disciples of "all nations" only now after Peter's specific encounter recorded in the book of Acts could be validated for them. What, if anything, does the timeline reveal? Peter first, then collectively.

By presenting this appearance of Christ to the Twelve as on a post Ascension timeline, one can see why the Teacher / Messiah would desire to reknit them together in a supernatural appearance in real time. Had not three of the twelve... Peter, James, and John... experienced a similar transformation event during the earthly ministry of Jesus? (Luke 9:28-36)

Back to Paul and 1 Corinthians 15. Paul does not allude to how... why the Twelve receive this appearance, or when, or where; only that it took place.

55
Back To The Multitudes

The Apostle Paul wrote of Jesus in 1 Corinthians 15:6, "...he appeared to more than five hundred of the brothers at the same time, most of whom are still living, though some have fallen asleep." Details are ambiguous. A statement without naming a specific location.

Amazing to realize Christ did appear either post Resurrection or post Ascension to "more than" five hundred at the same time. Not multiple appearances to different companies of fifty or even several groups of one hundred.

As for fear, or perhaps fearlessness, the reader has no way to glean knowledge whether these disciples were out in the open somewhere, or oppressed and in hiding. What does remain clear, a purpose-driven appearance just as important to Christ as any singular, duo, and/or smaller group appearances.

Accredited revelation remains allusive when considering this large group of brothers. Men? Male gender. Biblical fact, by number, stipulates the approximate head count. Speculation provides windows into potential answers. Raises questions, too.

In this scene, are women and children possibly there? Men only seems out of character with the revelation pattern established at the empty tomb. An even more looming question would be, if only men, why? One cultural reason, could simply be caution or avoidance...

against concern for an uproar or dangerous environment transformed by Roman or Jewish factions.

The feeding of loaves and fish happened to larger numbers during Jesus' miraculous multiplication of food on two occasions in His itinerant ministry, One time the feeding of four thousand included a documented head count of men, plus women and children. (Matthew 15:38) However in the feeding of five thousand only men were listed. (Luke 9:14) This becomes an important distinction.

To elaborate further on 1 Corinthians 15:6, brothers or brethren would be those who are righteous. Certain believers who had walked in the steps of Christ and His teachings. Paul gives a clear message: these individuals had received immediate benefit from the fulfilled prophecy of the Lord's death on the cross. An unusual precedent of His Resurrection life opens in practice before them.

The apostle adds that by the time of his writing to the Corinth Church, many years after his own conversion, some of these had fallen asleep, while most were living and breathing just like their family members and friends in the community. Dust to dust, in time became their final exit. Age or illness, natural or unnatural causes, had taken its toll; the expiration of physical life. Eternal life received in spite of the earthly jurisdiction on their bodies. No indication from Paul that these were caught up to heaven. His clarification was quite clear on that theme.

One cannot rule out a genuine two-fold possibility about this sequence where Jesus appeared to five hundred. First, one might suggest the appearance was a post Resurrection phenomenon. Or… a post Ascension revelation. Which is it?

Much earlier there was another event that happened, tied in with the moment of the crucifixion of Christ on the cross. In Matthew 27:52-53, the apostle writes, "The tombs broke open and the bodies of many holy people who had died were raised to life. They came out of the tombs, and after the Resurrection of Jesus they went into the holy city and appeared to many people." However, the many not defined as five hundred.

Graves opened, timed with the death of Christ, but only "after" His Resurrection did these people enter the city of Jerusalem. Where did the holy ones congregate or hibernate for three days and three nights? These were bodies, not just their spirits. What type of body enclosed their spirits? Mortal, resurrected, or heavenly type?

After the Resurrection of Jesus they make a strategic appearance in the city. Were these resurrected ones the "more than" five hundred Paul writes about? If so, Jerusalem became the exterior location. Right inside the city? Probable cause for an uproar might exist there. An interior location becomes an obvious unexplainable. However, the reader gleans no information about anything happening.

In Hebrews 11:35, the writer states, "Women received back their dead, raised to life again." In this faith chapter, the meaning has to have been mortal resurrection bodies; not eternal heavenly bodies. Recognizable too. This verse, corresponding with the "by faith" theme of the chapter, stands out. Could it be such a deep communal faith existed, that these women, united in prayer, brought a release of power manifesting the multiple resurrections?

Why men only in 1 Corinthians 15:6 and women only in Hebrews 11:35? On the other hand, Matthew 27:52-53, stipulates "many holy people" as a possible generic representation of sex and age. Does it seem to coincide with Paul's mention of the five hundred in 1 Corinthians 15:6? Perhaps self-explanatory to the early readers, but less clear in the twenty-first century.

Jesus and five hundred were in one place together without drawing attention either by being seen or heard. What possible location would have been selected? Happenstance or otherwise? The following offerings, provocative or not, prompt momentary need for exploration and reflection. Some apply more logical to post Resurrection, others could log into either timeline; including post Ascension.

The following list is not in any prioritized order:

Empty Tomb... a large group of people could gather to witness for themselves at the "by-now" famous location of the burial and Resurrection. An empty tomb in the garden might draw a curious crowd.

Galilee... the declared place of intended meeting, implication by angelic command, that He was going ahead and would meet the disciples there. Here the group of more than five hundred referenced meaning generic disciples, not apostles.

Note: In the second Ascension the "more than" five hundred would be seen by Jesus if He was high above on Mount Tabor. Or... In the third Ascension when the cloud was manifested in its awesome revelation... those more than five hundred would have seen Jesus high above them.

Sea of Tiberias... a favorite place in Galilee where Jesus often engaged in His life-changing healings and famous teaching, up-and-down along the shoreline areas.

Jerusalem... the temple where Jesus often taught. One of the few places where hundreds gathered at a large structure. Within the time frame of Christ's Resurrection and political systems of the day, both Roman and Jewish, a temple location post Resurrection would be unlikely. Nevertheless, it must be acknowledged or at least considered. What if Jesus appeared near-by on Pentecost following Peter's sermon?

Mount of Olives... a favorite place to come together with the apostles and the disciples in general. Anticipation could lead to a happenstance gathering.

Bethany... in the vicinity of the residence of Lazarus, Martha, and Mary where first-hand resurrection knowledge, practiced servanthood, and spiritual hunger were exemplified. A safe haven where questioners might congregate looking for potential answers.

Capernaum... known as the adopted community of Jesus, especially during His ministry years. The place He referred to as His second home.

Nazareth... would they believe now, that one of their own was a real prophet and the Messiah? Could the Lord have designated this location as a second chance opportunity?

During the earthly ministry of Christ, His itinerant teaching pattern kept expanding to larger numbers from time to time. Numbers ranged initially from one, two, three, twelve, to seventy, thousands or multitudes, culminating with undeclared numbers at the third Ascension (with 120 numbered on the day of Pentecost). Distinctive designations give insight into His methodology. Full circle, from one-to-many, then finally moving into multitudes especially since time was limited.

Chronological order seems relevant to Paul in 1 Corinthians 15:5-7. Is it? Or does a deliberate evasiveness surround Paul's lack of mentioning locations? Therefore, were these appearances post Resurrection as believed by most readers? Or post Ascension? Stunning thought? Of course, but one that requires contemplation.

Finally... to recap a perspective; recorded in Acts... Christ after His Ascension appears from heaven to Stephen... His whole physical presence revealed. Continuing in the book of Acts, to Paul, by Light and voice - Chapter nine; to Peter, by voice and vision - Chapter 10; to James, possibly this timing of an appearance prior to his violent death by sword - Chapter 12. There are several particulars and stories hidden within Scripture. When partially unwrapped these references shed light on some scenes in an effort to continue proclaiming the biblical sequence after the Resurrection and/or Ascension.

As for the material included here, in a seesaw explanation it is practical and reasonable for one to understand how difficult, with all accuracy, to logically place anyone alluded to in 1 Corinthians 15:5-7. Not only by location, but chronology, too.

One thing for certain, in the twenty-first century no one has an accurate and trust worthy perception from the Scripture concerning clear-cut revelation on timelines. The Lord Jesus Christ, whom the believer serves, gives only what one really needs to know, when one needs to know it. Truly, His mysterious ways and timing remain hidden till the appointed hour.

56
First Apostle Martyr

A reoccurring use of a common name can complicate the ability to discern whom the Scripture refers to even when the name is given. This complexity dealt with in an earlier chapter concerning the name, Simon; and it must evolve again covering the persons named James.

Peeling back the layers on this name, James, looks simplistic. Nonetheless, the process becomes complex the further one moves beyond the gospels, through the book of Acts, and into four other books in the New Testament. Three prominent James have leading roles, but only one became the second martyr in the New Testament and the first from apostolic leadership.

Below the three James are identified in mini cameos:

First… in Acts 12:2, Luke links James, the Apostle, to his brother John to establish without doubt the identity of the martyr. In the gospels, James remains distinctly tied to his sibling. He and his brother were nickname the Sons of Thunder because of their anger on one occasion when Jesus and the Twelve needed passage through a Samaritan village on their way to Jerusalem. As the result of the Samaritan's social and religious rudeness and refusal of entrance, James and John wanted to call down supernatural fire from heaven to destroy them in retaliation. Jesus rebuked His two disciples. The band of Twelve disciples along with the Lord then traveled through a different area. (Luke 9:51-55)

Zebedee, and his sons, James and John, were Galilean Jewish business men in the fishing industry around the Sea of Galilee (aka Sea of Tiberias) who had other connections. The sons personalities and entanglements existed even deeper; for they were peer partners of Simon (Peter) and Andrew. (Luke 5:10)

Second… a glimpse into the life of James, son of Alphaeus / Cleopus, nicknamed "the younger" in Scripture. Already definitive attention given in Chapter 2, therefore nothing needs to be restated other than this James, an apostle, was also one of the original Twelve.

Third… there was James, the step-brother of Jesus, who was conceived and born after Christ, to Joseph and Mary of Nazareth. Joseph, a carpenter had four sons and at least two daughters with his wife, Mary; plus being the step-father of Jesus on earth. Jesus being the firstborn conceived by the Holy Spirit to the then Virgin Mary; followed later by the natural conception of additional half-siblings, James, Joseph, Simon, and Judas, and all his sisters. (Matthew 13:55-56)

Unless one wants to take a different theological position, as some do, that these six step-siblings listed were from a previous marriage, prior to Mary, since Joseph is believed to have been much older. In the twenty-first century that theological theory less adhered to as valid. However, if true, then the percentage factor of this James being the one Paul refers to decreases.

As for James, the step-brother of Jesus, and James (the younger), son of Alphaeus, one of the Twelve apostles, there are few biblical reasons to claim the former one; and less reason to claim the latter, as having been the ones to be granted the privilege of seeing the Lord once again on the precise timeline.

Nonetheless, many theologians believe this step-sibling of Jesus wrote the book of James in the New Testament. Therefore necessary to mention Paul and James, the brother of Jesus spent purposeful time together. (Galations 1:19)

With the three James identified; the need to determine and validate who Christ appeared to in a one-to-one encounter requires further exploration. The Apostle Paul wrote in 1 Corinthians 15:7 about an appearance by Christ to James. Does interpretation in general define it as a post Resurrection appearance?

Can one assume it was post Resurrection; and not later, perhaps post Ascension? The placement of this chapter alludes to the belief it was more likely a singled-out post Ascension appearance. The reason… James the apostle, (brother of John the apostle) was about to be martyred. The timing… years after the birth of the Church to which James had given important initial apostolic leadership.

King Herod held the lead role in the death of James. This king, Herod Antipas, (a son of Herod the Great), was the ruling tetrarch of Galilee and Pernea. He functioned as a tyrant. (In Mark 3:6, the writer informs his readers of the king's plot early on in the itinerant ministry of Jesus… when some Jews and some Herodians conspired to bring about the crucifixion and death of Jesus.) Therefore, the Apostle James, a Galilean like Jesus, was under Herod's jurisdiction, not Pilate's.

By the time the Church had birthed and moved from infancy, King Herod Antipas, no stranger to a dominate stance on persecution had a pattern of arresting and persecuting believers, some in leadership roles. The possibility of James being well-known to Herod even as a child growing up in Galilee cannot be ruled out. The presence of James must have been enough of a threatening force, to motivate and compel the ruling king toward violence. By the sword, the king ended the life of James. (Acts 12:2)

The Jews showed their pleasure with King Herod's action and this encouraged the corrupt king to seize Peter too. Putting him in prison with the intent of providing a public trial after the Jewish Convocations… the Lord's Passover, the Feast of Unleavened Bread, and the Feast of Firstfruits had passed in that year. The earnest prayers of a united and powerful Church in Jerusalem changed the outcome of Peter's circumstance and personal destination at this time in the Church. (Acts 12:1-17)

Further explanation at this juncture turns toward the possible reason for the Lord's appearance to this specific James. The apostle had seen the Transfiguration of Jesus at one point in His itinerant ministry. (Luke 9:28-36) During that revelation James heard how Moses and Elijah spoke to the Lord about His departure soon to take place. This experience would prove to be an invaluable opportunity as a precursor to what James experienced as a post Ascension appearance of Christ in an open revelation to him before his murder by Herod. (As an angel strengthen Jesus in the Garden of Gethsemane; Christ also chose to minister to James.)

57
Apostles Believe In The Mission

Right after the Apostle Paul mentions James as having seen the Lord in 1 Corinthians 15:7, he acknowledges an appearance to all the Apostles. This classification, all, indicates in summation they were a complete group. Were they? Was James still alive? An actual collective number is not given.

The difficulty associated with chronology again comes in whether a post Ascension appearance. Speculation might fall under the category of debatable. Maybe? Maybe not?

In previous chapters, the Lord's appearances on the day of His Resurrection, Sunday, have been covered; in fact, both appearances in the locked residence first to the Ten, then to the Eleven. Therefore, this timeline of that day as an option really does not deserve further elaboration.

Post Resurrection, but many days before the Ascensions, might pose a possible consideration. However, the opportunity for this appearance becomes rather unlikely because of the other appearances throughout the thirty-nine days. If important, details would have surely been recorded by at least one of the four gospel writers: Matthew, Mark, Luke, or John. Nevertheless, it cannot be ignored what Luke writes in Acts 1:2-3, "...after giving instructions through the Holy Spirit to the apostles he had chosen… He appeared to them over a period of forty

285

days and spoke about the kingdom of God." Again, Luke called them apostles. Note the word "after."

Peter reaffirms this subject matter in Acts 10:41-42, "He was not seen by all the people, but by witnesses whom God had already chosen—by us who ate and drank with him after he rose from the dead. He commanded us to preach to the people and to testify that he is the one whom God appointed as judge of the living and the dead." The apostle references the association based on fellowship. Could Peter be referring to more than the closed door scenes and Sea of Galilee post Resurrection appearances? The timeline of events in this chapter of Acts becomes a central point of directional importance.

On the night before a post Ascension appearance might be justifiable. Could a legitimate possibility log in here? Perhaps the apostles were the first to embark on the short journey out to the Mount of Olives, the place of the third Ascension. The time being the evening before or the pre dawn morning hours of the actual Ascension.

Does this conceptional theory have little priority? The sight of the Lord leading them out would attract others to follow and opens the way for a major problem... lacking teaching intimacy. In theory, therefore time alone to discuss anything of importance, or to teach, seems unreasonable to ponder as legitimate. Especially when a distinct and detailed instruction would take place at that third Ascension event, when a whole group was present.

A post Ascension appearance specifically timed, would be extremely meaningful for the apostolic leaders. The reference in 1 Corinthians 15:7 follows the aforementioned named James, this notation in the list has legitimacy. What if James' death by sword struck overwhelming fear in the hearts of the Apostles? Christ might need to reaffirm their apostolic calling, the need for complete sacrificial surrender, and to assure them of the comforting power of the Holy Spirit. Without the apostles's suffering obedience to lead the Church through the years, the mission would falter.

For Paul to learn that the Lord had appeared to the apostles, after Stephen and James had died, would validate something of great importance to himself. Paul's own dramatic conversion through the miraculous appearance of Christ in "light and voice" to a persecutor of the Church would forever remain a statement to Paul that the Lord Most High calls whom He chooses.

A question or two surfaces. How, or when, does Paul know about the appearance to the apostles? And after mentioning an appearance to the "Twelve" why would Paul specifically set aside another appearance; calling or labeling them as "all the apostles?"

Paul, writing in Galatians 1:18-19, makes a statement that after his dramatic conversion he saw none of those in Jerusalem who were apostles; until three years later when he desired to become an acquaintance of Peter staying with him for fifteen days. He further alludes to important information by stating that even at that time he was not in the company of the other apostles, but only seeing James, the Lord's brother. By his own admission, it was fourteen years before Paul returned to Jerusalem. (Galatians 2:1)

The emergence of the apostolic Church leadership based in Jerusalem proves how in the beginning the new found faith of the disciples, after the Ascension of Christ and Pentecost, caused them to use the Resurrection as their reference point for the proclamation of the Gospel message far and wide. Events and times on the horizon would be difficult beyond belief. A post Ascension appearance from the Lord could cause them to be assured of one truth in particular… Jesus is faithful to those He called.

Years later, the Apostle Paul himself would write, "I want to know Christ and the power of his resurrection and the fellowship of sharing in his sufferings, becoming like him in his death, and so, somehow, to attain to the resurrection from the dead" (Philippians 3:10-11). Paul, and other martyrs, recognized not only the awesome supernatural power of the Lord, but the cost of association as well.

History confirms the apostles had a tumultuous spiritual journey. Life was neither comfortable for them, nor earthly death physically pain free. However, their convictions carried enough motivation, resilience, and courage to support them in the will of God. His grace and power sustained them beyond human comprehension.

Peter, Andrew and Philip were each crucified. James suffered decapitation, Nathanael died by being flayed, and James "the younger" succumbed to death by being sawed into fragments. John died, banished as a lonely exile on an island. Uncertainty about the means of death for Thomas, Matthew, Judas (not Iscariot), and Simon "the Zealot" remains, but consensus reigns they were martyred too. (Also, Mathias?)

In exploring different scenarios, one cannot be all-knowing about the timeline of the Lord's appearance to "all the apostles." Nonetheless, wherever or whenever, the appearance took place, the reader of Scripture becomes fully aware of the Lord's faithfulness to those whom He called. Nothing changes. Forever, He remains faithful.

58

The Lord's Faithful Presence

On this timeframe in the early Church nothing is stronger to the believers than the fulfillment of His words, "I am the resurrection and the life..." (John 11:25). Confirmation and validation of His Resurrection was solid in the hearts and minds of His servants. The band of Apostles knew it, but the overall count of disciples following the Lord also clung to this truth.

The Bible characters responded to the Lord within their complex behavioral patterns. In His post Ascension appearances Christ kept the early believers secure even as they struggle and strive to find their way. He, the author and perfecter of their faith, along with His protective watchfulness guarantees the Church's survival against the gates of Hades (hell). Therefore He remained a faithful presence through the power of the Holy Spirit, the Spirit of Truth, bringing comfort always in their many challenges. His eternal faithfulness accompanied by imparted revelation affirmed He was truly with them throughout life's daily events.

When going into the backstory of the New Testament, one sees the initial faithful presence came from God, the Almighty Father. For it was Jesus doing only those things shown to Him through His heavenly Father's divine direction. (John 5:19-20) In loving and compassionate obedience the Lord then met the needs of the people in His midst.

From the time of Pentecost, and beyond, the Lord Jesus Christ becomes the spiritual guiding presence in His Church, through the power of the Holy Spirit which involves relationship. Also, believers on the present day timeline show faithfulness to the Lord through obedience. This obedience to His commands keeps them from going astray in words and deeds throughout their daily happenings.

Jesus had imparted His loving direction through two commandments: The first of the two recorded as the most important one… "Love the Lord your God with all your heart and with all your soul and with all your mind and with all your strength" (Mark 12:30). The second of the two is this: "Love your neighbor as yourself. There is no commandment greater than these" (Mark 12:31).

In those early beginnings of Christianity the believers grew in steadfast character and in the spiritual gifts, leading to spiritual excellence. Their belief in His Resurrection motivated and sustained them on the straight and narrow road. As new Christians serving in troubled times, they matured in their relationship with the Lord.

Nevertheless, sometimes confrontation was necessary for believer and non believer alike. Tough love and decision-making happened through conversations, revelations, and in selfless actions. One such astonishing historical storyline unfolded in an unexpected manner. Godly intervention altered corrupt circumstances. It changed the course of the Church forever.

59

Suffer For Me

Known by Jews and Gentiles alike, Saul of Tarsus, had been a prime persecutor against the early Church. Consenting to Stephen's death as a standby participant, he kept sight over the robes of the executioners stoning the deacon. (Acts 7:57; 8:1)

When a reader of the New Testament first encounters Saul of Tarsus, he was out to destroy the Church. Those he could not scatter through fear he imprisoned. Saul had a Hebrew educational pedigree and familiarity with prominent Jews which enabled him to gain access and authority for reenforcing his violent and murderous threats against the disciples; thereby taking them as prisoners. Unable, or at least unwilling, to be uprooted, the Apostles hunkered down in Jerusalem. Many disciples who could not stand the persecution scattered; but they preached and proclaimed the personhood and deity of Jesus Christ far and wide. (Acts 8:1-3)

Known as, The Way, the Christians of 36 A.D. feared Saul. Even the Apostles knew their lives were in grave danger. However, by his own physical hand he never murdered any of the Apostles, at least none was documented.

Important Note: Jesus diid not change Saul's name to Paul. The apostle's name in Hebrew / Saul, and in Greek / Paul. Luke is the one who refers often to the man Saul, as Paul; thereby becoming the dominate person making the interchangeable cross referential use. Being a companion in ministry on missionary adventures, the physician, Luke, uses the twofold reference in his writing which fits in with their travel locations. The reader of Scripture learns of Luke's clarification in Acts 13:9.

In the New Testament, the largest volume of the literature has been accredited to the Apostle Paul. He became one of the esteemed and prolific apostles, writing at least fourteen books in the New Testament. It is not his epistles this chapter explores, but the supernatural appearance of Christ to Saul of Tarsus, a future disciple and apostle.

Saul's referenced conversion through an unusual post Ascension appearance of Christ (Christophany) has been documented in Acts 9:1-10. Repeated in commentary, Luke elaborates on it a second time in Acts 22:6-11; and a third reference, in Acts 26:12-18. Paul's supernatural encounter with Christ unfolded while this religiously trained and scholarly Jew had been on his way to Damascus.

Like any other Christophany, worthy of notation, the methodology of this post Ascension appearance opens a new precedent. Paul, traveling in the company of others, was on his way to bring chaos by raiding the synagogues in Damascus. On the open road in the vastness of creation, the Creator used the outside environment as His stage for the holy intervention.

Saul's day, life, and even future reference to his name were changed forever when, "a light from heaven flashed around him" (Acts 9:3). As Paul fell to the ground he heard the "voice of the Lord" calling out his name, "Saul, Saul." Though noon, or midday, the great and glorious Light was brighter than the sun's intensity.

Those "others" enveloped in fear, saw the "Light" only. The "voice" was beyond their spiritual receptive range. They heard not the dialogue of Jesus and Saul.

Seeing nothing, because the blindness had put him in physical darkness; the persecutor was reduced to being lead by the hand as the journey continued toward Damascus. Upon his arrival, the reader of the book of Acts learns, two coinciding visions would collide soon.

First, Saul resorted to praying; attempting to claw his way out of spiritual darkness through prayer and fasting. Second, Saul's previous harmful ways nearly caused the receiver of one vision, Ananias, to pull back in fear. His knowledge of Paul's authority from the chief priests to arrest, almost caused him to be disobedient to the vision and the command to "go." However, he responded in obedience and Paul's blindness was no more. He was filled with the Holy Spirit, and ordered to be baptized.

Ananias had a glimpse of what might be ahead for Paul. Jesus told Ananias, "I will show him how much he must suffer for my name" (Acts 9:16). Paul's divine appointment with Jesus of Galilee would be long term. Requiring obedience, suffering dedication, and resilient proclamation far above anything Paul had known.

His apostolic and evangelistic methodology was a call to witness and win others to Christ. His intellectual freshness as a religious philosopher, plus his rich spiritual character, and his evangelistic vision-casting catapulted him to prominence. By the power of the Holy Spirit he moved from guilt for persecution, through forgiveness into the grace of the Lord, and became a leadership guardian over portions of the Church. A tent-maker by trade, church planter by vocation, and above all a proclaimer of the Good News that Jesus is the Messiah.

A Pharisee by birth, Paul believed in the ultimate spiritual resurrection of the deceased. After the Damascus encounter with the living Messiah, Paul with zealous boldness proclaimed the Resurrection of Jesus. Paul was emphatic that Christ was raised from the dead.

Going back to the Garden of Eden where one man, Adam, sinned for all; Paul preached Christ as the firstfruits of those who had fallen asleep. Those who belong to Him, would be resurrected and be alive in Christ. Therefore, as there is a natural body, there is a spiritual body. As with Adam, an earthly perishable body (dust to dust) does not inherit heaven; but only in Christ, the imperishable heavenly body inherits eternal life. The dead in Christ will be raised imperishable because He has conquered death and brings believers through reconciliation to the Father in heaven. For Paul, this was a message burning within his heart beyond motivation of his Jewish intellectual knowledge.

In order for Paul not to be disobedient to the heavenly vision it would take willingness and determination on his part, coupled with grace and an anointing from the Lord. His original heartbeat and attempt was to evangelize his own Hebrews, the Jewish nation of Israel. Those personal heritage benefits and other human connections turn on the man once named Saul because the Jews conspired to kill him. They stirred up persecution against Paul as he preached in the same synagogues where he had once raised havoc. The persecutor becomes the persecuted. Expelled from the regional synagogues, Paul took the Good News to the Gentiles. An apostle to the Gentiles by default, yet in sovereign destiny. Closed doors often lead to a greater vocation elsewhere. How true in Paul's ministry.

Luke, a physician and a companion in the Gospel, went on Paul's three famous missionary journeys. Barnabas, the encourager, and others including Silas, John Mark, and even Timothy traveled extensively with the Apostle. Remaining true to the faith, plus enduring many hardships became part of the suffering they encountered as leaders. The Church throughout the region came to fear the Lord and not fear Saul any longer. Believers enjoyed a newfound peace after Saul's conversion. Short-lived, but real nonetheless.

The irony of "suffer for Christ" holds a repulsive connotation. If someone is suffering through injustice, the persecutor(s) are not moving, functioning, or walking in the Spirit of the Lord. If one is suffering, can one truly be effective? By traditional standards of success, no. Notwithstanding, the Bible clearly declares that if a believer does not suffer for Christ, they will not reign with Him. Does that mean martyrdom? Always? Of course not, but possible.

As a servant and as a witness, like Paul, the twenty-first century believer must follow the Lord wherever He leads. Often deprived of justice, and sometimes in a state of humiliation as Christ walked, a believer can be exploited, taken advantage of, and even endure physical and financial hardships for the name of Christ. Suffering cannot be compartmentalized for believers, but it does become a spiritual component on the way to resurrected life and eternal rewards.

This chapter could not conclude without stating that Paul did experience several revelations from the Lord throughout his life and ministry. Though these were important at the time for him, especially including being caught up to the third heaven; they are not included here. (2 Corinthians 12:1-4)

What those revelations make apparent for the student of the Bible is some may appear minor at the time, while others hold a major place of intensity in one's life. Levels of revelation by categories, experienced in the early Church, and beyond, were detailed in a previous chapter.

60
Exiled, But Love Remained

The stage lights come up and the spotlight focuses on the Apostle John. By now, the early Church has advanced across continents. No longer in the stages of infancy or adolescence, but progressing into a state of maturity through evangelistic church planting. The apostles and disciples have known Christ through the power of His Resurrection and in the fellowship of His sufferings.

John, a contributor to the New Testament, is known through his five books: the Gospel of John, and the epistles numbered: 1 John, 2 John, 3 John; and then, finally the book of Revelation. As a disciple in an earnest and unconditional relationship with the Lord, John drew others to Christ in his earlier writings as he lifted Him up for all to see. A reader of the Bible discovers and learns about the deity of Christ.

Then one reads in John's final record, in the book of Revelation, how the Lord God Almighty reigns. This outstanding supernatural revelation given and received post Ascension; with its historical documentation remains a spiritual precedent of overwhelming value to the Church in this present age.

Speculation could ask perhaps why John was chosen? He certainly was neither the oldest of the apostles, nor the most influential during the earthly ministry of Jesus. Actually John was possibly the youngest of the Twelve. The lack of being a prominent spokesman was probably caused by having been overshadowed by Peter's spontaneous verbalization; and then also John's own older brother, James' more subtle leadership skills.

The inner circle of Jesus consisted of three: Peter, James and John, with John later becoming the solo distinction by slipping into the number one position on receiving a long revelation and open post Ascension Christophany. However, he conveyed love unlike any of the Twelve. Dubbed the "apostle of love" by church theologians, John knew agape love on its highest level early-on. He described himself as the one Jesus loved. (John 13:23)

The greatest, holiest, and longest dramatic post Ascension appearance, one revelation in Scripture, called the book of Revelation, came to John on the Island of Patmos. The age sequence has shifted to a visual picture of John, as being a man advanced in years well beyond the age of those living in his century. His phenomenal written record of the Revelation has an approximate dateline of 90-95 A.D. The apostle's age, believed to be around one hundred years old, gives him a claim to longevity among the original Twelve. John is thought to have been the only apostle of the Twelve who died a natural death.

As for Patmos, one might think of it as a near equal to the United States twentieth century Alcatraz. The desolate island location of Patmos had become a place of exile established by the Romans for criminals and those who threatened the empire because of their personal witness through teaching, preaching, healing; an evangelism tract as they spoke and ministered in the power of the risen Christ. While exiled, John received, and in turn passes along to the Church, the amazing and awesome open Revelation.

A reader becomes privileged to know of it because of its inclusion in the New Testament. Often inappropriately referred to as the book of Revelations; incorrect in plural form. No "s" attached. Considered "one" revelation.

John entered the portal of heaven, through an open door, seeing among many observations a throne and the Lamb of God. (Revelation 4:11) The time span unfolds in the revelation, through conversation, interaction of angels and a brilliant scenic production with no lack of the glorious and holy presence of the Lord enveloping the earthly recipient.

A twenty-first century reader has little knowledge concerning what was required of John in both how long to receive or to write down in sequence the Revelation of Jesus Christ. The apostle, in the Spirit on the Lord's day, heard a loud "voice" like the sound of rushing waters. From the throne, the center of authority, different aspects are seen from the height of heavenly order. An example... like the one great street of gold in heaven. (Revelation 21:21) The glorious eternal picture opens as "one" Revelation. Also, the apostle was privileged to see the old order of things pass away.

In this chapter, without using an expository format, or teaching, or categorizing the chapters in the book of Revelation itself, reference must be made to this distinct post Ascension appearance of Christ. Important because it is the final Christophany in Scripture, and in the last book of the Bible.

Servanthood becomes a theme from the beginning for showing what must soon take place. God's set purpose was to show His current servant, John, and then all future servants who hear and receive. How awesome were the power, privilege and pictures that benefited the Apostle. Exiled, he remained a servant of the Lord in obedience through his writing. How selfless and faithful to share with each believer in Christ the message and leave it ready-at-hand for those not yet in the kingdom.

The revelation moves to a state of prophecy because it is futuristic. Like the Apostles, individual churches also have distinct personalities, quirks, idiosyncrasies, attitudes, gifts, callings and obedience levels shown through their words and deeds. Therefore, an equalizing theme compares, the Church and the world, what the Lord commends and condemns, expresses and exposes the conflict of good and evil, along with the eternal righteous, and the fallen wicked.

Resembling the temple curtain at the time of Christ's death on the cross, this Revelation also unveiled His reigning power. Through the Lord's patience and the process of His judgment, He unveils eternity for the establishment of the kingdom of God on earth to be seen. The government of established eternal order truly is upon His shoulders. (Isaiah 9:6) It explains the things which are about to happen by pointing out specifics which open the way of truth.

A threefold emphasis equalizes around the wrath of God, the compassion of Christ, and the sovereign will of God. Tribulations, agony, and wickedness from those who love falsehood and who through practice bring its evil effect upon the heads of the righteous; thereby causing thousands through the ages to be martyred. Out of the unexpected consequences and undeserved shame, one sees the compassionate Shepherd of martyrs, forever comforting the beloved, betrayed and banished. Hope eternal affirmed.

The inauguration of His reign, the hope of the world seen through a series of visionary events depicting heavenly order... a holy city comes because a Spirit of holiness triumphed over a spirit of evil. His love, always complete, is never finished; but His earthly wrath does cease. (Revelation 15:1) The process shown completed in eternal time; because nothing, absolutely nothing, can delay the fulfillment. Evil and evil doers banished to eternal damnation in the unrelenting fiery furnace in Hades (hell).

Through the ages, churches have been inundated with end-time prophecy in evangelistic preaching through pastoral emphasis, and even books with chapter by chapter exposition from the book of Revelation. Not to be ignored, nor to appear loathsome in attitude about some of these truths and expository insights, for many are valid; but sometimes the drone of preaching the terror of wrath seems to drain off the glory of His personhood and His majestic wisdom.

Christ is the Spirit of Prophecy; hence the book of Revelation in the New Testament resulting in believers receiving, from John, the Revelation of Jesus Christ. It is about the Lord. Often lost, or buried under end-time theology is the freshness, beauty, and the completeness of the Messiah, the King of kings, who came, and who will come again; and who reigns forevermore.

The time has come for believers to resurrect the last book of the Bible; to read and focus on His eternal story. To simply rest in its truth, and to breathe in the peace of Jesus as the Triumphant Overcomer, through His Resurrection, His Ascension, and His eternal Kingship.

Section Sixteen

God's Promise, An Eternal King

61
The Lineage Of The Eternal King

It all started... if one can use that phase... with God, the Father, and His Son, Jesus Christ. Not that simple really! The Bible opens with these words in the Old Testament in Genesis 1:1, "In the beginning..."

Without entering into a massive theological undertaking, believers in Christianity acknowledge that there was, and is, and will always be... God the Father, Jesus Christ the only begotten Son of God, and the Holy Spirit. All three, which most Christians refer to as... The Trinity, or the Three-in-One. Simple? Again, not really! Theologians have studied this eternal concept for centuries. Therefore it is not being explored in great detail here other than making the statement to recognize the eternal realm.

The three heavens consist of what some believe as: the first, the second, and the third heaven; already alluded to briefly in another chapter. Chaos broke out in the highest, the third heaven when Lucifer (an Archangel) determined he could be like God. A powerful dynamic ensued and Satan along with a third of the angels in heaven were subjected to Almighty God's event-filled action. Lucifer (Satan) and those angels (later characterized and referenced as demons) fell from unmerited favor into what is and will continue to be a judgement... Hades (hell); and still to be much later thrown into the lake of fire for eternity.

Important Note: Recorded in Luke 10:17-20, Jesus told seventy-two of His disciples whom He had sent out with His authority; and who upon returning reported in joyous puffed-up spiritual attitude, that even the demons were subject to them through the name of Jesus. The Lord admonished them... stating He had seen Satan fall from heaven because of his pride.

Next on the dominate theological events unfolding in Genesis, Chapters 2-3, finds the reader of Scripture in the Garden of Eden with Adam and Eve after their creation. Adam from the dust of the earth and Eve from the rib of Adam... created in the image of God. Once again sin pulled rank through disobedience known as the Fall from grace which caused them separation from their God, the Creator.

Why this Old Testament side trip? The whole creation concept within the hands of an eternal God, is understood as a doctrine of Christianity. One must make a decision to believe in faith in the words of The Holy Bible.

The content of this section provides a change of scenery on the stage. It would be amiss to ignore in the closing chapters of this book the theme about the King and His kingdom. Though vast in subject matter and comprehension, God's kingdom covered in brief here. Simple attention given to important spiritual truth.

A further look into the history and prophecies of the Old Testament, a reader discovers that a promise made by Jehovah (God) was that someone would sit forever on the throne of King David. (2 Samuel 7:16) This reference, to an ancestral and eternal ruler from the lineage of David, remained etched in the minds of the Hebrews throughout Israel for generations.

The divided nation of Israel experienced for centuries the leadership of Jewish kings in both its northern and southern regions. The kings and kingship in Israel faded away because of their disobedience; therefore captivity by the Assyrians and the Babylonians resulted. After the fall of northern Israel and southern Judah they became dominated by Assyria and Babylon respectively; leaving the people of Israel in exile and adrift. Eventually the Jews would return to their homeland.

(This is a limited description of the extensive backstory about kingship from the Old Testament.) By laying a brief foundation from the Old Testament, these sketches help to bring the reader forward into the context of New Testament theology.

Centuries later in the opening timeline of the New Testament, the fulfillment of God's promise to King David happens through a young virgin from Nazareth who gives birth to the Son of God / Son of Man while visiting in the village of Bethlehem. (Luke 1:26-35; 2:6-7) When one looks at the word "king" in the four gospels as it relates to Jesus there is a clear revelation and emphasis that exposes a spiritual tug-of-war. Also, in the natural, Israel's kingship was an important futuristic theme again at the time of the birth of the Messiah. The Jews were looking for a king; just not the One, God the Father sent.

62
Born A King, Died A King

Centuries later after King David; and in the timeline when Jesus was born in the town of Bethlehem, Herod the Great, the King of Judea reigned. The Roman empire had their kings who ruled over Israel. For centuries there had not been a Jewish ruling monarch in the land. An important emphasis as the historical relates to the spiritual.

The first mention in the New Testament of Jesus being referred to as the King of the Jews comes when the Magi have a conversation with King Herod the Great. These individuals had seen His star in the East and their travel to Judea had taken considerable time. No lack of intentional purpose. The men came to worship Jesus. (Matthew 2:1-2)

A speculative thought about the star injected here. The scientific and universal astronomy aspects, of course, have many ramifications; perhaps even less complex than the supernatural sight of a radiant, glowing star. Often the latter is not seen by all in the same area, but just a select few with important relational ties to the occurring event. A miraculous heavenly scene happened for the Magi. Was it the star of David?

King Herod was disturbed by a potential fulfillment of a king because he too had heard by word of mouth, through the years the prophecies from the Hebrew writings as proclaimed, taught, and discussed by the Jews. Warned in a dream, the Magi did not return to Herod to confirm where this infant child was because under false pretense the reigning king claimed a desire to worship Him. Also, on the timeline... Mary, with her espoused husband Joseph, and baby Jesus, escaped to Egypt because Joseph had been warned by an angel in a dream to leave Judea. (Matthew 2:13)

Protection by Herod, for himself, resulted in the deaths of male children being murdered by the king's own directive. He was ruthless. The horror of baby boys, two years old and under, being slaughtered echoed through the close knit region. The crying screams and sobbing meshed with the fears and tears in their mother's unconsolable weeping. (Matthew 2:16-18) Bethlehem was a small village. How many babies died remains unknown. This appears to be an isolated happening. Devastating nonetheless.

A Roman king's wicked attempt to destroy the King of kings was only the beginning. Later on the timeline, during Jesus advancing adult years... the Pharisees kept their observational focus on Jesus throughout His three years of itinerant ministry. The Sanhedrin (aka ruling council) would launch a premeditated and determined plan for carrying out an eventual death sentence on Jesus. (Matthew 12:14; John 11:45-53)

By this time in Israel a different Roman King, Herod Antipas, had been reigning in the Galilean region. He was one of the ruling sons of Herod the Great, the King who murdered the children when Jesus was an infant. (Another son of Herod the Great was, Archelaus, a tyrant, who ruled in Judea after his father had died and during the time when Joseph, Mary, and Jesus returned from exile in Egypt and went to Galilee to live in Nazareth.) Sections of the Jewish population had political allegiance and connections to the empire's leadership. Rejection of Jesus by His own people because of their jealousy, envy, and fears came through various modes and people groups. Jesus as an adult had become a threat to the well-intrenched religious and political systems.

Those same Jewish religious leaders neither comprehended, nor attempted to understand, the spiritual concept the Lord's kingship would not be in this physical world. For them... Jewish national kingship experienced earlier had been the ruling procedure throughout the land of Israel in previous centuries. In other words, no earthly king's dictating rulership wanted on their immediate sequential timeline. At least not that of Jesus, the Nazarene.

When looking at the disciples of Jesus only one of the future Twelve had the revelation of Jesus of Nazareth as a King. Nathanael openly confessed, "Rabbi, you are the Son of God; you are the King of Israel" (John 1:49).

The first, and only, biblical image of Jesus (in real time) as a coming king happens in the scene where He is honored by the people during the Triumphal Entry. They gave praise to Him as the coming kingdom of David. (Matthew 21:6-9; Mark 11:8-10) On this, His final trip into Jerusalem... the children's chants within the temple area singled Him out.

Before this spontaneous scene, Jesus had never acted like a king during His mission on earth even though He spoke often of the kingdom of God (aka the kingdom of heaven) coming not just in their midst, but within. His message to His followers forewarned that the kingdom had been forcefully advancing against evil and would continue. (Luke 16:16)

Fear escalated and advanced too. Some prophecies fulfilled affirmed the potential of Jesus becoming a designated ruling monarch in the land of Israel. (Isaiah 9:6-7) If a new governing sect was forming, its effect on many established leaders, Roman and Jewish alike, would bring unbelievable ramifications. Could this lowly man, Jesus of Nazareth, be crowned king? What a tremendous threat loomed on the horizon.

Moving on in the timeline, one finds Jesus on trial because of His capacity to draw disciples unto Himself, teaching with tremendous spiritual authority, and being the much needed LIGHT in the land. As Jesus stood before the Roman governor, in the palace, Pilate struggled with the truth of Jesus being the King of the Jews. (Mathew 27:11) Either intuition, or spiritual revelation, or the combination of both, enables divine insight and promptings that caused Pontus Pilate to question "Who" is this Jesus that stands before him?

Now it becomes a tug-of-war in heart and conscience along with the religious and political influence of power. In conversations with Jesus alone, and with the Jewish leaders, Pilate weighs the consequences of his own involvement in the clash between heavenly and earthly kingdoms. Of course, Pilate retains his allegiance to the ruling monarch, Herod Antipas. The mob crowd and their loud efforts gain precedence over truth. In the end, Pilate violates his own conscience. He succumbs to the external pressure brought by others. His own fears and motives rule. Jesus is led away to be crucified. (Matthew 27:26; Mark 15:15; John 19:16)

Nevertheless, in the interim situation between the circumstances of the post trial and the pending pre crucifixion scenes, Pilate enters into a final confrontation with the Jews. The latter lose. How? Why? A simple wooden sign attached to the crucifixion cross of Jesus Christ, located above His head, had the words: THE KING OF THE JEWS. (Mark 15:26) In three languages its silent proclamation speaks to all in attendance, at the crucifixion site on Golgotha outside of Jerusalem. However, the chief priests were appalled and protested to the governor about what he had ordered written. The simple phrase, THE KING OF THE JEWS, was exactly what these Jewish leaders complained about to Pilate, "Do not write, The King of the Jews, but that this man claimed to be king of the Jews" (John 19:19-21).

Looking at each of the four gospel writers, even though a slight difference appears, all stated in their conclusion... THE KING OF THE JEWS. Recorded in Scripture in capital letters: Matthew, Mark, Luke, and John, provide the reader with those words which were written in three languages… Aramaic, Latin and Greek. (John 19:20) The written notice described the charge against Jesus.

Matthew 27:37	THIS IS JESUS, THE KING OF THE JEWS
Mark 15:26	THE KING OF THE JEWS
Luke 23:38	THIS IS THE KING OF THE JEWS
John 19:19	JESUS OF NAZARETH, THE KING OF THE JEWS

Bible scholars know that Matthew and Luke drew from Mark's writings. The latter, Mark, being the earliest (60 A.D.) and the first to document in length the mission of Jesus on earth. Mark's expression is the simple, precise one. The other two writers attempt to define the man on the cross with more accuracy for their later readers around 65-75 A.D. John was the fourth of the writers to establish a written record through his gospel in approximately 80 A.D.

Why has the content of this chapter backtracked to the events... before the crucifixion... before the post Resurrection appearances... and before the post Ascension appearances... of Christ in Scripture? The truthful topic of the kingship of Jesus is relevant from the time of His birth to the time of His death. Even during the timeline of His actual crucifixion, the chief priests and the teachers of the law stood mocking Christ, calling Him the King of Israel. (Mark 15:32) Indeed He was King, for this reason He was born. Jesus said He would be sitting at the right hand of the Mighty One. (Mark 14:62)

It did not end there; but continued further as recorded in the Bible. The visual confirmation of a final completed post Ascension appearance in Scripture, in the book of Revelation, takes place in heaven and recorded as the heavenly revelation that the Apostle John received while exiled on the Island of Patmos. (Revelation 1:9)

63
The Kingdom Of God... Within

As Jesus traveled throughout Israel He often spoke about the kingdom of God (aka the kingdom of heaven). Prior to His crucifixion... the apostles, other disciples, and the Pharisees were not grasping the content and reality of His message concerning this subject. (Luke 17:20-21)

Jesus came to save His people. Therefore written... in Hebrew Yeshua, in Greek Joshua, in English Jesus; and all meaning in word form... Savior. The virgin Mary, told by Gabriel, the messenger angel, that the child soon-to-be within her was to be named Jesus. (Luke 1:31) Later her espoused husband, Joseph, was told in a dream that the child's name would be Jesus. (Matthew 1:21) Also in Matthew 1:23 a reference made about Jesus, as Immanuel, and meaning... God is with us. Sometimes spelt Emmanuel too.

Important Note: Comprehension of the coming salvation would be new to the Jewish people, at this time and in the homeland. Having been under the Mosaic Law for centuries, God's previous old covenant (Old Testament) endured.

The atonement for sin before God, both discernible and recognizable, in the practices in the Old Testament... required the spotless animal sacrifices through their shed blood for the people's sin. It took place in the Tabernacle, also referenced as the Tent of Meeting in the Bible; designed by God, with the complex instruction plan and assembly process given to Moses.

This place of ministering before God used by Moses' brother… Aaron, the High Priest, and his sons, the Levitical priesthood; took place in the huge portable sanctuary tent, transported in sections: the Outer Court, the Holy Place, and the Most Holy Place where God's holy presence would dwell. This place of worship for the Israelites remained available to them while they traveled in the wilderness for forty years.

Continuing thereafter at the first constructed Temple in Jerusalem by King David's son, King Solomon; and after its total destruction, the rebuilt second temple constructed in Jerusalem still in use in Jesus' adult years. (This is where Jesus threw over the money changers tables after upbraiding them as being… a den of robbers… rather than being a house of prayer. (Matthew 21:12-13)

The coming new covenant (New Testament) brought into existence through the crucifixion of Jesus as the sinless Lamb of God and being the redeemer by the shedding of His blood. He became the perfect sacrifice. However once Jesus was crucified, buried, and resurrected three days later, He fulfilled forevermore the redemption plan of His heavenly Father, Almighty God. Bringing humanity's ability to enter into the presence of God in prayer; due to the redemptive blood of the sacrificial Lamb, Jesus Christ.

Jesus told His disciples… if they obeyed His commandments they would remain in His love as He had in the same way with His Father's love while here on earth. (John 15:9-10) However after Pentecost the indwelling of the Holy Spirit resided within the believers and they were able to experience for the first time a three-fold relationship with the Godhead… God the Father, the First Person; Jesus the Son of God, the Second Person; and the Holy Spirit, the Third Person. (John 14:23)

The receiving of the power and the presence of the Holy Spirit completed the availability for every person to be changed and conform to the image of God as intended from the foundation of the world.

In the eternal realm, the Three-in-One had created man in their own image. Humanity became a spiritual being; with a spirit, with a soul (intellect and emotions), within a physical body.

Backstory again… In the Old Testament: One man, Adam, brought sin into the world through his disobedience causing separation from God for all of humankind. In the New Testament: One Man, Jesus Christ, brought justification through His obedience and shed blood on the cross to provide redemption with God for humanity. The message of the Bible… God's love and salvation for His creation; provides the believer future access to live eternally in the presence of God. (1 Corinthians 15:45-50)

This redemptive work of Jesus Christ was once for all. Grace given to each person (a sinner) who confesses in a simple prayer, their sin and acknowledges they believe in Jesus Christ as their Savior, as the Son of God / Son of Man.

Accepting by faith one's need for a Savior opens the door fully to eternal salvation. In the New Testament, in the book of Romans 10:9-10, "That if you confess with your mouth, Jesus is Lord, and believe in your heart that God raised him from the dead, you will be saved. For it is with your heart that you believe and are justified, and it is with your mouth that you confess and are saved."

Christians refer to this as being "born again" and similar to what Jesus told Nicodemus. Recorded in John 3:5-7, Jesus said, "I tell you the truth, no one can enter the kingdom of God unless he is born of water and the Spirit. Flesh gives birth to flesh, but the Spirit gives birth to spirit. You should not be surprised at my saying, you must be born again." (This is the same Nicodemus, who later became one of the two compassionate pallbearers for the deceased body of Jesus of Nazareth.)

Jesus' words spoken to Thomas (on the Sunday one week after the Resurrection) were… "Stop doubting and believe" (John 20:27). For some reading now, those words may apply. If so, take hold of the eternal hope Jesus provided as an anchor of the soul. Believe in Jesus.

Be open to asking for the infilling of the Spirit. Let the Holy Spirit lead you as you walk and serve the Lord wherever He has you living. Purchase a New International Version (NIV)... of The Holy Bible; or another translation... in a print size for easy reading. Start with one or two chapters a day in the New Testament. Especially with the four Gospels... Matthew, Mark, Luke, and John, who tell of the Lord's life and mission. Follow Jesus around as if you were right there. Focus your eyes, mind, and heart on Him.

In heaven it is well. Is it well within your spirit and soul?

64

Heaven's Unspeakable Glory

Back to those heavens again. However... attention drawn only to the third heaven where the eternal kingdom of God always reigned... yesterday, today, and forever. Angels eternally participate around the vast throne of Almighty God and proclaim His glory. As celestial beings, their created purpose is to worship and to sing praise. What does this view look like? Scripture gives at least four insights into the presence of the glorious eternal throne.

First... in the Old Testament, in the book of Isaiah, the prophet Isaiah saw into the heavenly realm and seeing One, "...seated on a throne, high and exalted, and the train of his robe filled the temple" (Isaiah 6:1). He gave the reader of Scripture an awesome revelation of the glory of God. Captivated by the overwhelming presence of seraphs (angels) Isaiah continues in Chapter 6:3 with them calling to one another,

> "Holy, holy, holy is the Lord
> Almighty;
> the whole earth is full of his
> glory."

Second... in the New Testament, in the book of Acts, Chapters 6-7, the story of Stephen's anointed life, as a deacon, leads to the unfolding of his untimely death. This revelation of seeing into the third heaven happened post Pentecost and after the Church had increased in numbers and in many locations.

At his impending death and without any reservation, he declares he sees Jesus in heaven. Written in the book of Acts 7:55, it states, "But Stephen, full of the Holy Spirit, looked up to heaven and saw the glory of God, and Jesus standing at the right hand of God." An apparent revelation given only to him in the final moments of his crisis. He describes nothing further... than the all-knowing revelation that Jesus' completed Ascension had taken Him into the presence of His heavenly Father. The revelation affirmed Steven's trust and servanthood relationship too.

Third... in the New Testament, in 2 Corinthians 12:2-4, the Apostle Paul tells of a man (himself?) caught up to Paradise in a moment in time. Where he experienced how unspeakable his extensive visionary view of heaven became for him. Not only seeing but hearing, "... inexpressible things, things that man is not permitted to tell."

In other words, the awesomeness beyond human speech remains confidential. Unspeakable! No dramatic insight provided, nor any conclusion drawn why he chose to disclose ever-having seen the grandeur of the God-given revelation. Nothing about the presence of angels, even though he appears to be overwhelmed with the sights, sounds, words, and colors of the open revelation granted to him.

Fourth... in the New Testament, in the book of Revelation, the Apostle John under a special anointing of the Spirit leaves in his writing the largest of all documentation of the heavenly realm where peace, and glory, and majesty reigns forevermore. Recorded in Revelation 4:8,

"Holy. holy, holy
is the Lord God Almighty,
who was, and is, and is to come."

Going further in Revelation 5:11, John says, "Then I looked and heard the voice of many angels, numbering thousands upon thousands, and ten thousand times ten thousand." Continuing in Revelation 5:12, he states they encircled the throne….and In a loud voice they sang:

"Worthy is the Lamb, who was slain,
to receive power and wealth and
wisdom and strength
and honor and glory and praise!"

The four Bible characters referenced here… Isaiah, Stephen, Paul, and John, have told of the glory awaiting believers as they join Jesus Christ in the heaven-lies. Glimpses only… nothing which reveals fully what God has prepared for those who love Him, and are called according to His purpose. (1 Corinthians 2:9)

Of course, the lengthly revelation throughout the book of Revelation encompassed many more amazing and awesome descriptions of the Lord Jesus Christ. Also, large portions of the Revelation reveals end-time eschatology to be fulfilled; but neither elaborated on here, nor pertinent for this chapter. (Eschatology means the study of the end-times and the final destiny of souls.)

65
The King's Second Coming

The hour had come indeed, but not fully. The King also, but not the way the Jews perceived Him, or by the multitudes of people who followed Jesus, or even His Twelve Apostles. Nevertheless, the Lord Jesus Christ was born, crucified, resurrected and ascended as a King.

The question needing to be asked of Christians today... Do they believe the Lord Jesus Christ is the resurrected and ascended King of kings? Then if He is King, the lives of believers should reveal it through both verbal testimony and silent witness.

Let's examine an image of kingship in the twenty-first century:

First... let an image appear in your mind... a king sitting on his throne. Any unnamed, unknown king. Pause for a moment! What do you see? How regal is he? His clothes, the throne, the scepter, the scene? Who else is there with him in the room? Does he have the power to do good? Or evil?

Second... dethrone and dismantle that earthly image of a king.

Third... place the King of kings on His heavenly throne. What changes do you now realize in truth and perception? Do you see His "throne" as the totality of the "third heaven" or perhaps even beyond?

Fourth... what do the statements and teachings recorded in Scripture that Jesus made about His kingdom mean to you? Has any new insight and clearer understanding of His message, as seen through the four gospels and spoken by Him, been enlarged through your amazing and interesting new thoughts?

Fifth… in your new scene with Jesus on the throne how does it renew your spiritual life and your concepts of… Salvation, Lordship, and Kingship? How does the phrase, the kingdom of God is within you, become spiritually realized? It will be different for everyone depending where one is in their current relationship with the Lord Jesus Christ. The image of the awareness of Him… will and should change, and increase for each person through the years; but has never changed from the beginning in eternity.

Sixth… what rules you? Self-sufficiency? Who is on the throne of your heart? You? Or another human being? Or a tangible item? If Jesus is your Lord; He should be the One there! The kingdom of heaven ruling within.

There is extreme difficulty in conveying a heavenly vision to mortal souls. The greatness and vastness of the kingdom of God in the heights of heaven is beyond any believer's full comprehension… nothing this side of eternity compares as a plum line of reality.

Important Note: Jesus, during His itinerant ministry, spoke about Himself being the gate into the eternal realm through a relationship with Him. (John 10:9) Is He the gate on earth; the door in heaven? In the book of Revelation in the Bible… John, the Apostle, describes his entrance into heaven as entering through a door standing open before him. (Revelation 4:1)

In an attempt to expound on a third heaven where Almighty God dwells one thing seems certain. There is no throne room. What? The word "room" does not appear in the Bible (NIV) connected to, or following, the word throne. Therefore the throne appears to be the entire vast third heaven! When Christians try in their finite minds to categorize it, one verse in particular helps to open insight concerning vastness. Again the importance of the reference from Revelation 5:11 when John saw, "and heard the voice of many angels, numbering thousands upon thousands, and ten thousand times ten thousand."

In eternal reality… these were encircling the throne which reveals the vastness of the throne in heaven.

Christians need to remember God is Spirit. A whole different eternal dynamic has been created, evolved, and is contained in the unseen realm believers refer to as God in the heaven-lies. Jesus promised He will come again. (Revelation 22:7) As an infant in a humble birth? No! Of course not! Every eye shall see Him in all His power and glory and coming with the clouds… and all the angels with Him. (Matthew 25:31; Mark 13:26; Revelation 14:14) Really? How possible? A speculative thought about the heaven-lies injected here… the first and second heavens will part as if non existent through a type of scroll roll-back; and the whole earth filled with people will see upward into the glorious massive third heaven and beyond! Remember… it could be an omnipotent supernatural event and omnipresence revelation.

Important Note: In the Old Testament, the parting of the Red Sea was at ground level. (Exodus 14:15-22) This time… at the Second Coming of Christ is it the parting of the heaven-lies?

However, in the New Testament, in the book of Hebrews, the writer makes several statements that spiritualize and depict a heavenly picture which includes the King. He who entered the third heaven brought with Him the crown that is glory and honor because of His being the ultimate spiritual victory. (Hebrews 2:9) Jesus, the Messiah… did the will of the Father to the end… thereby being the Victorious Overcomer!

Righteousness is the scepter of His kingdom. (Hebrews 1:8) Grace is the white throne. (Revelation 20:11) The One who sits on the great white throne is the radiance of God's glory. He has the power over life and death, Heaven and Hades (hell). He rules… because He reigns eternal. Earth is His footstool. (Matthew 5:35)

Hopefully the reader of Scripture has a greater appreciation and celebration of the Lord's Resurrection; but also for what His disciples encountered and emphasized about His post Resurrection appearances and post Ascension appearances.

The truth and encouragement of Scripture imparts hope. Not just the everyday kind, but eternal hope. Jesus said, "I am the way and the truth and the life" (John 14:6).

The stage has been prepared, everything continues to search for its time and place. The cast of characters have not all arrived yet, but they will. Then the final curtain will open on a more complete and fuller revelation of eternity.

The Apostle John wrote because he wanted his readers to believe that, "Jesus is the Christ, the Son of God..." (John 20:31). As the Messiah...

Through His Crucifixion... Jesus, the Savior.
Through His Resurrection... Jesus, the Lord of lords.
Through His Ascension... Jesus, the King of kings.

The Lord Jesus Christ spoke truth many-times-over about Himself. Below are just two of those numerous proclamations:

Jesus said, "... I am the light of the world ... the light of life" (John 8:12).

Jesus said, "... I am the resurrection and the life" (John 11:25).

Christianity began when the disciples of Jesus proclaimed His Resurrection after Pentecost. Can twenty-first century believers do any less?

His glorious LIGHT shines forever!

Three Crosses And Three Crowns

On the back cover of the book... a composite illustration of three crosses and three crowns reveals a timeline in the life of Jesus.

The cross on the lower left connects the Son of God / Son of Man in lineage. The Jewish star placed on a crown, with no indication of glory signifies the Savior's humble birth; and God's promise to King David that one of his descendants would sit on the throne forever. A manger turned toward the crucifixion cross indicates the baby born, Jesus, would die as the Heavenly Father's future redemption plan for humanity.

On the lower right, the cross with the crown of thorns and blood droplets is kept simple. Nothing this side of eternity conveys the true image of the overshadowing darkness and horror Christ experienced during His crucifixion death as the Lamb of God for the sins of the world. The sign on the cross... The King Of The Jews... proclaimed the message of grace and truth to those who initially rejected Him and His dying for their salvation.

In the center, the largest cross wrapped in lilies is symbolic of His glorious Resurrection... and links the other crosses heavenward. Above the cross, the gold crown with purple gems indicates in color both royalty and Resurrection; and honors Christ's eternal redemptive work as the Son of God / Son of Man.

The overall radiance streaming... a symbolic affirmation of the King's glorious Ascension; the Light that shines for all eternity and welcomes believers into heaven.

About The Author

As a dedicated believer in the Living Word… the Lord Jesus Christ, and the Written Word… the Holy Bible; both have been Bonnie's focus in her heart and life for decades. She received Jesus as Savior, at eight years old when an elderly female neighbor took her to Vacation Bible School; and has served Christ as Lord since thirty-one years of age. She is an ordained elder who loves searching the Scriptures and teaching. Also as an avid reader, who reads widely on various subjects, she believes in lifelong learning.

The remaining productive years of her life will continue taking a much more decisive and active turn toward teaching through a full-time writing ministry. Another book underway, her third, to be published in late Summer 2025. Her passion is teaching biblical concepts that have potential to enlighten and equip church leadership and enable believers to reach their full potential.

Bonnie has been married 62 years to her husband, George; and they have always lived in the Toledo Ohio metropolitan area. They have four children, nine grandchildren, and five great-grandchildren.

Social Media Platform
Bonnie J. Smith

E-mail:
bonjsmi@aol.com

Vocational and Professional:
bjs4christianbooks.com
LinkedIn.com/in/bonniejsmith1/